From the Cold War to Detente

edited by

Peter J. Potichnyj
Jane P. Shapiro

The sixth of eight volumes of papers from the first international conference sponsored by the American Association for the Advancement of Slavic Studies, British National Association for Soviet and East European Studies, British Universities Association of Slavists, and Canadian Association of Slavists.

General Editor: Roger E. Kanet

From the Cold War to Detente

PRAEGER SPECIAL STUDIES IN INTERNATIONAL POLITICS AND GOVERNMENT

Praeger Publishers New York Washington London

Library of Congress Cataloging in Publication Data

International Slavic Conference, 1st, Banff, Alta., 1974.
From the cold war to detente.

(Praeger special studies in international politics and government)
Includes bibliographical references and index.
1. Detente—Congresses. 2. United States—Foreign relations—Russia—Congresses. 3. Russia—Foreign relations—United States—Congresses. 4. International relations—Congresses. I. Potichnyj, Peter J. II. Shapiro, Jane P. III. American Association for the Advancement of Slavic Studies. IV. Title.
JX1393.D46I58 1974 327.73'047 75-19808
ISBN 0-275-56200-X

PRAEGER PUBLISHERS
111 Fourth Avenue, New York, N.Y. 10003, U.S.A.

Published in the United States of America in 1976
by Praeger Publishers, Inc.

Printed in the United States of America

GENERAL EDITOR'S FOREWORD

Roger E. Kanet

The studies published in this volume were selected from those presented at the First International Slavic Conference, held in Banff, Alberta, Canada, September 4-7, 1974. The conference, which was attended by approximately 1,500 persons, was sponsored by the American Association for the Advancement of Slavic Studies, the British Universities Association of Slavists, the British National Association for Soviet and East European Studies, and the Canadian Association of Slavists. Although the sponsorship of the conference was limited to the four major English-speaking Slavic associations, attendance and participation were much broader and included numerous scholars from continental Western Europe, Asia, Africa, Latin America, and Oceania. In addition, a substantial number of scholars from the Soviet Union and Eastern Europe participated in the deliberation of the conference.

Among the more than 250 papers presented, a relatively large number have been selected for publication in two series of conference volumes. Papers in the social sciences are included in the series of volumes being published by Praeger Publishers of New York; those in the humanities are appearing in the series of books being published by Slavica Publishers of Cambridge, Massachusetts.

As general editor of both the Praeger and Slavica series of Banff publications, I wish to express my sincere appreciation to all the individuals and institutions that made the conference possible, including the numerous government and private organizations that provided financial assistance, the members of the International Planning Committee who prepared the conference, and the participants themselves. Finally, I wish to thank the editors of the individual volumes in the two series and the authors of the essays for their major contributions.

CONTENTS

Page

GENERAL EDITOR'S FOREWORD v
Roger E. Kanet

LIST OF TABLES x

INTRODUCTION xi
Peter J. Potichnyj and Jane P. Shapiro

PART I: THE COLD WAR IN RETROSPECT 1

Chapter

1 AMERICAN POLICY AND THE ORIGINS OF THE COLD WAR IN CENTRAL EUROPE: 1945-47 3
Walter C. Clemens, Jr.

United States Initiatives, 1945-1946 3
The Soviet Critique, 1946 10
Soviet Counterproposals, 1947 15
Out of Phase or Different Tracks? 20
Notes 22

2 DID THE UNITED STATES USE ATOMIC DIPLOMACY AGAINST RUSSIA IN 1945? 26
Thomas T. Hammond

Act I: The Strategy of an Immediate Showdown 29
Act II: The Strategy of a Delayed Showdown 30
Alamogordo and Potsdam 32
Act III: American Diplomacy Takes the Offensive 37
Bulgaria 39
Rumania 42
The London Conference 44
Did the United States Use Atomic Diplomacy? 46
Conclusions 49
Notes 51

Chapter		Page
3	SOVIET POLITICS AT THE START OF THE COLD WAR: THE SOVIET PARTY REVIVAL REASSESSED William O. McCagg, Jr.	57
	Paradox or Trick?	57
	The Wartime Relaxation	58
	The Party's Revival	63
	Stalin Challenged?	67
	Conclusions	74
	Notes	75
4	AMERICAN FOREIGN AID AND YUGOSLAV FOREIGN POLICY Stephen C. Markovich	78
	Aid after the Expulsion	79
	Aid after the Rapprochement	85
	Conclusions	92
	Notes	94
	PART II: SPECULATIONS ABOUT DETENTE	
5	DETENTE "MYTHS" AND SOVIET FOREIGN POLICY Robert C. Horn	99
	Myth I: Detente Precludes Conflict or Competition	100
	Myth II. The Soviet Regime and Its Policies Are Monolithic and Single-Minded	103
	Myth III: Hard-line Ideological Statements Reveal the True Nature of Soviet Foreign Policy	104
	Myth IV: Detente Has Been and Is Being Pursued by the USSR out of Offensive Motives	108
	Myth V: Results of Detente Have Been Assymetrically Favorable to the USSR	113
	Conclusions: Detente Revisited	117
	Notes	118
6	SOVIET POSTWAR FOREIGN TRADE POLICY: STABILITY AND METAMORPHOSIS Steven Rosefielde	122
	Introduction	122
	Specialization	123

Chapter		Page
	Nomenclature and Specialization Policy	124
	Adjusted Factor Costs	125
	Domestic Cost Conversion Coefficients	126
	The Specialization Index	127
	Empirical Findings	128
	Metamorphosis: Soviet-COMECON Trade Policy in the 1970s	138
	Conclusions	141
	Notes	141
7	TOWARD A COMPARATIVE FOREIGN POLICY OF EASTERN EUROPE Zvi Gitelman	144
	East European Foreign Policy: The Case of Poland and the Federal Republic of Germany	150
	Diversity and Deviance in East European Foreign Policies	159
	Conclusions	161
	Notes	162
8	ACTUAL PROBLEMS OF POLITICAL RELATIONS BETWEEN THE USSR AND THE GDR Peter C. Ludz	166
	The GDR's Political Position within the Eastern Alliance	166
	The Security Motives of the SED Leaders	170
	Problems of the GDR within COMECON	172
	The Foreign Policy Functions of Domestic Policy	174
	The GDR's Lack of Legitimacy	176
	Modernization and the Capacity of the System to Adapt	178
	Conclusion	180
	Notes	180
9	DETENTE AND CZECHOSLOVAKIA George Klein	181
	Bases of Czechoslovak Foreign Policy	183
	The Dimensions of Internal Politics	186
	Economic Factors	187
	Detente and the Federal Republic of Germany	190

Chapter Page

The United States and Czechoslovakia 193
Detente and the Vatican 194
Conclusions 196
Notes 197

10 HUNGARY'S ROLE IN DETENTE 199
Richard C. Gripp

Internal Reforms 201
Foreign Trade and Foreign Policy 203
Hungary and Detente 208
Notes 211

NAME INDEX 214

SUBJECT INDEX 217

ABOUT THE EDITORS AND CONTRIBUTORS 222

LIST OF TABLES

Table		Page
3.1	Purge of Oblast First Secretaries September 1948-December 1949	69
6.1	Soviet-Comecon Commodity Specialization 1955-1968	130
6.2	Net Soviet-Comecon Exports (Foreign Trade Ruble Prices)	131
6.3	Net Soviet-Comecon Exports (12 Percent AFC Prices)	132
6.4	Specialization Ratios for Soviet Trade with Selected COMECON Nations (Foreign Trade Ruble Prices)	134
6.5	Specialization Ratios for Soviet Trade with Selected COMECON Nations (12 Percent AFC Prices)	135
6.6	Dispersion of Commodity Specialization in Soviet Trade With COMECON Member States	136
7.1	Policy Issues of the Federal Republic of Germany	159
8.1	GDR Foreign Trade 1960-1973	173
10.1	Hungarian Foreign Trade in 1960 and 1972	206

INTRODUCTION

FROM THE COLD WAR TO DETENTE

The ten studies that comprise this volume were originally presented at the First International Slavic Conference, "Banff '74." These were selected from nearly 30 essays which dealt with the general theme of Soviet and East European foreign policies and international relations. They divide into two rather clearly defined categories: a review of the origins of the cold war in perspective; and an investigation of the influence of detente upon the present and future relations among Communist states and between Communist states and the capitalist world. Some of the studies which were submitted had to be excluded because they did not relate to these issues; others unfortunately were excluded because of space considerations. Studies which had been committed for publication before this volume was compiled were not considered for inclusion.

What were the main factors underlying the inception of cold war? What kinds of limitations and restraints were imposed upon the leading policy makers in both the United States and the USSR at the close of World War II? Was the cold war inevitable? Walter C. Clemens examines the intricacies involved in fashioning American policy toward the Four-Power agreement in Germany and suggests that advisers to President Truman frequently perceived wrongly and miscontrued Soviet interests and intentions. Thomas T. Hammond reviews the shift in foreign policy after Roosevelt's death in 1945 and the actual influence that the exclusive atomic monopoly exerted over American policy toward the USSR. William O. McCagg scrutinizes the configuration of Stalin's political power in the early postwar years and concludes that there were distinct limits to his power which necessarily influenced the course and shape of Soviet domestic and foregin policy making. Stephen C. Markovich considers the impact of American foreign aid on Yugoslavia after 1948 and concludes that at best the United States had limited success in restraining Yugoslavia from following one or another policy of which it did not approve.

What is the nature of U.S.-Soviet relations in the era of detente between East and West? What impact has detente had upon relations among Communist states? What are the limits of sovereignty in foreign policy making for the East European states? Zvi Gitelman looks at Communist Eastern Europe in its totality and concludes that there is a growing complexity and differentiation among these states in regard to bilateral relations with the USSR, with one another, and with the West, all requiring closer examination. Richard C. Gripp, George Klein, and Peter C. Ludz examine the impact of detente on the particular cases of Hungary, Czechoslovakia, and the GDR, respectively. Robert C. Horn deals with a number of commonly accepted American assumptions about detente and dissects them critically, while Steven Rosefielde reviews the changing nature of Soviet-East European economic relations within the broader framework of East-West trade.

The editors wish to thank McMaster University, the Russian Institute of Columbia University, and Manhattanville College, for their generous assistance in the preparation of this volume.

PART I

THE COLD WAR IN RETROSPECT

CHAPTER

1

AMERICAN POLICY AND THE ORIGINS OF THE COLD WAR IN CENTRAL EUROPE, 1945-47

Walter C. Clemens, Jr.

The year 1975 marked the 30th anniversary of a proposal for an East-West security pact which, if enacted, might have helped forestall or temper the intensity of the cold war. As it happened, the American proposal and Soviet response became part and parcel of the snowball momentum taking both sides toward a serious confrontation in East Central Europe and other parts of the globe.

Was the cold war inevitable? The four-power pact proposal, on the face of it, had much to recommend it to all four powers occupying defeated Germany. Was it inevitable that the narrow interests and objectives of each side came to outweigh their common or parallel interests in perpetuating the wartime coalition? What roles were played by the personalities involved, the material and ideological conditions within each country, and the opportunities and challenges resulting from the defeat of Nazi Germany?

UNITED STATES INITIATIVES, 1945-1946

The most concrete proposal for an alliance between Moscow and the major Western powers derived, ironically, from a speech just prior to the Yalta Conference by a Republican senator, Arthur H.

This chapter is part of a larger study on U.S.-Soviet relations since 1917, supported in part by the Graduate School, Boston University.

Vandenberg, until that time known as a leading isolationist and noninterventionist. On January 10, 1945, Senator Vandenberg proposed that "a hard and fast treaty between the major allies" be signed immediately that would obligate them to move automatically against any new German or Japanese aggression. A premise of the proposal was that "Russia's unilateral plan appears to contemplate the engulfment, directly or indirectly, of a surrounding circle of buffer states, contrary to our conception of what we thought we were fighting for in respect to the rights of small nations and a just peace." Russia's announced reason for this plan, however, was "perfectly understandable" to the Senator, that is, "never again to be at the mercy of another German tyranny. The alternative," he argued, "is collective security."[1]

The tone of Vandenberg's address, however, was rather anti-Soviet, and hardly calculated to inspire the Kremlin to forgo hard-won domination in Poland and other potential buffer states for a set of paper assurances.* Indeed, over one year later, while commenting negatively on the U.S. draft treaty for the demilitarization of Germany, Soviet Foreign Minister Molotov noted in his report to the Soviet press on the results of the Paris meeting of the Council of Foreign Ministers, May 27, 1946 that it was advanced "in the spirit of the generally known proposals of Senator Vandenberg."[2] There was no consistency when, in 1948, Senator Vandenberg introduced a resolution by which the U.S. Senate urged American participation in what became the NATO alliance and called on the president to strengthen the United Nations in ways that would skirt the veto.[3]

The particulars of the Vandenberg proposal were not discussed at the Yalta Conference, although the notion of great power rule through the Security Council was endorsed by all parties. Nevertheless, the idea of a security treaty linking the Big Three appealed to several men in the U.S. Cabinet.[4] As a result of this interest, the State Department prepared a memorandum recommending that the president sound out both Churchill and Stalin at the Potsdam Conference to determine whether they might join the United States in a treaty to enforce the

---

*(Arthur H. Vandenberg, Jr., ed., pp. 130, 128.) The Private Papers of Senator Vandenberg (Boston: Houghton Mifflin Co., 1952). Reflecting on his proposal in 1948, Vandenberg recalled that he had possessed in 1945 "the deep conviction that it was time to anticipate what ultimately became the 'Moscow menace' and to lay down a formula which would make postwar Soviet expansionism as illogical as it would be unnecessary (except for ulterior purposes)." And in 1946 Vandenberg recalled that Roosevelt's attitude to the Russians "had not been encouraging" so that the Senator felt the need to challenge the "President on the eve of his departure for Yalta."

"permanent demilitarization" of Germany. In language that combined the psychological insights of arms controllers in the 1960s with the logic of Senator Vandenberg, the memorandum contended that,

> If the demilitarization of Germany is secured by such a commitment, no combination of European powers could effectively threaten the Soviet Union and the latter could afford to adopt a more liberal policy, particularly in Eastern Europe, thus making it possible to break the vicious circle in which [the Soviet Union] moves to insure its own security and which tends to bring about the very combination of powers against it that it is seeking to avoid.

Such a treaty, the memorandum argued, would have many advantages: As a "safeguard against any further German aggression," it would also "strengthen the relationship between the Allies and eliminate or minimize other conflicts which might arise between them. It would greatly reduce Soviet fears that Germany might one day be permitted to regain its strength and be used by the Western Powers in an anti-Soviet combination." Another utility of the treaty, the State Department noted, was that it "would also counteract the threat of both [the] British and Soviet governments to establish spheres of influence" by eliminating the justification for maintaining such spheres. Further, the treaty would "strengthen the influence of the United States in European affairs as it would go far to remove the fear that within a very few years the United States might again turn its back on Europe and once more resort to a policy of isolation."[5]

At Potsdam, however, as at Yalta, the United States seems not to have discussed the projected treaty with British or Soviet representatives. Only in September 1945 did Secretary of State Byrnes raise the matter with Molotov. Byrnes was encouraged by Molotov's interest, but heard no more from him on the subject. He decided, therefore, to discuss the project when he visited Stalin in December. Following a toast-laden dinner on Christmas Eve, 1945, Byrnes and Stalin, accompanied only by the Soviet interpreter, moved into the drawing room for coffee. Byrnes chose that moment to tell of his disappointment that he had not heard again from Molotov about the treaty they had discussed in London. To this, Stalin replied that his Foreign Minister had mentioned the treaty, but the questions Stalin then posed led Byrnes to infer that "no serious consideration had been given to the proposal."[6] "Such a treaty would give all European states assurance that the United States would not return to a policy of isolation," Byrnes argued. According to Byrnes' notes, Stalin replied: "If you decide to fight for such a treaty, you can rely on my support."[7]

With this conversation in mind, Byrnes began to prepare a draft treaty immediately upon his return from Moscow. This document, completed in February 1946, seemed to reflect much of the thinking contained in the State Department memorandum on a four-power pact prepared before the Potsdam Conference, for the draft treaty endeavored to maximize the advantages and to minimize the disadvantages noted in that document. It also attempted to follow as closely as possible the language of the Allied declaration of June 5, 1945, on the demilitarization of Germany during the occupation period.

The treaty's objectives were staggeringly comprehensive: (a) to disarm and disband all German armed forces and paramilitary organizations, and their staffs; (b) to prevent the manufacture or importation of military equipment including "all arms, ammunition, explosives . . . "; "all fissionable materials . . . except under conditions approved by the high contracting parties"; all naval vessels of all classes . . . "; "all aircraft of all kinds . . . and equipment for anti-aircraft defense"; and (c) to prevent the establishment or operation of all military installations, factories, and laboratories designed for military production. The treaty partners would determine the conditions under which civil police units could be formed and equipped with small arms, and explosives could be imported for peaceful economic purposes.

To implement the treaty, a system of four-power inspection was envisaged, "which shall become operative upon termination of the Allied occupation of Germany." A Commission of Control through its commissioners and agents, would be able to make such inquiries and investigations as it deemed necessary. For the duration of the occupation period, the treaty partners agreed that they would enforce disarmament and demilitarization. Moreover, acceptance by Germany of the four-power inspection system would be "an essential condition to the termination of the Allied occupation. . . . " The treaty was to last twenty-five years.[8]

The draft treaty was quickly endorsed by President Truman and—at least in principle—by key U.S. senators of both political parties. In February 1946, Byrnes sent copies of the proposed treaty to France (now replacing China as the fourth party), Great Britain, and the USSR. Paris replied sympathetically, but with reservations; Moscow indicated "serious objections," which Molotov said he would discuss with Byrnes in Paris; only London expressed unequivocal support for the U.S. initiative.[9]

Despite the forethought and respect for Soviet as well as Western interests embodied in the draft treaty, the trend of world politics was not conducive to either superpower's placing great reliance upon a paper assurance from the other. While the origins of the cold war can be traced back to 1917 or even to British-Russian rivalry in the 19th century, many observers took Stalin's preelection speech on February 9, and Churchill's "Iron Curtain" address on March 6, 1946 as virtual declarations of renewed and implacable hostilities—declarations made just before and after the circulation of the draft four-power pact.[10] Events and actions, of course, spoke more loudly than words, but these two addresses seemed to give formal and public recognition to what many in Moscow and in the West probably took to be a new and somewhat lasting phase of international struggle.

Even a liberal such as Justice William Douglas regarded the Stalin speech as a "declaration of World War III."* Such an interpretation, however, seems to reflect a basic ignorance of Soviet history and an insensitivity to Soviet politics after the world war. Stalin's speech might better be interpreted as defensive—both internally and externally—rather than as portending aggression. It began by recapitulating the Leninist thesis that war among capitalist states was inevitable, due to their uneven development and need for markets. But Stalin said nothing about the likelihood of war between the capitalist and socialist systems, though he asserted that the USSR's economic development would be directed so as to "ensure against any eventuality." While a new five-year plan was being developed to rebuild the damage done by World War II, "perhaps three new Five-Year Plans . . . if not more" would be required to achieve a level of development that would, in fact, provide such assurance of peace. True, Stalin omitted any mention of Russia's responsibility for World War II, but the entire thrust of his speech was to justify and defend the Soviet system against criticism: its economy, he argued, had performed remarkably since 1928 despite predictions that it was unworkable; its multinational federation, he boasted, had not collapsed under the strain of war; its Red Army, despite the misgiving of many recognized authorities on the art of war abroad, "had routed the German army and converted foreign misgivings to praise for the high qualities of the Soviet armed forces and their leaders." Stalin's concluding remark was that, having struggled together in World War II, "the bloc of Communist and non-Party

---

*This comment is recorded in Walter Millis, ed., <u>The Forrestal Diaries</u>, (New York: The Viking Press, 1951), p. 134. According to Millis, James Forrestal, then Secretary of the Navy, often cited the Stalin speech thereafter; it "came close to convincing him that there was no way, as Walter Lippmann had hoped, in which democracy and Communism could live together." From this time on "he felt increasingly that policy could not be founded on the assumption that a peaceful solution of the Russian problem would be possible."

persons" was joined in a "natural and common cause," making the "distrust" earlier felt toward non-Party persons unnecessary.[11] Molotov's electoral speech of the same week took a somewhat firmer line.[12]

The hostile character of the Stalin and Molotov speeches paled next to the address made by Winston Churchill in Fulton, Missouri, on March 6, 1946. True, he had not cleared the address with the Labor government in London, but he had discussed it with then President Truman, who accompanied him to Fulton and applauded the address. The "war talk" about which Molotov had warned was a leitmotiv of Churchill's speech. The former Prime Minister granted that the Soviet leaders did not want war, but only "the fruits of war and the indefinite expansion of their power and doctrines." "Tyranny " was a second danger against which Churchill warned, noting that an "iron curtain" had descended subjugating all the peoples "from Stettin in the Baltic to Trieste in the Adriatic" (an area that excluded East Germany) to an "increasing degree of control from Moscow." Security could not be had on the basis of "narrow margins," he declared, but required a preponderance of power against the USSR. The United Nations offered the best hope for peace, but it would be ineffective unless there developed a "fraternal association of the English-speaking peoples." It would be imprudent for the United States, Great Britain and Canada to turn over their atomic bomb to the United Nations while the international organization was still in its infancy.

Churchill denied, however, that war was inevitable or even imminent. And he called for "a grand pacification of Europe. . . . " In words that may have been intended to nudge the United States toward a still more conciliatory policy toward Germany, Churchill proclaimed: "The safety of the world requires a new unity in Europe from which no nation should be permanently outcast."[13]

Although Secretary of State Byrnes and others in the State Department refused to associate themselves with the speech—Undersecretary Dean Acheson even refusing to attend a dinner scheduled for Churchill—the effects on the minds of the Soviet leadership could not easily be undone. In Moscow, according to Brooks Atkinson, the speech had the effect of "electrifying and depressing everyone." A Pravda editorial entitled "Churchill Rattles the Sword" compared him to Goebbels, noting that it was very characteristic that he spoke not in England, where he had just been defeated in a reelection campaign stressing the "Red danger," but in the United States. Stalin, in an interview, declared that Churchill's speech was a dangerous act, one calculated to sow dissension. Comparing Churchill with Hitler, Stalin asserted that the British leader "also begins the work of unleashing a new war with a race theory, asserting that only English-speaking nations are full fledged nations . . . called upon to decide the fortune of the entire world."[14]

Assuming that Moscow's response to Churchill's address was at least partially genuine rather than feigned, this development would naturally affect the Kremlin's attitude toward the draft four-power pact circulated by the State Department just before the Fulton speech. The British leader's call for building up Western power and unity—a theme that he repeated throughout 1946—would naturally increase the Kremlin's diffidence about reliance upon a system of paper assurances.

Molotov might be forgiven if he sensed the "spirit of Vandenberg" when Secretary Byrnes put the four-power pact on the agenda of the Foreign Ministers meeting in Paris in April-May 1946, for the Republican senator from Michigan was in the U.S. delegation together with Democratic Senator Tom Connally. Indeed, the headlines of C. L. Sulzberger's New York Times report (April 30, 1946) repeated the theme of the January 1945 Vandenberg address: "Puts Russians' Aims to Test." And the article quoted an unnamed member of the delegation as saying,

> This should determine whether the Soviet Union really wants to cooperate on the international scene. . . . If they are sincere in their intentions toward the rest of the world, they must sign. If they are not and refuse to sign, it will make them appear an outlaw nation before the eyes of the world.

The language of Sulzberger's quotation is similar to that in Vandenberg's diary, except that the latter is much starker. The entry for April 29, 1946, when the four-power pact was first debated at the Paris conference, begins "Bad day! The Russkies were themselves again! All spirits are low tonight." Molotov, Vandenberg said, was "maddeningly obdurate, and refused even to understand the proposition."[15]

The father of the four-power pact concept, Senator Vandenberg, claimed personal credit for the harder inflection in U.S. policies toward Moscow in 1946. Whereas Secretary Byrnes had been "loitering around Munich" in 1945, according to Senator Vandenberg, Byrnes had gone "on the march" commencing with a firm speech on February 28, 1946. This address, immediately following a Vandenberg statement highly critical of the administration, was dubbed by some reporters the "Second Vandenberg Concerto." By July 1946 Vandenberg wrote that "almost everybody . . . concedes to me the major influence in changing the American attitude from 'appeasement' to firm resistance."[16] Within less than a week of Byrnes' February speech, Churchill delivered his "Iron Curtain" address at Fulton, Missouri.

THE SOVIET CRITIQUE, 1946

When the Council of Foreign Ministers met again in Paris, Byrnes asked Molotov, over dinner on April 28, what were the Soviet objections to the four-power pact. The Soviet Foreign Minister replied, both at dinner and at the council meeting the next day, that the treaty appeared to postpone the question of German disarmament until after the occupation. An agreement already existed, Molotov said, that Germany should be disarmed immediately and he proposed that a commission be appointed to verify how it was being carried out. When this investigation was completed, he added, the question of future controls could be embodied in a separate treaty.

In reply to Molotov's call for a special commission to investigate the state of Germany's demilitarization, Byrnes and Bevin pointed out that there already existed an Allied Control Council to supervise German disarmament, making another commission superfluous. Typical of French diplomacy in this period, Bidault took a middle position: He backed Molotov's proposal for an extra-special commission, but also praised the Byrnes plan. Many diplomats at Paris, according to a report by Harold Callender in The New York _Times_ on April 30, felt that Moscow was "missing no bets in extending its influence in Germany and lining up German political parties in the Russian zone."

Whether genuinely or by contrivance, Byrnes and Molotov mirrored the charges each made against the other. Thus, at their dinner meeting on April 28, Byrnes warned Molotov that "there are many people in the United States who are unable to understand the exact aim of the Soviet Union—whether it is a search for security or merely expansion."[17] A treaty like the one proposed regarding Germany and a similar treaty for Japan, Byrnes asserted, "will effectively take care of the question of security." Several weeks later, in a statement to the Soviet press, on the results of the Paris meeting, Molotov proved that there were two sides to this argument, declaring that

> It is sometimes said that it is difficult to draw a line between the desire for security and the desire for expansion. And, indeed, it is at times difficult. For instance, what security interests of the United States dictate the demand for military bases in Iceland. . . . Certain circles in the United States, leagued with their friends in Great Britain, are seeking to establish naval and air bases in all parts of the globe—on Pacific and Atlantic islands and on the territories of states in the Western and Eastern hemispheres.[18]

At a ministers meeting on May 16 Molotov had asked what was the connection between the Byrnes proposal and the task of reaching a peace treaty with Germany before the end of 1946. Molotov observed that Byrnes' February 1946 circular letter had not included a detailed treaty draft. and argued that there was still "plenty of time to study the question," since the U.S.-proposed treaty would be concluded after the peace settlement with Germany. Moscow felt it more urgent to investigate the implementation of joint agreements already reached on German disarmament.[19]

When Byrnes recalled Stalin's support for the treaty during their meeting in December 1945, Molotov replied that nothing more than an exchange of opinions had taken place, without a draft text as a basis for discussion. Moreover, according to Molotov, the subject considered in December was a mutual assistance pact against German or Japanese aggression—not a mere disarmament agreement that would undermine the stronger obligations already undertaken at Yalta and Potsdam. (On this count, Molotov's memory differed radically from Byrnes' notes, which could be due either to some failure of communication or a deliberate distortion.)[20]

Responding to Molotov's criticisms of the U.S. treaty, Byrnes frequently affirmed that nothing in the proposed treaty would "delay or prevent" the completion of total demilitarization and disarmament of Germany.[21] Further, to meet Molotov's complain about lack of action on the existing demilitarization agreement, Byrnes proposed that the Allied Control Commission in Berlin appoint a commission to visit the four occupation zones and report on the progress of demilitarization, a step to which Molotov agreed in May 1946.[22]

In a major address on July 9, Molotov reaffirmed that "the disarmament and long-term demilitarization of Germany" were "absolutely essential"—not just for 25 years, as suggested in the draft treaty, but for at least 40.

Although Secretary Byrnes and others inferred that the USSR objected to the U.S. draft treaty because it postulated the continued presence of American troops in Europe,[23] Molotov denounced the treaty for envisaging "the possibility of terminating the Allied occupation of Germany." Molotov declared that allied occupation of Germany had three aims: (1) disarmament, (2) democratization, and (3) the assurance of reparations deliveries. "So long as these objectives have not been achieved," the USSR held that "the presence of occupation forces in Germany and the maintenance of zones of occupation are absolutely essential."[24]

Byrnes, in reply, stated that Washington was willing to extend the proposed treaty for 40 years, and denied that Allied occupation would necessarily terminate after the treaty expired. He pointed out that the draft language on demilitarization and disarmament had been lifted from a June 5, 1945 agreement signed by military leaders of the four powers—Zhukov, Eisenhower, Montgomery, and De Lattre de Tassigny. The American proposal did not purport to settle political and reparations questions. "It merely tried to carry out for twenty-five years agreements which had been reached between the Generals on the demilitarization of Germany."[25]

Molotov proposed on July 10 that the Allied Control Commission set up a Special Commission to control the implementation of decisions of the allied governments regarding disarmament and the liquidation of all Germany military and paramilitary organizations in all zones of occupation. A second commission would prepare a plan, with agreed time limits, "to liquidate any branch of German industry which can be' used for German war production and armaments." Byrnes agreed to the first commission, but called for an investigation of the plan already agreed to on June 5, 1945 for the destruction of German military potential. The United States, he added, was complying with the 1945 directives. Indeed, Byrnes had reported on the previous day that he had telephoned the U.S. Deputy Military Governor in Germany, Lucius Clay, in reponse to Molotov's charges that the Western governments were not carrying out their disarmament obligations. Clay had told him that Soviet occupation authorities wanted to limit investigations to disbandment of German troops and to exclude any look at demilitarization of German industry. More generally, they opposed visits by Western representatives in the Soviet zone. The British and French occupation authorities, supported by the United States, were insisting that the commission examine not only the disbandment of armed forces but also the utilization of plants designed for war production. There were charges that the war items were still being produced in the Soviet zone. But the Russians wanted to limit the commission's frame of reference,[26] and agreed to permit industrial inspection in their zone only in October 1946, with the understanding that only 15 percent of declared war plants would be subject to inspection, with a maximum of nine plants per tour, and that the tours were to take place two or three months apart. Thus, opportunities would exist to dismantle or conceal factories, or even to alter their production schedules. The first inspection took place in January 1947.[27]

Molotov's July 10 proposal seemed to cater to the German Communists by picturing the USSR as the champion of German economic development, contrasted with the Anglo-Americans, dedicated to "agrarianizing" the country.[28] His remarks harmonized with a shift in Soviet reparations policy during the summer of 1946 away from dismantling German industry for removal to Russia and toward extraction from current production. The Kremlin may well have decided that attempts to transplant German factories were inefficient and that the more profitable procedure would be to restore German industry to productive uses and withdraw reparations mainly from this source. This procedure, however, was interpreted by the Western powers as a violation of the Potsdam agreements, which they said allowed only for capital transfers.*

Already, in April and May 1946, parallel with the Foreign Ministers' meetings in London and Paris, the United States had inflicted pressure on a sensitive Soviet nerve—the issue of reparations. On May 3, 1946, General Lucius Clay advised the Coordinating Committee of occupying powers that the United States was stopping all further reparations from her zone until a broader set of problems had been resolved. The issue of reprations was one of several matters on which the United States sought to utilize her economic strength to gain political concessions from Moscow. Each pursuing its own goals, the great powers failed to agree in 1945-1946 (or later) on the precise amount and kinds of reparations to be extracted from Germany. The USSR, for her part, claimed reparation amounting to $10 billion, while the West maintained that this sum had been agreed on only as a "basis" of discussion. The USSR proceeded to remove fixed capital equipment from her zone and to extract reparations from current production, but without making any accounting on the value of these items. Further, in Western eyes, the USSR was violating the Potsdam agreement to treat Germany as an economic whole and to utilize export proceeds to pay for essential imports. Soviet failure to comply with these accords exacerbated living conditions in the Western zones, forcing the United States to spend $200 million per year to support the people in her zone. Clay's decision to halt reparations payments came after the Soviet representative reaffirmed that there would be no pooling of resources until there was a balanced economy and refused to make any accounting on plant or productive output removed from eastern Germany. This decision, as General Clay understood, "was certain to have a lasting effect on our relationship with Russia." After it was announced, "the threatening storm had broken. . . ."[29]

The shift in Soviet policy toward extracting reparations from current German production made it logical for Moscow to court Germany's good will and enhance her productivity, even while claiming a major share of this output. The Soviet strategy for attaining

---

*See Documents on Germany, 1944-1961 (Washington, D. C.: U. S. Government Printing Office, 1961), pp. 9, 34. In fact, the Potsdam accord seems to have been ambiguous, but earlier in 1945, the Yalta agreement specified that reparations would come from three sources: a) removal of capital equipment; b) "annual deliveries of goods from current productions for a period to be fixed"; and c) "use of German labor." The relevant portions of each agreement are given.

these somewhat incompatible objectives was implicit, as Clay observed, in Molotov's speech of July 10. Indeed, the Soviet foreign minister began by stressing that "the spirit of revenge is a poor counsellor" when considering the future of Germany. The two premises of his speech were: (1) that "Germany is an important link in the whole system of world economy," and that (2) "more than once this industrial might has served as the base for the arming of aggressive Germany." Our purpose, Molotov said, "is not to destroy Germany, but to transform her into a democratic and peace-loving state which, alongside of agriculture, would have its own industry and foreign trade, but which would be deprived of the economic and military potentiality to rise again as an aggressive force." He opposed any proposal to turn Germany into an "agrarian" state without industrial centers.

While Molotov rejected the U.S. treaty proposal in its present form, the British and French foreign ministers supported it, even though they kept open the possibility of offering amendments at a later date. Bidault, in his statement, declared it necessary to destroy the "militarist Prussian character" of Germany, and held that the U.S. treaty should constitute "the crown of the edifice."[30]

Molotov's statement on the proposed German peace treaty confirmed for Byrnes

> our fears that unless forced by world opinion to do so, the Soviet Union would not agree to a treaty of peace with Germany for years to come. They would utilize their veto power on the Allied Control Council and in the Council of Foreign Ministers to secure adoption of their conception of a "democratic" government; to secure a part in the control of German industry, the industries of the Ruhr in particular, and to enforce the payment of $10 billion of reparations.[31]

Nevertheless, Molotov's statements on July 9 and 10 put the United States on the defensive and Byrnes responded by deciding to formulate a major address outlining U.S. policy to Germany, in part so as to refute the image of a power determined to impoverish the country. This address was delivered at Stuttgart, on September 6, 1946. Byrnes, like Molotov, declared his opposition to harsh and vengeful measures, and expressed determination to rid Germany of militarism. More generally, he stated, "It is not in the interest of the German people or in the interest of world peace that Germany should become a pawn or a partner in a military struggle for power between the East and the West." While calling for execution of the Potsdam agreements on demilitarization and reparations so that Germany's war industry was eliminated, Byrnes opposed reparations from current production and added that the United States would not agree to greater reparations payments than those agreed on at Potsdam. The Allies should lay down rules "under which German democracy can govern itself." But, he emphasized, "Security forces will probably have to remain in Germany for a long period. . . . We are not withdrawing. We are staying here and will furnish our proportionate share of the security forces."[32]

Before making the Stuttgart address, Byrnes discussed it with General Clay, expressing particular concern over the sentence: "As long as an occupation force is required in Germany, the army of the United States will be part of that occupation force." Byrnes tried to clear the sentence with President Truman, first by phone and then by cable, but received no reply. Clay, however, encouraged Byrnes to include it "because it would be the most welcome part of his speech, not just in Germany but throughout Europe." Byrnes proceeded without Truman's specific authorization to make what Clay termed "the first expression by a high American official of our firm intent to maintain our position in Europe."[33]

As Barrington Moore, Jr., has written, the Stuttgart speech, coupled with Molotov's earlier remarks, "might be regarded as the unofficial funeral of the Potsdam agreement and the overt beginning of a race for Germany between the Western powers and the USSR, although the roots of the split can be traced back to the divergent policies of the various powers from the first days of the occupation."[34] As Byrnes himself pointed out with pride, the fact that at Stuttgart he threw the weight of the United States on the side of Germany in the question of the return of the "eastern territories" compelled the Soviets to choose between the Poles and the Germans, thus undermining Soviet prestige in Germany.[35]

SOVIET COUNTERPROPOSALS, 1947

One of James F. Byrnes' last moves as secretary of state (before being replaced in January 1947 by George C. Marshall) was to introduce at the December 1946 meeting of foreign ministers in New York a proposal to reduce occupation forces in Germany and other East Central European countries to certain specified levels as early as April 1947, with additional cuts to take place in the following year.[36] But no detailed negotiations on this proposal or on the four-power pact took place until the Council of Foreign Ministers reconvened in Moscow for a session lasting from March 10 to April 24, 1947, with Germany and Austria as the main items on the agenda.

The prospects for agreement at Moscow were hardly enhanced by the general thrust of world politics. Two days after the conference opened, President Truman announced economic and military aid to Greece and Turkey. According to press reports, the president told congressional leaders that "What we are doing will strengthen

[Marshall's] hand in Moscow." And James Reston wrote on March 11 that Secretary Marshall had "not gone to Moscow primarily to make peace with Germany, but to emphasize the cost of not making peace with the United States." The mood in Washington was summed up by D. F. Fleming in this way: "It was even expected that a dose of real toughness would bring hard-boiled Russian leaders to terms. If not, well and good, since the Administration did not attach much importance to the conference anyway."[37]

Fleming's interpretation seems more extreme than the evidence permits, but not by much. The only mention of the 1947 Moscow meeting of foreign ministers in Truman's memoirs is buried in the many pages dealing with the origins of the Truman Doctrine and the Marshall Plan. Secretary Marshall went to Moscow, Truman piously notes, "with the hope that he could persuade the Russians that the United States was working for peace. The Russians, however, were interested only in their own plans and were coldly determined to exploit the helpless condition of Europe to further Communism rather than cooperate with the rest of the world." As a result, when Marshall returned home on April 26, "he arrived in a pessimistic mood." The report that Marshall made on the meeting confirmed Truman's "conviction that there was no time to lose in finding a method for the revival of Europe."[38]

Once the foreign ministers were assembled in Moscow, the task of eliminating Germany's military potential returned again to center stage, but it was embroiled in a whole series of other issues. Thus, when Marshall tried the first day to put onto the agenda the Byrnes troop-ceiling proposal of December 1946, Molotov linked Russia's approval to Western acquiescence in his call for a report by each government on fulfillment of earlier pledges regarding China.[39] But demilitarization of Germany was discussed the following day (March 11), Moscow demanding economic disarmament. Molotov charged that no Western plan for industrial disarmament had as yet been set out. Further, according to Western reports, 81,358 German soldiers in the British zone and 9,000 in the American zone were serving as auxiliary units under military organization of their former officers. More, in these two zones were undisbanded military units of Yugoslavs, Poles, and Ukrainians who refused to be repatriated.

To correct this situation, Molotov proposed four steps: (1) to work out by July 1, 1947, a plan for eliminating German's war-industrial potential, with special attention to liquidation of cartels and trusts; (2) to expedite destruction of German war materials and installations by the end of 1949; (3) to disband and liquidate by June 1, 1947, all extant German military formations including auxiliary units; and (4) to dissolve all units and organizations among non-Germans who by decision of the Control Council were subject to being disbanded and repatriated.[40]

Great Britain and the United States replied that complete economic disarmament was not feasible. Marshall denied that it was possible to distinguish war production potential so clearly as Molotov implied, and proposed instead heavy reliance on a four-power pact. Bevin said the powers could not proceed much further in the destruction of Germany's war potential without a working accord on a unified German economy.[41] Responding to earlier Molotov demands about German prisoners under British administration, Bevin asked for a report on German POWs "still held in Allied territory."[42]

Bevin and a small British delegation visited Stalin on March 24, 1947. Stalin's tone, judging by the British report, was conciliatory, He was well informed on the debate over centralization of the German government, but appeared confused when Bevin asked him about the four-power pact proposal. At first he seemed to think this referred to a treaty <u>with</u> Germany. After consulting with Molotov, however, he replied that the USSR would probably welcome such a pact if it contained revisions of the kind suggested by the Soviet delegation to the Paris Council of Foreign Ministers in 1946. On a related matter, Stalin expressed confidence that the allies could exert sufficient force to keep Germany from reclaiming any of the territories of which she had been deprived in the peace settlement.[43]

Not until late in the conference—April 14—did the foreign ministers focus their discussions on the four-power pact proposal. All three Western governments agreed to name negotiators to draft a final text based on the U.S. draft and all other suggestions.[44] On the same day, Molotov presented the Soviet position in a draft treaty "On the Demilitarization and Prevention of German Aggression", which reflected the criticisms of the U.S. draft that he had expressed in July 1946 and in the earlier sessions of the March-April 1947 meetings in Moscow.[45]

The Soviet amendments to the U.S. draft treaty stirred a negative response in the U.S. delegation. General Marshall held that the amendments "would have completely changed the character of the pact, making it in effect a complicated peace treaty"—one that would include in the amendments most of the points regarding the German problem on which disagreement was already registered at the Moscow meeting. The U.S. secretary of state inferred that the Kremlin utilized this procedure because it "either did not desire such a pact or was following a course calculated to delay any immediate prospect of its adoption." The United States, he said, "should adhere to its present position and insist that the pact be kept simple and confined to its one basic purpose—to keep Germany incapable of waging war."[46]

Molotov replied that his amendments were aimed at implementation of the four-power pact and represented an effort to meet the West half way. He asked for an agreement in principle on the four-power pact and also suggested that a special committee consider all drafts and amendments and report to the next Council of Foreign Ministers, adding that the committee must refer to the relevant decisions of the Yalta and Potsdam conferences.

On the following day, April 15, Marshall finally paid a courtesy call on Stalin, which lasted from 10:00 to 11:20 p.m.[47] The U.S. secretary of state had been in Moscow over a month and, as Ambassador Smith later noted, "Secretary Marshall's call could no longer be delayed without discourtesy." The British and French foreign ministers had made their visits some three weeks earlier. The available documents give no clue why Marshall put off this visit so long (or why, if he was so devoted to the four-power pact, he let the opportunity pass to see whether Molotov's counterproposals might be whittled down to an acceptable compromise).

Marshall's only explanation of the delay was his apology to Stalin that he had been busy with the conference, and had hoped for some "real subjects" to discuss with him. The secretary presumed that he should speak first, and proceeded to make what Smith termed a "quiet but forceful review" of East-West relations since the Potsdam Conference. Marshall said there had been a "serious and steady deterioration in public regard toward the Soviet Union" from the high esteem and admiration of the wartime period. This had resulted from many acts or failures to act on the part of the USSR—many matters relatively unimportant in themselves, "but the sum total [of which] had created a most unfortunate impression, particularly among the section of the public who were uninformed on such matters."

Throughout Marshall's soliloquy, according to Smith, Stalin "did not comment, or interrupt, and only exchanged a quick whispered word with Molotov" when Marshall mentioned a Soviet delay or failure to respond. When Marshall concluded, Smith reported, Stalin began "in an equally quiet and friendly tone."

"It is wrong," he said, "to give so tragic an interpretation to our present disagreements."

> He looked upon our differences like a quarrel within a family. With reference to the present conference, and the problem of Germany, the differences which had developed were "only the first skirmishes and brushes of reconnaissance forces" on this question. Differences had occurred in the past on other questions, he went on, and as a rule "when people had exhausted themselves in dispute, they recognized the necessity for compromise.
>
> It was possible, he said, that no great success would be achieved at this session, but he thought that compromises

> were possible on all the main issues, including the demilitarization of Germany, its political structure, reparations and economic unity. It was necessary to have patience, and not to become pessimistic.

On the question of Germany's political structure (centralized or federalized?), Stalin made the interesting suggestion that, if the four occupying powers could reach no agreement, they should let the Germans decide by plebiscite how much power to give the Laender!

Two days later Marshall reported to Truman that he was "not certain the Soviets may not compromise sufficiently to make possible a four-power pact, though I feel certain they do not desire such a pact and tried to kill it with amendments including every disputed issue." He thought the meeting with Stalin was beginning to yield results, and that an Austrian treaty might be achieved in this session.[48] (The Austrian State Treaty was finally signed in 1955, whereas a comparable German treaty and a four-power pact have not been signed.)

On the last day of the Moscow meeting, April 24, Marshal succeeded in getting the Council to consider the proposal introduced by Byrnes in December, 1946, for troop ceilings. For occupation forces in Germany, Washington proposed a ceiling of 140,000 for Great Britain and for the United States; 70,000 for France; and 200,000 for the USSR. Each of the four occupying forces in Austria could maintain 10,000 men there, while the USSR would be limited to 20,000 men in Poland and 5000 in Hungary and also in Rumania. These levels would be further reduced in 1948.

The Soviet delegation replied with a demand for virtual parity with the Western forces. The USSR, according to Molotov, needed 200,000 troops in her zone, and held that the British and U.S. forces combined should also total this number, and the French 50,000. To this, Mr. Bevin replied that he had been instructed to agree to 145,000 men for the British zone; Bidault said that the French government could not permit a figure less than 70,000 for its zone; while Marshall rejected the idea of combining U.S. and British forces to equal a Soviet total. Unable to agree on these matters, the ministers solemnly referred the issue to the Allied Control Commission in Germany, Washington insisting that it report by June 1 on strengths required as from September 1, 1947.[49]

As Soviet-Western differences seemed increasingly irreconsilable, the Western governments increased the momentum toward unification of their occupation zones. The stage was set for the first major confrontation in Germany, the Berlin blockade.

General Marshall summarized after the conference his understanding of why no agreement was reached: "The Soviet Union insisted upon proposals which would have established in Germany a centralized government, adapted to the seizure of absolute control of a country which would be doomed economically through inadequate area and excessive population, and would be mortgaged to turn over a large part of its production as reparations, principally to the USSR. In another form, the same mortgage upon Austria was claimed by the Soviet delegation." The U.S. delegation, Marshall reported, concluded that the Soviet program "not only involved indefinite American subsidy, but could result only in a deteriorating economic life in Germany and Europe and the inevitable emergence of dictatorship and strife."[50]

OUT OF PHASE OR DIFFERENT TRACKS?

Stalin's remarks to Marshall in April were reminiscent of his November 1944 speech in which he warned that differences among allies were to be expected, but could and should be kept within the bounds of a viable coalition.[51] As late as April 1947—in the face of the Truman Doctrine, the refusal of the U.S. delegation to consider the amended treaty submitted by Molotov as a possible basis for discussion, and the somewhat haughty behavior of the U.S. delegation—Stalin seemed to retain a perspective that would diminish the real and imagined slights of day-to-day politics if it had been reciprocated.

Failure to agree on a common approach to the problems of Germany and arms control was occasioned by far more than communications failures or excessive propaganda manipulation. Although the occupying powers appeared in 1945-47 to be genuinely concerned to prevent a resurgence of German militarism, their efforts to unite on this goal foundered on a number of competing interests:

	Soviet Interests		Western Interests
1.	To increase soviet influence in Eastern Europe;	versus	To prevent Sovietization of Eastern Europe;
2.	To gain reparations from all of Germany including the Ruhr;	versus	To develop a viable German economy without massive subsidies from the United States (although France, like the USSR, put more priority on reparations than on such viability, and wanted to absorb parts of Germany for her own purposes);

3. To form an all-German central government, (a) without discrimination against the Communist Party and (b) with competence to assure reparations in payments;	versus	To form a federal German structure, to thwart either a fascist or a Communist takeover;
4. To prevent unity of the United States, Great Britain, and France—among themselves and/or with Western zones of Germany;	versus	To establish working unity of Western Allies and their zones of occupation;
5. To replace cartels and large landowners with socialist institutions in all of Germany.	versus	To support free enterprise as the most effective route to a viable German economy.

Still, the possibility that one or both sides were misreading eachother's intentions cannot be excluded. Moscow probably underestimated the extent to which Western policies were anxious responses to a perceived threat from Soviet probings in Central and Eastern Europe and in the eastern Mediterranean. The Western nations, as Shulman has written, believed that a new balance of power was in the making, and that no fundamental stabilization of relations with the USSR was likely until the power relations in Europe had been defined afresh. Western actions, which began to reverse "the process of military demobilization, appeared in turn to confirm Soviet expectations of 'capitalist hostility' and were followed by a new and more militant phase of Soviet policy."[52]

The most problematic portions of the Soviet counterproposal centered on demands for Germany's industrial disarmament. A major priority for Soviet foreign policy in these years was to obtain material means for rebuilding the USSR—through reparations, credits, loans, or whatever other instruments might become available. As Washington and London stiffened their resistance to reparations at Potsdam and after, the Kremlin increased its effort to obtain controls over the German economy that would give it assured access to the capital plant and production from the Western zones.

Though the trade-off was never made explicit by Soviet spokesmen, one can only wonder whether the USSR would not have accepted the narrower type of security treaty proposed by the United States if Washington had been more forthcoming on some economic dimension: if not reparations, then credits; if not credits, then reparations. Receiving nothing on any of these fronts, Moscow was the more dogged in its pursuit of Germany's economic disarmament.

There were also sharp differences in the interests and ideological approaches of Washington and its non-Communist associates, divergences so significant that General Clay found it "difficult" in July 1946 "to place all blame" on the USSR.[53] Like France, the Netherlands, Belgium, and Czechoslovakia were all seeking hidden reparations in the form of trade concessions from Germany,[54] while Clay believed Great Britain to be working for a complete socialization of the German economy along lines unacceptable to the American public.[55]

Acceptance and implementation of the American version of the four-power pact would have forestalled rearmament in either part of Germany, and might have helped efforts to treat the country's economy as a unified whole. The Soviet counterproposal, if accepted in its entirety, would probably have delayed Germany's economic recovery, and to that extent, the reconstruction of Western Europe. Left to themselves, Soviet authorities continued to exploit East Germany's economy until the early or mid-1950s.[56]

The Western proposals, we conclude, offered far more to the mutual advantage of all parties than those of the USSR. The tragedy was that Moscow did not respond positively to the Byrnes overtures in 1946, and that the Western governments did not explore more deeply the potential for compromise in Molotov's counterproposal of April 1947. By the time Moscow brought forward its own draft treaty, the United States and her allies were much more disposed to seek means for Western unity than to rekindle the erstwhile coalition with the USSR.

We cannot be sure that the positions of both sides on such issues would ever have been harmonized. Perhaps they were deliberately out-of-phase for purposes of psychological warfare. We cannot know with certainty that mutual accommodation was possible unless a specific agreement was reached and observed. But neither can we be sure that meaningful accords were fatalistically precluded.

NOTES

1. For text of Vandenberg's speech, see Congressional Record, vol. 91, pt. 1, pp. 164-67; long excerpts also in Arthur H. Vandenberg, Jr., ed. The Private Papers of Senator Vandenberg, (Boston: Houghton Mifflin Co., 1952), pp. 132-38.

2. V. M. Molotov, Problems of Foreign Policy (Moscow: Foreign Languages Publishing House, 1949), p. 46.

3. Vandenberg, op. cit., pp. 399-420.

4. Stimson Papers: Stimson Diaries, 11.1.45. Cited in Gerhard Wettig, Entmilitarisierung und Wiederbewaffnung in Deutschland,

1943-1955 (Munich: R. Oldenbourg Verlag, 1967), p. 141. A major Soviet work tilted in the opposite direction is P. A. Nikolaev, Politika Sovetskogo Soiuza v germanskom voprose, 1945-1964 (Moscow: Nauka, 1966).

5. "Briefing Book Paper, Memorandum, Top Secret (Washington), June 27, 1945; Subject: Treaty for Demilitarization of Germany with Commitment to Use United States Forces" in Foreign Relations of the United States, Diplomatic Papers, The Conference of Berlin-1945, 2 vols. (Washington, D.C.: U.S. Government Printing Office, 1960), 1: 450-52.

6. James F. Byrnes, Speaking Frankly (New York: Harper and Brothers Publishers, 1947), p. 171.

7. Ibid., pp. 171-72. No record of this conversation has been left in U.S. government archives, according to Foreign Relations 1946 (Washington, 1970) 2: 66.

8. Text in New York Times, April 30, 1946 and in Foreign Relations 1946, 2: 190-93.

9. Byrnes, op. cit., p. 173.

10. For a survey of the literature reporting different views on the dating of the cold war, see Paul Seabury, The Rise and Decline of the Cold War (New York: Basic Books, 1967), pp. 6-10.

11. Text in the New York Times, February 10, 1946, pp. 1, 30.

12. Speech at meeting of voters of the Molotov electoral area, February 6, 1946, in Molotov, op. cit., pp. 26-36.

13. Randolph S. Churchill, ed. The Sinews of Peace: Post-War Speeches by Winston S. Churchill. (Boston: Houghton Mifflin Co., 1949), pp. 93-105.

14. New York Times and Keesing's Contemporary Archives quoted in D. F. Fleming, The Cold War and Its Origins, 2 vols. (Garden City, New York: Doubleday and Co., Inc., 1961), 1: 351-56. The only place in President Truman's memoirs where the Iron Curtain speech is discussed comes at the bottom of a paragraph—one of many—given over to the rising crisis resulting from the continued Soviet military presence in Iran and U.S. efforts to dislodge it. (Memoirs by Harry S. Truman, 2 vols. [New York: Doubleday and Co., Signet Ed., 1965], 2: 117.) Earlier in the year, embittered by what he saw as Soviet intransigence, Truman told Byrnes, "I'm tired of babying the Soviets." (Ibid., 1: 606. This phrase occurs a second time on the same page, with Truman's comment: "I meant it.")

15. Vandenberg, op. cit., pp. 267-68.

16. For documentation, see John Lewis Gladdis, The United States and the Origins of the Cold War, 1941-1947 (New York: Columbia University Press, 1972), pp. 305-06.

17. Byrnes, op. cit., p. 173.

18. Molotov, op. cit., p. 49.

19. Foreign Relations 1946, 2: 426-33.

20. Molotov, op. cit., p. 37; Byrnes, op. cit., p. 175.

21. Byrnes, op. cit., pp. 174-75.

22. Ibid., p. 174; Foreign Relations 1946, 2: 432.

23. Byrnes, op. cit., p. 176.

24. Molotov, op. cit., p. 62.

25. Foreign Relations 1946, 2: 847-50.

26. Ibid., 2: 878-98, 848; see also Clay to Oliver P. Echols, 23 May 1946 in Jean Edward Smith, ed. The Papers of General Lucius D. Clay: Germany, 1945-1949, 2 vols. (Bloomington, Indiana: Indiana University Press, 1974), p. 211.

27. Wettig, op. cit., pp. 153-54; Lucius D. Clay, Decision in Germany (Garden City, New York: Doubleday and Co., 1950), p. 128.

28. Clay, Decision, pp. 128-29.

29. Clay, Decision, pp. 120-22, 128-29; Byrnes, op. cit., p. 175.

30. Byrnes, op. cit., pp. 175-76.

31. Ibid., p. 181.

32. Ibid., pp. 188-91; see also Documents on Germany, 1944-1961, pp. 52-62.

33. Clay, Decision, p. 79

34. Barrington Moore, Jr., Soviet Politics—The Dilemma of Power (Cambridge, Mass.: Harvard University Press, 1950), p. 378.

35. Byrnes, op. cit., p. 192.

36. Foreign Relations 1946, 2: 1466-67.

37. Fleming, op. cit., 1: 466.

38. Truman, Memoirs, 2: 136.

39. Marshall from Moscow to Acheson in Washington, March 10, 1947, in Foreign Relations 1947, 2: 239-40.

40. Molotov, op. cit., The Demilitarization of Germany. Statement made at the sitting of the Council of Foreign Ministers, March 11, 1947, pp. 343-48.

41. Marshall to Acheson, March 11, 1947, in Foreign Relations 1947, 2: 243.

42. Marshall to Acheson, March 12, 1947 in ibid., 2: 245.

43. Ibid., 2: 278-84.

44. Marshall to Truman, Vandenberg, Connally, Acheson, April 14, 1947, in ibid., 2: 331-33.

45. Text in Molotov, op. cit., pp. 601-08; see also Molotov's statement on the draft treaty on April 15, 1947, in ibid., pp. 443-48 and his reply to comments by the U.S. delegation, pp. 443-48 and 448-50.

46. Marshall to Acheson, April 15, 1947, in Foreign Relations 1947, 2: 334-36.

47. The following account is based primarily on Marshall's report in ibid., 2: 337-44; on the testimony of Walter Bedell Smith (My Three Years in Moscow [Philadelphia: J. B. Lippincott Co., 1950], pp. 221-22); and on excerpts of Stalin's remarks repeated by Marshall in his radio broadcast in the United States, April 28, 1947, text in Documents on Germany, 1944-1961, pp. 74-82, at 81.

48. Marshall to Acheson for delivery to President's eyes only, April 17, 1947, in Foreign Relations 1947, 2: 351.

49. Marshall to Acheson, April 25, 1947, in ibid., 2: 388-90; for background, see Foreign Relations 1946, 2: 1466-67.

50. Radio broadcast, April 28, 1947, in Documents on Germany, 1944-1961, pp. 74-82, at pp. 80-81.

51. See Joseph Stalin, The Great Patriotic War of the Soviet Union (New York: International Publishers, 1945), pp. 127-43, at pp. 137-42.

52. Marshall D. Shulman, Stalin's Foreign Policy Reappraised (Cambridge, Mass.: Harvard University Press, 1963), p. 14.

53. Clay to McNarney, July 23, 1946 in The Papers, 1: 243-44.

54. Clay to Marshall, May 2, 1947, ibid., 1: 346-49.

55. Clay to Noce, April 28, 1947, ibid., 1: 341-43.

56. See "Joint Communique of the Negotiations Between the Soviet Government and the Government Delegation of the German Democratic Republic, 20-22 August 1953," August 22, 1953, in Beate Ruhm von Oppen, ed. Documents on Germany Under Occupation, 1945-1953, (New York: Oxford University Press, 1955), pp. 592-94 and related documents at pp. 488-90, 585-90, 597-98.

Paul Marer has estimated that East Germany's total reparation-type deliveries to the Soviet Union amounted to about $19 billion during the first eight years after the war—from one-fifth to one-third of East Germany's GNP for these years. See his "Soviet Economic Policy in Eastern Europe," in Reorientation and Commercial Relations of the Economies of Eastern Europe, a Compendium of Papers submitted to the Joint Economic Committee, U.S. Congress (Washington, D.C.: Government Printing Office, 1974), p. 139.

CHAPTER

2

DID THE UNITED STATES USE ATOMIC DIPLOMACY AGAINST RUSSIA IN 1945?

Thomas T. Hammond

> I do not consider the atom bomb such a serious force as some statesmen are inclined to. Atom bombs are designed to frighten those with weak nerves, but they cannot decide the outcome of wars because for this there definitely are not enough atom bombs. Of course monopoly possession of the secret of the atom bomb constitutes a threat, but against this there are, in any case, two remedies: (a) the monopoly possession of the atom bomb cannot last long; (b) use of the atom bomb will be outlawed.
>
> Joseph Stalin, September, 1946.

> The atom bomb is a paper tiger which the U.S. reactionaries use to scare people. It looks terrible, but in fact it isn't.
>
> Mao Tse-tung, August, 1946.

The cold war has produced yet another war—a war among historians, a war over the question of who is to blame for bringing about the hostility that characterized Soviet-American relations after World War II. Scholars and journalists have divided into two camps: The orthodox writers argue that the cold war was caused mainly, or entirely, by the Russians, especially Stalin, while the revisionists

---

The author wishes to express his appreciation to George F. Kennan, Arthur Schlesinger, Jr., Cyril E. Black, Robert H. Ferrell,

contend that the guilt belongs to the West, particularly the United States and its president, Harry Truman. This battle of the books has been steadily escalating during the past decade, with a new barrage of publications appearing almost every week. Historians have loaded their fountain pens, manned their typewriters, shot off books at one another, and attempted to wipe out the other side with volleys of atomic adjectives, nuclear nouns, devastating details, fissionable footnotes, explosive explanations, and thermonuclear theories.

The war goes on with no peace in sight and with no clear indication as to which side will emerge victorious. Initially the orthodox forces dominated the field of battle almost without challenge. But in the 1960s the revisionists began an all-out assault and in the years since then they have won more and more recruits. The generals in the orthodox camp have usually scorned the revisionists and refused to engage them in direct conflict, assuming that the correctness of the orthodox cause would eventually be obvious to all except a few fanatics. Meanwhile, the revisionists have attacked one orthodox position after another, have won increasing respectability, and have converted a growing number of supporters to their ranks. Even some of those who are generally orthodox in viewpoint have at times accepted revisionist arguments uncritically, without subjecting them to careful examination.

A case in point is the book by Gar Alperovitz, *Atomic Diplomacy: Hiroshima and Potsdam; The Use of the Atomic Bomb and the American Confrontation with Soviet Power*.[1] Despite fundamental deficiencies, this book received many laudatory reviews, has been widely used in college courses, is quoted in several collections of readings on the cold war, and is still cited with approval by numerous writers. It has been praised not only by revisionists but also by others. Its theses are rather commonly accepted, and it is believed by many to be a work of superb scholarship. That it continues to be regarded with respect is demonstrated by the fact that as recently as October, 1974, *American Historical Review* published a review article which contained a vigorous attack on one of Alperovitz's detractors, but included not one word of criticism for Alperovitz.[2]

Robert J. Maddox, Charles Maier, Roy M. Melbourne, David Powell, Norman Graebner, Paul Gaston, Martin J. Sherwin, and William R. Tanner. Thanks are also due to Sharane Morgan and Debra Bryant for typing the manuscript, to John Kneebone and John Copely for research assistance, and to the Thomas Jefferson Center for Political Economy and the University of Virginia Research Committee for financial aid.

Yet despite the great impact of Atomic Diplomacy and despite its controversial interpretations, it has never been subjected to lengthy, detailed analysis. Robert James Maddox wrote a ten-page critique of Alperovitz's scholarship,[3] but no one, surprisingly, has made a careful examination of Alperovitz's theses. The present article attempts to do just that, while at the same time taking a new look at the whole question of atomic diplomacy in 1945, and employing new sources that have become available since Alperovitz's book was written.

Alperovitz's theses can be summarized as follows:

1. American foreign policy "shifted radically after Roosevelt's death." Truman quickly abandoned his predecessor's "conciliatory course" and adopted "a tough policy aimed at forcing Soviet acquiescence to American plans for Eastern and Central Europe" (p. 13).

2. Soon thereafter, however, Truman shifted to a "strategy of delayed showdown," postponing the confrontation with Russia until the atom bomb had been tested in New Mexico. Later he decided to delay the showdown until after the bomb had been publicly demonstrated on Japan.

3. Once the bombs had been used on Hiroshima and Nagasaki, Truman was ready for a showdown with Russia. He and Byrnes used "atomic diplomacy" in "a powerful foreign policy initiative aimed at reducing or eliminating Soviet influence from Europe" (p. 13).

4. These policies of the Truman administration helped bring about the Cold War.

I am skipping Alperovitz's thesis that the bombs were used to frighten the Russians because he does not take a firm stand on this issue himself. In Atomic Diplomacy, p. 14 , he says: "I believe more research and more information are needed to reach a conclusive understanding of why the atomic bomb was used." And on page 236 he says much the same thing.

On the positive side it can be said that Alperovitz made a valuable contribution by bringing to our attention the fact that the atom bomb influenced the thinking of American leaders in 1945, a point which had not been given sufficient attention by earlier writers. However, he tried to prove too much. Like most all-inclusive theories, Alperovitz's hypothesis is consumed by its own explanatory appetite. *

---

*For this felicitous expression I am indebted to Professor Martin J. Sherwin of Princeton University. Although Prof. Sherwin kindly gave assistance on this article, this does not imply that he agrees with its conclusions.

There are, as we shall see, several fundamental flaws in his argumentation, particularly in his contention that, encouraged by the bomb, Truman "aimed at reducing or eliminating Soviet influence from Europe."[4]

Alperovitz's book is like a three-act play with no third act. The first two acts build up to a great climax: Truman, Byrnes, and their colleagues are plotting to use the atom bomb in order to force their will on Stalin. Concealing their plans, they bide their time through the first two acts, waiting for the bomb to be finished. Just as soon as the bomb is ready, they will use atomic diplomacy to drive the Russians out of Central and Eastern Europe. But the third act comes and the showdown never takes place. The atomic bomb proves to be a dud.

The three acts of the Alperovitz drama can be labeled as follows, using the titles of chapters in his book: Act 1: "The Strategy of an Immediate Showdown," Act II: "The Strategy of a Delayed Showdown," Act III: "American Diplomacy Takes the Offensive." Let us now examine Act I.

ACT I: THE STRATEGY OF AN IMMEDIATE SHOWDOWN

One of the most widely debated issues about the cold war is the question of whether or not Truman reversed Roosevelt's policies toward Russia. Alperovitz is not only certain that Truman changed Roosevelt's conciliatory policy to a tough policy; he even fixes the precise date when a "strategy of an immediate showdown" was supposedly adopted. "The actual decision," he says, "was taken just before Molotov's meeting with the President on April 23."[5]

The immediate showdown strategy as Alperovitz sees it, was implemented in the following weeks in several ways. First of all, Truman talked tough to Molotov. Second, Truman made unwarranted demands regarding the reorganization of the Polish government.[6] Third, he attempted to exert economic pressure on Russia by ordering an abrupt cutback in Lend-Lease.[7] And fourth, he tried to force concessions from Stalin by refusing to withdraw American troops from the Soviet zone of occupation in Germany.[8]

Alperovitz does not say that these four moves by Truman or the policy of "immediate showdown" itself were prompted by his knowledge that he would soon have the atom bomb. In fact, Alperovitz points out that before Roosevelt died several of his top advisers had already come to the conclusion that a firm policy toward Russia should be adopted.[9] Hence these moves in the "immediate showdown" do not fall under the scope of "atomic diplomacy," and the present author does not feel it necessary to comment on them. This does not, however, imply agreement with Alperovitz's specific charges or with his general contention that American policy toward Russia "shifted radically after Roosevelt's death."

While the "immediate showdown strategy" was supposedly being carried out, what were the thoughts of the top American leaders about the future use of atomic diplomacy against the Russians? As Alperovitz admits, "there is very little direct evidence available regarding Truman's personal view of the atomic bomb during April and May."[10] There is a bit of information about the views of James F. Byrnes during this period, however. In May Byrnes had a conversation with Leo Szilard, the atomic scientist, who reported it as follows: "Byrnes was concerned about Russia's having taken over Poland, Rumania and Hungary, and so was I. Byrnes thought that the possession of the bomb by America would render the Russians more manageable in Europe."[11]

Meanwhile, according to Alperovitz, by early May "the immediate showdown strategy had reached an impasse. . . . With Stalin failing to respond to increased pressure, American policy makers had to consider their course of action."[12] In Alperovitz's view, the failure of the immediate showdown made Truman receptive to a different strategy which Stimson recommended, and which Truman supposedly adopted—the strategy of a delayed showdown.[13]

ACT II: THE STRATEGY OF A DELAYED SHOWDOWN

As has been shown, Alperovitz is able to cite several events which, if interpreted a certain way, support the view that Truman instituted an immediate showdown during the first weeks of his administration. Soon, however, Alperovitz must face up to other instances where Truman gave in to Russian demands, made conciliatory moves, and refused to exploit opportunities to exert pressure on the Russians. How to explain these? How to interpret Truman's rejection of Churchill's plea that American forces liberate Prague before the Red Army? Or Truman's decision in June to withdraw American troops from the Soviet zone of Germany? Or Truman's move to send Harry Hopkins, the living symbol of Roosevelt's policies, to settle disputes with Stalin? And, finally, how to explain Truman's choice of Joseph E. Davies (of all people!) to discuss Russian matters with Churchill?

Alperovitz admits on page 272 that Truman made some "sudden conciliatory efforts after the showdown with Molotov." He supplies his explanation and the explanations of other writers on pages 272-75. Other conciliatory moves by Truman are described on pages 85-86.

Alperovitz might have concluded that, since Truman was new to the job and had little knowledge about world affairs, he had difficulty in deciding on fixed policies toward the USSR.

Professor Cyril E. Black of Princeton made the following comments in a letter to the author dated February 27, 1974:

> Policy in the last months of the war develped in response to immediate crises rather than as part of a long-term plan. . . . It is a mistake to look too closely for general policies and clear thinking. They didn't exist. It was a matter of pragmatically working out policies on a day-to-day basis, with no great sense at all of political support on the part of the public for any policy except a return to prewar normalcy in the U.S. . . .We never had a policy in 1945 of opposing a Soviet sphere of influence in Eastern Europe—a policy in the sense of allocating resources . . . or taking risks to this end, despite all the bluster.

Black was an Auxiliary Foreign Service Officer in the State Department during World War II, served in Bulgaria in 1944-45, visited Rumania, Russia, and Bulgaria as a member of the Ethridge Mission from October to December, 1945, and was an Advisor to the U.S. Delegation of the U.N. Commission Concerning Greek Frontier Incidents in 1947.

But Alperovitz evidently is convinced that Truman was antagonistic toward the Soviet Union from beginning to end. How then can he explain the fact that on a number of occasions Truman made concessions and demonstrated an eagerness to reach agreements with the Soviets? To solve this problem, Alperovitz devised the theory of the "delayed showdown." According to this theory, Stimson pointed out to Truman that, after the atom bomb was completed, the United States would be in a much stronger bargaining position. As Stimson put it in his diary, "We shall probably hold more cards in our hands later than now."[14] So, says Alperovitz, Truman adopted a "strategy of delay," postponing "any confrontation with the Russians until the atomic bomb had been proved and demonstrated."[15]

Here Alperovitz seems to have relied too much on his imagination. Even if Stimson had favored a policy of delayed showdown, there is no proof either that he advised the President to adopt such a policy or that Truman adopted it. Alperovitz admits on one page that "we do not have precise information on the exact date on which Stimson advised the President to postpone diplomatic confrontations with the Russians."[16] But on another page he asserts that "all the evidence suggests that the April 25 meeting was the crucial date on which Truman accepted Stimson's line of advice."[17] No evidence is supplied, however. The only accounts of this meeting (by Truman, Stimson, and General Leslie R. Groves) say nothing at all about a strategy of a delayed showdown or anything remotely similar. In fact, Stimson opposed any showdown with Russia at all, then or later.[18]

Not only is there lack of evidence that Truman adopted a policy of "delayed showdown," there is considerable evidence that he did not. If Truman had wanted to postpone decisions in Eastern Europe until the bomb had been demonstrated, he would have done this especially in regard to Poland, the most important country in the area. Instead Truman did just the opposite. He sent Harry Hopkins to Moscow, and Hopkins finally disposed of the Polish dispute by acceding to Stalin's demands.* This agreement left Poland firmly in Communist hands. In spite of this, Truman established diplomatic relations with the Polish government on July 5.[19]

For Alperovitz the Polish accord poses a problem because it is in obvious conflict with his theory of the "strategy of delay." Alperovitz attempts to solve this problem by saying that Truman viewed the Hopkins agreement as only a temporary accommodation:

> The President and his advisers regarded Hopkins's diplomacy as a delaying action, not a defeat. It matters little that the strategy eventually failed. What is important is that in the thinking of American policy makers final determination of the Polish issue and of other problems in Eastern and Central Europe depended upon the results of the atomic test. An early showdown had failed, but a later one—if necessary—would probably succeed.[20]

Unfortunately for Alperovitz's theory the later showdown never took place. After dropping the atom bombs, Truman made no effort to reverse the Hopkins agreement on Poland.

ALAMOGORDO AND POTSDAM

It may be that Truman postponed Potsdam in the hope that by the time he met with Stalin and Churchill he would know the results of the bomb test at Alamogordo. Truman told both Stimson and Davies

---

*In Atomic Diplomacy, p. 141, Alperovitz admits that "Hopkins had yielded on the Polish question." And on page 230 he says that Truman "was forced to yield the substance of the point at issue in the Polish controversy."

that he had delayed Potsdam because of the test, but he told others who knew about the bomb that the delay was for other reasons.[21] At any rate, on the eve of Potsdam we find a statement by Truman which seems to indicate that he expected the bomb to strengthen his bargaining position with Russia: "If it explodes, as I think it will," he said, "I'll certainly have a hammer on those boys." Alperovitz uses the quotation without any qualification, the implication being that "those boys" meant the Russians and only the Russians. But when one checks the original source, Jonathan Daniels' biography of Truman, he finds that the succeeding sentence (omitted by Alperovitz) reads as follows: "He [Truman] seemed to be referring not merely to the still unconquered Japs but to the Russians with whom he was having difficulty in shaping a colloboration for lasting peace."[22] So the object of Truman's hammer is ambiguous; he probably had in mind the Russians as well as the Japanese, but we cannot be certain.

On July 16, the day before the formal opening of the Potsdam Conference, the first atomic device was tested in Alamogordo, and Stimson immediately informed the President. Five days later Stimson read Truman a detailed report from General Groves. According to Stimson, "The President was tremendously pepped up by it [the report of the successful test] and spoke to me of it again and again when I saw him. He said it gave him an entirely new feeling of confidence."[23] Alperovitz claims that Truman was "pepped up" because now he would be able to use atomic diplomacy against Russia in Eastern Europe. As Alperovitz puts it, "Thus, the first effect of the atomic bomb was a simple, yet profoundly important one—it confirmed the President's belief that he would have enough power to reverse Roosevelt's policy and attempt actively to influence events in the Soviet sphere of influence."[24]

It is easy to believe that Truman was "pepped up," but there may have been many reasons other than a desire to reverse Roosevelt's policies in Eastern Europe. First of all, the bomb meant that the war with Japan could be ended more quickly. Second, Russian aid against Japan was no longer essential, and Truman would not have to make further concessions to the Russians to ensure their participation.[25] In addition, Western Europe could be defended from Russian domination even if American troops were withdrawn. * Furthermore, unreasonable demands by Stalin in other areas could be resisted. The bomb would serve as an "equalizer," counter balancing the huge Red Army. As Stimson expressed it,

---

*The American leaders were worried that if they recognized a Soviet sphere of influence in Eastern Europe, this might encourage Stalin to extend it further, into Western Europe, the Mediterranean,

> The news from Alamogordo . . . made it clear to the Americans that further diplomatic efforts to bring the Russians into the Pacific war were largely pointless. . . .
>
> The Russians at Potsdam were not acting in a manner calculated to increase the confidence of the Americans or the British in their future intentions. Stalin expressed a vigorous and disturbing interest in securing bases in the Mediterranean and other areas wholly outside the sphere of normal Russian national interest, while Russian insistence on de facto control of Central Europe hardly squared with the principles of the Atlantic Charter. . . . These extravagant demands were backed by the Red Army, which was daily increasing in its relative strength in Europe, as the Americans began their redeployment for the Pacific attack. Naturally, therefore, news of the atomic bomb was received in Potsdam with great and unconcealed satisfaction by Anglo-American leaders. At first blush it appeared to give democratic diplomacy a badly needed "equalizer."[26]

It has been said that after Truman got the news of the bomb test he not only was "pepped up" by it but that the next day he "bossed" the meeting of the Big Three. This view was expressed by Churchill, as reported by Stimson in his diary.[27] The American and Russian records of that meeting do not, however, confirm Churchill's account; Truman clearly talked less at that session that either Stalin or Churchill, and he certainly did not "boss" it.[28] Herbert Feis's description of Truman's behavior at Potsdam seems correct.

> His knowledge that the bomb had been tested did make Truman firmer in his refusal to cede some of the more grasping Soviet claims at Potsdam and after. But the American Government did not change its policies or expand its claims because it had acquired the bomb; it faithfully followed the course defined by officials who had known nothing about the bomb until it was exploded on Hiroshima.[29]

---

and the Middle East. See Philip E. Mosely, The Kremlin and World Politics (New York: Random House, 1960), pp. 194-95; U.S. Department of State, Foreign Relations of the United States, 1945: The Conference of Berlin 4, pp. 407-08, and 5, p. 637.

The records of the Potsdam Conference also indicate that the United States did not follow a hard line on Eastern Europe. As one scholar put it,

> Allied conflict over the political future of Rumania, Bulgaria, and Hungary was clearly not resolved during the Potsdam discussions. None of the governments showed any willingness to back down. . . .
>
> Given the impossibility of resolving the conflict, Secretary Byrnes undertook to prevent a public break. He systematically withdrew all recommendations for implementation of the principles of the Declaration on Liberated Europe to which the Soviet Union objected. He finessed every issue on which the possibility of a break existed. . . . American officials at Potsdam did not sustain pressure for Allied supervision of the holding of free elections. . . . The Declaration on Liberated Europe was not even mentioned in the final Potsdam communique.[30]

How does Alperovitz explain the failure of the Americans to take a tough stand on the Balkans, even after the atomic test? And why didn't they use atomic diplomacy at Potsdam? This would be the first (and last) meeting of Truman with Stalin; if ever there was an opportune moment for atomic diplomacy, this was it. Churchill wanted to use atomic diplomacy at Potsdam.[31] If Truman had been planning to use atomic diplomacy, he would have announced the results of the Alamogordo test with great fanfare, would have provided Stalin with all of the frightening details and then, with the Russian leader sufficiently intimidated, would have proceeded to dictate American terms.

Truman, of course, did just the opposite. He carefully concealed the Alamogordo test from public view. Then he waited eight days and "casually mentioned to Stalin" that the United States "had a new weapon of unusual destructive force," but gave no details and did not reveal that it was an atomic weapon.[32] The opportunity to use atomic diplomacy was completely by-passed. Why this behavior? Because Truman wanted to keep the secret of the bomb's manufacture safely in his hands until an international committee of control could be set up. Truman and Stimson were concerned that at Potsdam Stalin might demand information on how the bomb was produced; if he did, it would be awkward to refuse an ally.[33]

How does Alperovitz explain the failure of the Americans to use atomic diplomacy at Potsdam? Once again his imagination has full play. Whereas earlier he said that the American leaders had decided to delay the showdown with the Russians until a bomb had been tested,* now he says that they had decided to delay the showdown until a bomb had been dropped on Japan. According to Alperovitz, this decision was made in a conversation between Stimson and Truman on June 6:

> In the first week of June, Stimson advised that mere knowledge of the success of the atomic test would not be enough to influence the power realities; it would first be necessary to publicly demonstrate the weapon by "laying it on Japan" before Stalin could be expected to be greatly impressed. If the heads-of-government meeting took place before the battle demonstration there would be "the greatest complication."
>
> Truman's agreement with this new recommendation had profoundly ironic complications. . . . By the end of June it was certain that the bomb would not be "laid on Japan" until early August. Thus, Truman's twice-postponed meeting still would occur a few weeks too early for the atomic bomb to strengthen his diplomatic hand. . . .
>
> The President now had no alternative but to go ahead with the arrangements for a mid-July heads-of-government conference. But it was clear that he could not yet press his diplomatic demands to a showdown. Ironically, the logic of his position ensured that the much heralded confrontation with Stalin could only be a <u>modified continuation of the strategy of delay</u>![34]

Almost every sentence in this statement is fallacious. It is based on gross distortions of Stimson's diary for June 6. It is not true, as Alperovitz claims, that "Stimson advised that mere knowledge of the success of the atomic test would not be enough to influence power

---

*In <u>Atomic Diplomacy</u>, p. 57, Alperovitz says "The key to the Secretary's [Stimson's] view was a consistent judgment . . . that the atomic bomb would add great power to American diplomacy once it was developed. . . . He believed it 'premature' for the United States to raise diplomatic issues in the Far East until the bomb had been tested." On page 59 he says "The Secretary advised that a heads-of-government meeting be delayed until the atomic bomb had been tested early in July."

realities." He said nothing remotely similar to that. Nor did he say that "it would first be necessary to publicly demonstrate the weapon by 'laying it on Japan' before Stalin could be expected to be greatly impressed." Stimson said nothing about Stalin or about publicly demonstrating the bomb. Nor did Stimson say that "if the heads-of-government meeting took place before the battle demonstration there would be 'the greatest complication.' "[35]

Alperovitz says that "by the end of June it was certain that the bomb would not be 'laid on Japan' until early August," and here he is right. But it does not follow, as he claims, that Potsdam still would "occur a few weeks too early for the atomic bomb to strengthen his [Truman's] diplomatic hand." As indicated above, Truman could have used the Alamogordo test to strengthen his hand at Potsdam if atomic diplomacy had been part of his plans. If Truman had really been intent on frightening Stalin, he could have invited Soviet observers to the New Mexico test, as General Marshall had suggested.[36] There they would have seen the explosion first-hand, whereas no Russians witnessed the dropping of the bombs on Japan. And if atomic diplomacy based on Alamogordo didn't work, it still could have been used after the bombing of Hiroshim and Nagasaki.

To summarize, Alperovitz's theory of the "modified continuation of the strategy of delay" seems to be based on a wholesale misreading of Stimson's diary. Like the "strategy of delay" itself, it appears to be a product of Alperovitz's imagination.

ACT III: AMERICAN DIPLOMACY TAKES THE OFFENSIVE

The bombings of Hiroshima and Nagasaki brings us to Act III. If it were true, as Alperovitz contends, that Truman hoped "to force Soviet withdrawal from Eastern Europe,"[37] one would no expect to find him making demands along this line. Once the atom bomb had been publicly demonstrated, one might expect to find the Russians pulling their armies out of Eastern Europe and allowing the Communist-dominated governments to be removed. According to Alperovitz, this is precisely what Truman tried to bring about.

In fact Truman's objectives were considerably more limited. Apparently he and Byrnes were greatly encouraged by the success of the bomb and hoped that now they could get the Russians to live up to the Yalta Declaration on Liberated Europe. But they did not aim at "eliminating Soviet influence from Europe" (to use Alperovitz's phrase); instead they merely tried to prevent this area from falling 100 percent under Soviet influence.[38]

Alperovitz claims that the aims of the United States and Great Britain were much more ambitious. He describes Western policies toward Eastern Europe after Hiroshima as an "Anglo-American diplomatic offensive," an "Anglo-American assault," and "a campaign of dirct intervention in the internal politics of Hungary, Bulgaria, and Rumania."[39] According to him, the first step in this offensive came on August 9, when Truman publicly declared that Bulgaria, Hungary, and Rumania "are not to be spheres of influence of any one power." Alperovitz maintains that this declaration was one of the key events in the start of the Cold War.

> This statement of American opposition to Soviet domination of the Balkans was of major political significance. Here was the first open and public break in the wartime alliance. And immediately the President and his Secretary of State demonstrated that the declaration meant what it said: The United States demanded that the government subservient to Soviet influence be removed.[40]

From Alperovitz one gets the impression that Truman made a major declaration devoted solely to Eastern Europe, but it turns out that he delivered a "Radio Report to the American People on the Potsdam Conference," a speech eleven and one-half pages long, with only two short paragraphs, on page eight, devoted to the Balkans. The section of Truman's address from which Alperovitz picked his quotation reads as follows:

> At Yalta it was agreed . . . that the three governments would assume a common responsibility in helping to reestablish in the liberated and satellite nations of Europe governments broadly representative of democratic elements in the population. That responsibility still stands. We all recognize it as a joint responsibility of the three governments.
>
> It was reaffirmed in the Berlin Declarations on Rumania, Bulgaria, and Hungary. These nations are not to be spheres of influence of any one power. . . . Until these states are reestablished as members of the international family, they are the joint concern of all of us.[41]

The only part of this quotation that was new or "tough" was the sentence that reads "These nations are not to be spheres of influence of any one power." But other parts of the speech gave the impression that Soviet-American relations were most cordial. Truman said that "it was easy for me to get along in mutual understanding and friendship with Generalissimo Stalin. . . . There was a fundamental accord and agreement upon the objectives ahead of us." And he closed with these stirring words: "The Three Great Powers are now more closely than ever bound together in determination to achieve . . . peace. . . . We shall continue to march together to a lasting peace and a happy world!"[42]

Still the sentence declaring that Rumania, Bulgaria, and Hungary "are not to be spheres of influence of any one power" would have had great importance if it had been followed by concrete action to implement such a policy. But such was not the case. Maynard B. Barnes, the U.S. political representative in Bulgaria, summed up the situation accurately in a telegram to the Secretary of State:

> No one could be more delighted with or convinced by such evidence of power of the US as the President's radio speech on Berlin Conference than General Crane and myself. . . . To the skeptical Balkan mind, and . . . for Russians, something more concrete than words—even the words of President of the US—is necessary to be convincing.[43]

As we shall see, it was precisely the failure of the United States to follow up Truman's speech with "something more concrete than words" that robbed the speech of any significance for the Balkans.

So much for the first step in the "Anglo-American diplomatic offensive." What about Western actions in specific countries?

Alperovitz devotes only one paragraph to the "offensive" in Hungary, so we can skip that subject. The Soviets permitted free elections in Hungary in 1945, and the Western powers had relatively little to complain about at that time.

BULGARIA

Here is Alperovitz's account of the supposed beginning of atomic diplomacy in Bulgaria:

> Truman's need to wait for the atomic bomb had complicated the problems he faced in Bulgaria.
>
> To make up for his own delay, therefore, the President first had to attempt to postpone the Bulgarian election to allow time for serious campaigning. . . . Four days after Nagasaki, Secretary Byrnes moved speedily to the task, forcefully unveiling the full

extent of the American demands. . . . On August 13, Byrnes sent an open letter to Prime Minister Georgiev. He demanded that the elections scheduled for August 26—now less than two weeks off—be postponed. Byrnes also gave notice that the United States would not recognize the Bulgarian government until it had been radically reorganized.[44]

This argument is full of inaccuracies. First, Byrnes' letter was sent on August 18th, not the 13th. Second, Byrnes did not "demand that the elections . . . be postponed." Third, he acted not "speedily" but slowly; if he had waited much longer, the elections would have been over. Fourth, Byrnes acted not "forcefully" but weakly; he did about the least he could have under the circumstances. Fifth, Byrnes did not ask that the Bulgarian government be "radically reorganized."[45] Alperovitz gives the impression that Byrnes, emboldened by the success of the atom bombs on Japan, put forward new and sweeping demands regarding Bulgaria. In fact, Byrnes simply restated what he and Truman had said at Potsdam and on other occasions—that the United States would not recognize the Bulgarian government until free elections had been held.

Byrnes' statement had no apparent effect, so further steps were taken by Maynard Barnes and by the U.S. representative on the Allied Control Council (ACC), General John A. Crane. Without approval from Washington, Barnes asked Crane to tell the Soviet chairman of the ACC that the United States and Great Britain wanted the elections to be postponed, which Crane did on August 23.[46] This brought Barnes an immediate reprimand from Secretary Byrnes:

> Dept is not making representations to Moscow nor can it support your actions in requesting Gen Crane to make the communications to the Chairman ACC. . . .
>
> . . . before taking further steps Dept should have been consulted. The views expressed in Deptel 260, August 18 did not contemplate our making specific request for postponement of elections and Dept has consistently felt the formation of a representative democratic Government in Bulgaria is matter for Bulgarians to undertake.[47]

But the request by General Crane had already been made and, surprisingly, it produced results. Stalin personally telephoned the

Soviet commander-in-chief in Bulgaria and told the astonished general that the elections should be postponed.* Byrnes did not gloat over this Soviet retreat; instead he tried to help the Russians save face. On August 25 he issued the following press release:

> I am gratified to learn that the Bulgarian Government has announced the postponement of the national elections originally scheduled for August 26.
>
> It is especially gratifying to me that the representatives in Sofia of the Soviet Union, British and United States Governments were unanimously in accord with the decision of the Bulgarian Government. This is a striking demonstration of the unity of purpose of the three nations to work together to assist the liberated peoples of Europe in the establishment of democratic governments of their own choice.[48]

With Byrnes insisting upon a policy of "great caution," the interventions made earlier by Barnes, Crane, and the British had no long-run effect. The Communists continued to use terror against the opposition, and it soon became clear that the November elections would not be free. The United States proposed that they be postponed once more, but this time the Communists refused. So the elections were held on November 18.

According to Alperovitz, the cancellation of the August elections "could only be attributed to the atomic bomb."[49] But if Stalin succumbed to atomic diplomacy in connection with the August elections, why did he fail to do so with the November elections? Alperovitz says that "the failure" to change the Bulgarian government seemed a sign that the diplomatic offensive which had scored so brilliantly might be losing its force."[50] But why atomic diplomacy should lose its force so quickly he does not explain.

Cyril E. Black, who was a State Department officer in Bulgaria in 1944-45, casts further doubt on the use of atomic diplomacy in that country.

---

*Malcolm Mackintosh, who was present when this took place, has described it in Thomas T. Hammond, ed., The Anatomy of Communist Takeovers (New Haven, Conn.: Yale University Press, 1975), pp. 239-40 . The Soviet major who first answered the telephone was so startled to hear Stalin's voice that he was unable to speak!

> The atom bomb played no role at all in the Balkans in 1945 to the best of my knowledge. It was never mentioned. The Russians ordered the Bulgarians to postpone the election in August, 1945, because they wished to have U.S. recognition of Bulgaria. The only bargaining power we used was the threat of withholding recognition. . . . Byrnes and Truman did not take a firm stand with the Russians on the Balkans.[51]

Alperovitz ends his account of Bulgaria with the November elections, which means that he fails to describe how atomic diplomacy, if it was ever used there at all (which is doubtful), was quickly abandoned. At the Moscow Conference in December, 1945, Byrnes made a deal with Stalin: the United States would grant diplomatic recognition to Bulgaria if two democratic leaders were given posts in the cabinet.[52] Stalin promised to "advise" the Bulgarian government to admit two non-Communists, but when the Bulgarians worked out an agreement along these lines, he vetoed it, and no democratization of the Bulgarian government ever took place.[53] Nor were free elections ever held. Thus the net effect of Alperovitz's "atomic diplomacy" in Bulgaria was zero.

RUMANIA

In Rumania, as in Bulgaria, one finds no evidence that Truman and Byrnes adopted a "tough" line designed to eliminate Soviet influence. In March 1945, King Michael had been forced by the Soviets to approve a Communist-dominated government, headed by Petru Groza. Early in August, however, the final communique of the Potsdam Conference gave Michael grounds for hope that the Groza regime would finally be removed. The communique said that peace treaties would be signed with "recognized democratic governments," which seemed to imply that no such treaty could be signed by Rumania until its government had been approved by America and Great Britain.[54] Michael therefore demanded that Groza resign and appealed to the Soviet, American, and British governments "to give their assistance with a view towards forming a government which . . . may be recognized by the three principal Allied Powers."[55]

The Soviets assumed that Michael's action was part of an American plot, but there seems to be no real evidence to support this view. Henry L. Roberts, who was an OSS officer in Rumania, says:

> As far as I know, American action in Rumania did not extend beyond informing King Michael that the Groza regime was unacceptable, a fact generally known, and indicating approval of measures taken to broaden it. The United States did not have, perhaps unfortunately, a positive, thought-out plan of action.[56]

Meanwhile, the Soviets gave Groza full support. With their encouragement he refused to resign, and when Michael went "on strike," Groza simply ruled without him. Byrnes, for his part, would not go beyond his earlier statements that the Groza government was unacceptable. He even ordered the American political representative to avoid any further contact with democratic leaders or the King.

> Principal concern of US Govt at present jucture is, as you know, to keep the road open to a solution of Rumanian political crisis which will be acceptable to all three Allied Govts. We hope no action will be taken which might seem to give ground for Soviet suspicion that crisis was brought about by "Anglo-American intervention." Contact with Rumanian political leaders should be avoided at present stage.
>
> In this connection we do not think that any advice or assurances should be given to the King regarding his present difficult position vis-a-vis Groza and Soviet officials or regarding contingencies which may arise with respect to his political future or personal position . . . though you may apprise him of this Govt's hope that measures which might further provoke Soviet officials will be avoided.[57]

The King, understandably, felt he had been deserted. As his biographer says:

> It appeared as though Britain and America, after encouraging him to defy Russia and create a deadlock, had abandoned him. . . . All the King knew was that not one official word of encouragement had come in answer to his appeal. It seemed to him that he was expected to stand alone and if need be fall alone, invoking the vaunted Four Freedoms while the great democracies watched apathetically.[58]

Thus Alperovitz's picture of Byrnes and Truman, intoxicated by atomic power, undertaking an "offensive" in Rumania does not hold up. Byrnes seems to have wanted Groza's removal only if it could be achieved in agreement with the Soviets, not by unilateral action against the Soviets.

The stalemate over the Rumanian government continued during the London meeting of the Council of Foreign Ministers, where Molotov again demanded that the United States grant recognition to the Groza regime, and Byrnes once more insisted on free elections.[59] Finally, at the Moscow Conference in December, 1945, Byrnes produced a compromise that abandoned democratic principles and gave the Russians what they wanted—complete domination of Rumania—while at the same time granting token representation to the non-Communist majority. Byrnes got Stalin to agree that "one member of the National Peasant Party and one member of the Liberal Party should be included in the Government"[60] Unlike his promise regarding Bulgaria, Stalin lived up to this agreement. Two members of the democratic opposition were admitted to the cabinet, and Truman granted diplomatic recognition on January 7, 1946. But the addition of two powerless ministers had no effect on Communist control of the country. To use George Kennan's expression, the Soviet concessions were merely "fig leaves of democratic procedure to hide the nakedness of Stalinist dictatorship."[61]

As with Bulgaria, the Truman administration apparently came to the conclusion that—despite the atom bomb—there was nothing the United States could do to prevent the establishment of a Communist dictatorship in Rumania. There is no real evidence that the atomic bomb played a role in Rumania. Certainly it is an exaggeration to say, as Alperovitz does, that Truman and Byrnes plotted to drive the Russians out of Rumania. During the first wave of enthusiasm following Alamogordo, the American leaders apparently thought that the atom bomb would frighten Stalin and make him eager to cooperate. Byrnes, for example, had predicted at Potsdam that "in the final analysis" the bomb "would control."[62] But Stalin apparently was not afraid of the bomb and refused to relax his domination over Rumania. Faced by Stalin's recalcitrance, Byrnes gave up and abandoned Rumania as a hopeless cause.

THE LONDON CONFERENCE

This brings us to the final scene of Act III—Secretary of State Byrnes setting off for London in September 1945, for the first meeting of the Council of Foreign Ministers. Alperovitz sets the stage for the meeting by quoting the most incriminating statement made by any member of the Truman administration on atomic diplomacy.

> Now, in late August, as Byrnes prepared for his meeting in London, the Secretary of State made it clear that the bomb continued to play a predominant role in his calculations. In a long discussion with Byrnes, Assistant Secretary of War McCloy found him "quite radically opposed to any approach to Stalin whatever" to attempt to establish international control of atomic energy—"He was on the point of departing for the foreign ministers' meeting and wished to have the implied threat of the bomb in his pocket during the conference."[63]

The London meeting would presumably provide Byrnes with a wonderful opportunity to practice atomic diplomacy. Since this was the first Allied get-together after the dropping of the bombs on Japan, one would expect Alperovitz to discuss the meeting in great detail, explaining how Byrnes used atomic diplomacy on the Russians and attempted to force them out of Eastern Europe.

Yet, surprisingly, Alperovitz ends his account at precisely this point. He doesn't describe the London conference. What logically could have been the scene of the greatest triumphs of atomic diplomacy is almost completely ignored. The reason is obvious—there were no triumphs. Byrnes may have had "the implied threat of the bomb in his pocket during the conference," but either he didn't try to use it, or he didn't know how to use it, or it didn't work.

At the conference Molotov showed no signs of being frightened by the bomb; indeed, he was even more difficult than usual. He rejected all compromises and seemed to go out of his way to treat the bomb as a joke. At a reception he offered a toast: "Here's to the Atom Bomb," and added, "We've got it."[64] In a conversation with Stettinius shortly before the conference ended, Byrnes said that he had expected Molotov to ask the United States to share the secret of the bomb. Stettinius reports Byrnes' comments as follows:

> In view of the way the Russians were behaving now, as emphasized in this Council of Foreign Ministers, he [Byrnes] would be opposed to giving the secret to anybody at the present time. He thought Molotov would have raised the matter here in these talks but he had not. If he had raised the question of the atomic bomb, Byrnes would have said to Molotov that General Marshall had tried on many occasions during this War to exchange military secrets with Russia and Russia had always refused.[65]

Byrnes had counted on the "implied threat of the bomb" to make the Russians more "manageable." Instead he found them more obstreperous than ever. A "new Russia," he told Stettinius, was taking an unreasonable and aggressive stance.

> Secretary Byrnes told me generally the state of affairs he was faced with in the Council of Foreign Ministers. They were at a deadlock on most everything they discussed. They were getting nowhere and it was most discouraging. . . .
>
> Secretary Byrnes then stated there was no question but that we were facing a new Russia, totally different than the Russia we dealt with a year ago. As long as they needed us in the War and we were giving them supplies we had a satisfactory relationship but now that the War was over they were taking an aggressive attitude and stand on political and territorial questions that was indefensible.[66]

Despite the fiasco at London, Byrnes was still determined to negotiate a settlement with the Russians on Eastern Europe. Soon after his return from London, he told Joe Davies that the United States had already made compromises on Finland, Poland, and Hungary, and that he would attempt to make similar compromises on Rumania and Bulgaria.[67] This is precisely what he did. In December Byrnes journeyed to Moscow and worked out a deal with Stalin whereby the United States made some pro forma (but meaningless) concessions to Russian demands for a role in the governing of Japan, while Stalin in return made some pro forma (but meaningless) concessions to Western demands that the governments in Bulgaria and Rumania be democratized. This was old-fashioned bargaining, not atomic diplomacy. Instead of a policy "aimed at forcing the Russians to yield in Eastern Europe,"[68] this was a policy of the Americans yielding in Eastern Europe.

DID THE UNITED STATES USE ATOMIC DIPLOMACY?

As indicated above, there were three ways in which atomic diplomacy could have been practiced against Russia: (1) as an explicit threat, (2) as an implied threat, and (3) as a bargaining chip.

As has been noted, there seems to be no evidence that an explicit threat was used. The atom bomb, precisely because it was so powerful, was useless—useless, that is, except in the most desperate circumstances, when national survival itself was threatened. And no crisis so far has been considered that serious. As Louis J. Halle remarked, "one does not use a hand-grenade to kill mosquitoes."[69] The Russians saw this as clearly as the Americans did. Any explicit threat by Truman to use the bomb over Eastern Europe would have lacked credibility because the Russians knew that the United States did not have a vital interest in that area. The establishment of Communist regimes in Eastern Europe was, from the American point of view, undesirable, but it was not worth going to war over.

What about use of the bomb as an implied threat? Actually, the bomb was an implied threat whether the Americans consciously used it in that way or not. The United States had the bomb, the Russians knew it, and that made it a threat regardless. The only way in which the Americans could have prevented it from being an implied threat would have been to share their atomic secrets, and their bombs, on an equal basis.

To argue that Truman should have done this, however, is to overlook the fact that the Red Army was also an implied theat. With the rapid withdrawal of American forces, Western Europe was left at the mercy of the Soviet military machine—except for the bomb. The American bomb and the Soviet army tended to counterbalance one another: if the United States had bombed Russia, the Red Army could have retaliated by occupying Western Europe; while if Russia had invaded Western Europe, the United States could have retaliated by dropping atom bombs on Russia. As Stephen Ambrose has noted, "the Red Army was just as effective a deterrent as the atomic bomb."[70]

Most Americans who had dealt with the Russians considered them difficult and unreasonable and it was hoped that the bomb would make them less so. It did not, however. The probable reason was summed up by Leo Szilard in describing a conversation with Byrnes.

> Byrnes was concerned about Russia's having taken over Poland, Rumania and Hungary, and so was I. Byrnes thought that the possession of the bomb by America would render the Russians more manageable in Europe. I failed to see how sitting on a stockpile of bombs, <u>which in the circumstances we could not possibly use</u>, would have this effect, and I thought it even conceivable that it would have just the opposite effect.[71]

Szilard was right. Molotov presumably knew, as Szilard had, that the United States could not use the bombs against Russia, so the implied threat did not work at London, or anywhere else.

This is not to say that the atom bomb had no influence at all on American foreign policy. Apparently it gave Truman at Potsdam "an entirely new feeling of confidence." It encouraged him to resist such "extravagant demands" by the Russians as "bases in the Mediterranean and other areas wholly outside the sphere of normal Russian national interest."[72] It probably gave him renewed determination to try to get the Soviets to abide by the terms of the Yalta agreements. And Byrnes went to London with the deliberate intention of using the "implied threat of the bomb" to improve his bargaining position with Molotov. In general the American leaders believed that the bomb would make the Russians easier to deal with.

Since American possession of the bomb made it an implied threat in any case, the key question is what the Truman administration tried to obtain with this implied threat. This is where Alperovitz makes his biggest mistake, since he insists that the bomb brought about a fundamental change in American objectives. Over and over again he argues that, armed with the bomb, Truman & Co. attempted to drive Russia out of Eastern Europe. For example, he says that

> far from following his predecessor's policy of co-operation, shortly after taking office Truman launched a powerful foreign policy initiative aimed at reducing or eliminating Soviet influence from Europe. . . . I believe new evidence proves not only that the atomic bomb influenced diplomacy, but that it determined much of Truman's shift to a tough policy aimed at forcing Soviet acquiescence to American plans for Eastern and Central Europe.[73]

Elsewhere he says

> Byrnes had been quite explicit; his policy always aimed at forcing the Russians to yield in Eastern Europe, and in mid-1947 he still continued to argue that the United States had it in its power to force the Russians to "retire in a very decent manner."[74]

And on the next page he refers to "the attempt to force Soviet withdrawal from Eastern Europe."[75]

Undoubtedly Truman and Byrnes would have been pleased to see the Soviets withdraw from Eastern Europe, but there is no evidence that they undertook such an ambitious goal or that they believed such a goal was obtainable, even with the atom bomb. Their aims were much more modest. Truman and Byrnes did not change the objectives of their foreign policy because of the bomb. Rather for a few months they pursued with greater confidence and determination the objectives that they (and Roosevelt) had earlier decided upon. They did not attempt to roll back Soviet power, but rather to contain it. They did not try to get Russia to give in to new demands but rather to live up to old agreements. And not even full compliance with old agreements was asked for. Token compliance with the Declaration on Liberated Europe—enough to satisfy American public opinion—was all that was required. And when even this was not granted in some countries, they settled for less.

Far from attempting to "eliminate" Soviet influence from Eastern Europe, the United States accepted Soviet dominant influence, while attempting to retain some minimum American influence. For example, one of the briefing papers for Potsdam read as follows:

> While this Government may not want to oppose a political configuration in Eastern Europe which gives the Soviet Union a predominant influence in Poland, neither would it desire to see Poland become in fact a Soviet satellite and have American influence there completely eliminated.[76]

By the end of 1945 it became clear that Stalin intended to have American influence "completely eliminated" from those countries occupied by the Red Army, and the United States, realizing it could do nothing about it short of war, gave in.

What about the third possible form of atomic diplomacy—did the United States ever use the bomb as a bargaining chip, asking that Russia make concessions in return for atomic secrets? In June 1945, Stimson and Truman discussed the possibility that Russia be offered partnership on an international committee to control atomic weapons in return for "settlement of the Polish, Rumanian, Yugoslavian, and Manchurian problems."[77] Apparently no such proposal was ever made to the Russians, however. Suffice it to say that there was talk in Washington about using the bomb as a bargaining chip, but it remained just talk.

CONCLUSIONS

Like most books which offer a new, dramatic thesis, Atomic Diplomacy has attracted considerable attention, and it has won numerous supporters at a time when Americans are more inclined than usual to be critical of their country's foreign policy. As Samuel L. Sharp said, "it is a bad book, written at the right time." It simply does not stand up under careful analysis. Its main theses are either implausible, exaggerated, or unsupported by the evidence. The chief contribution of the book was to draw our attention to the fact that for a few months in 1945 Byrnes, Stimson, and Truman hoped that possession of the bomb would improve their bargaining position with the Soviets. But by exaggerating the effect of the bomb on American policy the book has misled many unsuspecting readers into believing that atomic diplomacy played a much more important role in 1945 than was the case. All things considered, the book ought to have had a different title, maybe something like Atomic Diplomacy: How America Made a Half-hearted, Short-lived and Unsuccessful Attempt to Use the Atom Bomb in its Relations with Russia.

Unfortunately, Atomic Diplomacy also fails to meet the basic standards of scholarship. Although skillfully written and equipped with an impressive number of footnotes, it proves on close examination to be highly unreliable. The author frequently uses quotations out of context or omits portions that fail to support his preconceptions. When ellipses appear in his quotations, the words excised often weaken or contradict the thesis he is trying to prove. Like Humpty Dumpty in Through the Looking Glass, quotations for Alperovitz mean just what he chooses them to mean, neither more nor less.

Sometimes the source Alperovitz refers to in a footnote says precisely the opposite of what he indicates.[78] On other occasions he sees things in a source which simply are not there. And some of his speculations are not only unsupported by the facts but are also illogical in their reasoning. Alperovitz's thesis may be dramatic, but when compared with the evidence it falls to pieces. What we have then is a case of a beautiful theory being murdered by a gang of brutal facts.

* * * * * *

Looking back on it today, it seems almost incredible that the United States did not take fullest advantage of its atomic monopoly in 1945. One would think that America's exclusive possession of atomic weapons in 1945 would have permitted it to impose its will anywhere in the world. Among other things the United States could have used "its atomic monopoly to preserve its atomic monopoly."[79] But American leaders simply did not think in such terms in 1945. Soon after Nagasaki, Americans began to suffer pains of guilt over having used the bomb on an enemy, and using it on an ally was out of the question. Thus atomic diplomacy was not a policy but merely a hope—a hope that American possession of the bomb would prevent Russia from embarking on a program of further expansion, would force it to abide by its promises, and would cause it to cooperate in building (to use the favorite phrase of the time) "a just and durable peace."

NOTES

1. Gar Alperovitz, Atomic Diplomacy: Hiroshima and Potsdam: The Use of the Atomic Bomb and the American Confrontation with Soviet Power (Princeton, N.J.: Princeton University Press, 1973).

2. Warren F. Kimball, "The Cold War Warmed Over," American Historical Review, 79, no. 4 (1974): 1129-31. Kimball attacks the book by Robert James Maddox, The New Left and the Origins of the Cold War (Princeton, N.J.: Princeton University Press, 1973), but gives no hint that there might be any defects in Alperovitz, op. cit.

3. Robert James Maddox "Atomic Diplomacy: A Study in Creative Writing," Journal of American History 59, no. 4 (1973): 925-34. This article was later reprinted in Maddox's book, The New Left and the Origins of Cold War, op. cit.

4. Alperovitz, op. cit., p. 13.

5. Ibid., pp. 28-29. Truman's account is in his own Year of Decisions (Garden City, N.Y.: Doubleday, 1955), pp. 77-79. To support his contention that Truman favored a tough approach Alperovitz says on page 231 "The President's attitude is best summed up in the statement he made eight days after Roosevelt's death: He 'intended to be firm with the Russians and make no concessions.' " A check of Truman's memoirs discloses that Alperovitz left out the last part of the sentence. Truman said he "intended to be firm with the Russians and make no concessions from American principles or traditions in order to win their favor." Truman, op. cit., p. 71.

6. See Appendix I in Alperovitz, op. cit., pp. 243-69; see also pp. 34-35.

7. Ibid., pp. 34-39. For a convincing refutation of Alperovitz's views on Lend-Lease see George C. Herring, Jr., Aid to Russia, 1941-1946: Strategy, Diplomacy, the Origins of the Cold War (New York: Columbia University Press, 1973).

8. Alperovitz, op. cit., pp. 41-49.

9. Ibid., pp. 26-28, 51. Alperovitz's chief source of information about the stiffening of attitude toward Russia under Roosevelt is Stimson's diary for April 2, 3, and 23, Stimson Papers, New Haven, Conn., Yale University Library.

10. Alperovitz, op. cit., pp. 62-63.

11. U.S. News & World Report 49, no. 7 (Aug. 15, 1960): 69.

12. Alperovitz, op. cit., p. 64.

13. Ibid., pp. 64-66.

14. Stimson Diary, May 16, 1945.

15. Alperovitz, op. cit., pp. 57, 58.

16. Ibid., p. 59. On p. 270 he says much the same thing.

17. Ibid., p. 272.

18. Truman, op. cit., p. 87; Stimson Diary, April 25, 1945; Henry L. Stimson and McGeorge Bundy, On Active Service in Peace and War (New York: Harper, 1947), pp. 635-36; Groves, "Report of Meeting with the President, April 25, 1945," in Records of the Chief of Engineers, Manhattan Engineer District, Commanding General's File Folder 24, Box 8, National Archives, Record Group No. 77; Martin J. Sherwin in "The Atomic Bomb and the Origins of the Cold War," American Historical Review 78, no. 4 (1973): 963-64, says

> If, as another historian [Alperovitz] has claimed, this meeting led to a 'strategy of delayed showdown,' . . . there is no evidence in the extant records of the meeting that Stimson had such a strategy in mind or that Truman misunderstood the secretary's views.
>
> "What emerges from a careful reading of Stimson's diary, his memorandum of April 25 to Truman, a summary by Groves of the meeting, and Truman's recollections is an argument for overall caution in American diplomatic relations with the Soviet Union: It was an argument against any showdown. Since the atomic bomb was potentially the most dangerous issue facing the postwar world and since the most desirable solution of the problem was some form of international control, Soviet cooperation had to be secured.

The author is indebted to Sherwin for a copy of the Groves report. Groves was the head of the Manhattan Project. For Stimson's attitude toward Russia see also his diary for April 2, 3, and 23, 1945.

19. U.S. Department of State, Foreign Relations of the United States 1945, The Conference of Berlin (hereafter FRUS 1945), 1, pp. 733-35. For Harriman's views regarding the Hopkins agreement on Poland, see ibid., pp. 727-28.

20. Alperovitz, op. cit., p. 89.

21. Stimson Diary, June 6, 1945; Davies Diary, May 21, 1945; FRUS, 1945, 1, pp. 11, 13, 14. On Potsdam one must agree with John L. Gaddis that "the question of whether the bomb influenced Truman's timing thus remains inconclusive." The United States and the Origins of the Cold War, 1941-1947 (New York: Columbia University Press, 1972), p. 232n.

22. Alperovitz, op. cit., p. 130. The original source is Jonathan Daniels, The Man of Independence (Philadelphia: J. B. Lippincott, 1950), p. 266. Daniels does not give the date of this remark, but does indicate that it was made at Potsdam but before Alamogordo.

23. Stimson Diary, July 21, 1945, p. 2. Byrnes also was encouraged by the bomb test. He told Joe Davies that "the success of

the Atomic Bomb . . . gave him confidence that the Soviets would agree" on the reparations issue. Davies Journal, July 29, 1945, Davies Mss, Box 19. The next day "Byrnes was disgusted with Molotov's stubbornness," but he added that the bomb "had given us great power, and that in the final analysis, it would control." Ibid., July 29. Martin Sherwin generously supplied these citations.

24. Alperovitz, op. cit., p. 151.

25. Stimson and Bundy, op. cit., p. 637.

26. Stimson and Bundy, op. cit., pp. 637-38.

27. Stimson Diary, July 22, 1945, p. 2. Churchill was shown Groves' report on July 22, and he was referring to the meeting of the Big Three on July 21.

28. FRUS, 1945 2, pp. 203-21; Robert Beitzell, ed., Tehran, Yalta, Potsdam; The Soviet Protocols (Hattiesburg, Miss.: Academic International, 1970), pp. 192-208.

29. Herbert Feis, From Trust to Terror (New York: W. W. Norton, 1970), pp. 93-94.

30. Lynn Etheridge Davis, The Cold War Begins (Princeton, N.J.: Princeton University Press, 1974), pp. 296-97.

31. Stimson Diary, July 22, 1945, p. 2.

32. Truman, op. cit., p. 416. Alperovitz is correct when he says: "Since Truman did not tell Stalin of the atomic bomb [at Potsdam], it could not yet be expected to play a major role in Soviet-American relations." Alperovitz, op. cit., p. 233. Stalin probably knew, as a result of Soviet espionage, what Truman was talking about, but naturally he could not admit it. Stimson suspected that Soviet spies had found out about the bomb project, and he may have conveyed his suspicions to the President.

33. Stimson's memo of conversation with Truman, June 6, 1945, Stimson Papers, Box 421, and Stimson Diary, June 6, 1945.

34. Alperovitz, op. cit., pp. 144-45. Alperovitz cites no source, but the only known source for the June 6 meeting is the memorandum that Stimson dictated and then repeated in his diary. Stimson Papers, Box 421; Stimson Diary, June 6, 1945. The differences between the memo and the diary are few and insignificant. It is clear that the June 6th meeting is what Alperovitz has in mind because he speaks about "the first week of June" and earlier on the same page refers specifically to June 6. Also, the two preceding footnotes in Atomic Diplomacy refer to Stimson's diary for June 6.

35. Stimson Diary, June 6, 1945, p. 3.

36. Richard G. Hewlett and Oscar E. Anderson, Jr., The New World, 1939-1946 (University Park, Penn.: Pennsylvania State University Press, 1962), p. 357. For a critique of the "strategy of delay" see Gabriel Kolko, The Politics of War (New York: Random House, 1968), pp. 421-22, 538-43.

37. Alperovitz, op. cit., p. 235.

38. FRUS, 1945 1, pp. 360-61, 715, 727-28.

39. Alperovitz, op. cit., pp. 203, 204, 205.

40. Ibid., p. 202.

41. Public Papers of the Presidents, Harry S. Truman, April 12 to December 31, 1945, (Washington, D.C.: G.P.O., 1961), p. 210.

42. Ibid., pp. 204, 214.

43. Telegram of August 11, 1945, FRUS, 1945 4, p. 282. General John A. Crane was U.S. representative on the Allied Control Council in Bulgaria.

44. Alperovitz, op. cit., pp. 211-12.

45. The letter is in FRUS, 1945 4, p. 294. Byrnes had sent a similar letter to Barnes on August 11; ibid., pp. 282-83.

46. Ibid., p. 305.

47. Dispatch from Byrnes, August 24, 1945; ibid., pp. 308-09.

48. FRUS, 1945 4, p. 311. See also Byrnes' messages of August 25 and 30 on pp. 312 and 316-17.

49. Alperovitz, op. cit., p. 216.

50. Ibid.

51. Letter to T. T. Hammond, February 27, 1974. Black served in Bulgaria from October, 1944 to September, 1945, and again in November, 1945.

52. FRUS, 1945 4, p. 417.

53. Robert Lee Wolff, The Balkans in Our Time (Cambridge, Mass.: Harvard University Press, 1956), pp. 298-99. For a perceptive account of the Communist seizure of power in Bulgaria, see Nissan Oren, "A Revolution Administered: The Sovietization of Bulgaria," in Hammond, op. cit., pp. 321-38.

54. FRUS, 1945 2, pp. 1509-10.

55. FRUS, 1945 5, p. 575. Michael's appeals were presented on August 21. On August 11 Byrnes had wired the U.S. Political Representative in Bucharest that he could tell Rumanian leaders that the United States would not recognize Groza; ibid., pp. 565-66. The King was so informed on Aug. 14; ibid., pp. 566-67.

56. Henry L. Roberts, Rumania: Political Problems of an Agrarian State (New Haven: Yale University Press, 1951), p. 301n. See also Arthur Gould Lee, Crown Against Sickle: the Story of King Michael of Rumania (London: Hutchinson, 1950), pp. 121-24.

57. FRUS, 1945 5, p. 594.

58. Lee, op. cit., pp. 129-30.

59. FRUS, 1945 2, pp. 194-202, 243-47, 267-69. It is not true, as is commonly said, that free elections in any of the East European countries would have produced anti-Soviet regimes. Free elections in Finland, Czechoslovakia, Austria, and Hungary did not produce that result, and if free elections had been held in Bulgaria and Yugoslavia,

the results in these two Russophile countries probably would not have been anti-Soviet regimes either.

60. FRUS, 1945 2, p. 821. See also Elisabeth Barker, Truce in the Balkans (London: Percival Marshall, 1948), pp. 70-72.

61. George Kennan, Memoirs, 1925-1950 (Boston: Little, Brown, 1967), p. 284. See also Barker, op. cit., p. 72, and Hugh Seton-Watson, The East European Revolution (New York: Praeger, 1956), pp. 207-11. C. L. Sulzberger reports that Burton Berry, the American Political Representative in Rumania, told him that "the Moscow conference was a sell-out and the American mission staff in Bucharest wanted to resign en bloc but decided it would do no good." C. L. Sulzberger, A Long Row of Candles (New York: Macmillan, 1969), p. 292.

62. Davies Journal, July 29, 1945, Davies Mss, Box 19; cited in Gaddis, op. cit., p. 264.

63. Alperovitz, op. cit., pp. 224-25; Stimson Diary, August 12-September 3, 1945. Byrnes made a similar comment to Stimson; Stimson Diary, September 4, 1945.

64. Feis, op. cit., p. 98, citing the diary of Chancellor of the Exchequer Hugh Dalton for October 5 and October 17, 1945. See also Lisle A. Rose, After Yalta (New York: Scribner's, 1973), pp. 123-24.

65. Calendar Notes, Sept. 28, 1945, pp. 12-13, Edward R. Stettinius, Jr., Papers, Box 247, University of Virginia Library.

66. Ibid., p. 3.

67. Davies' memo of conversation with Byrnes, October 9, 1945, Davies Mss, Box 22; cited in Gaddis, op. cit., pp. 275-76.

68. Alperovitz, op. cit., p. 234. Alperovitz does not discuss the Moscow Conference. To have done so would have greatly weakened his case.

69. Louis J. Halle, The Cold War As History (New York: Harper & Row, 1967), p. 173. This point is also well expressed by Stephen Ambrose in his Rise to Globalism (Baltimore, Md.: Penguin, 1971), p. 129.

70. Ambrose, op. cit., p. 129. Halle, op. cit., p. 170, says: "Moscow held West Europe as a hostage, thereby effectively deterring an atomic attack by the United States."

71. Leo Szilard in U.S. News & World Report 49, (August 15, 1960): 69. The conversation took place at the end of May, 1945. Alperovitz uses the quotation from Szilard but omits the words after "I failed to see how." Alperovitz, op. cit., p. 203 fn.

72. Stimson Diary, July 21, 1945, p. 2; Stimson and Bundy, op. cit., pp. 637-38.

73. Alperovitz, op. cit., p. 13.

74. Ibid., p. 234.

75. Ibid., p. 235. See similar statements on pp. 127-28, 131, 203, 204, 205, and 240.

76. FRUS, 1945 1, p. 715. A similar statement can be found on pp. 360-61. See also Harriman's evaluation of the Hopkins agreement on Poland, pp. 727-28. In a speech on October 31, 1945, Byrnes indicated that he sympathized with the Soviet desire to have a sphere of influence in Eastern Europe because of Russia's "special security interests in those countries." However, he objected to Russia's apparent determination to "deny their neighbors the right to be friends with others." That is, he opposed "spheres of exclusive interest." Department of State Bulletin 13, no. 332 (November 4, 1945), p. 710.

77. Stimson Diary, June 6, 1945.

78. For example, see Alperovitz, op. cit., p. 208 where it is said that in Bulgaria "a small dissident faction" of the Social Democratic Party opposed the Communist-dominated government, and the footnote refers to Seton-Watson, op. cit., p. 214. Yet Seton-Watson clearly states that it was the majority faction that opposed the government.

For additional cases where Alperovitz has misused his sources, see Maddox, The New Left; Arthur Schlesinger, Jr., "Origins of the Cold War," Foreign Affairs 46, no. 1 (1967): p. 24n, and Robert H. Ferrell, "Truman Foreign Policy: A Traditional View," in Richard S. Kirkendall, ed., The Truman Period as a Research Field; A Reappraisal, 1972 (Columbia, Mo.: University of Missouri Press, 1974), p. 31n.

79. Halle, op. cit., p. 169.

CHAPTER

3

SOVIET POLITICS AT THE START OF THE COLD WAR: THE SOVIET PARTY REVIVAL REASSESSED

William O. McCagg, Jr.

PARADOX OR TRICK?

It is useful to think of Stalin as "statist." Such a tag implies, quite properly, that Stalin's major accomplishments were his economic and political consolidation of the Soviet state, and his brutal retreat from the value system which Lenin's party had propagated before 1917. It hints at why Stalin murdered the old Bolsheviks during the 1930s, and flaunted the banners of tsarist nationalism during his last years. And to think of Stalin as having been thus against the Communist Party highlights a certain paradox midway in his career. *

At the end of the war, the Soviet Communist Party briefly resumed its erstwhile leading role within the Soviet system. With Leninist abuse of imperialism it encouraged the Red Army and Communist parties abroad to press revolutions, which in the end nearly doubled the expanse of world socialism. The paradox seems the greater because Stalin himself in those early postwar years continued to issue

---

* John A. Armstrong, The Politics of Totalitarianism (New York: Random House, 1961), chs. 11-15 . The only scholarly study which reviews in any detail the whole range of Soviet politics in the immediate postwar period. Armstrong has also written "An Essay on Sources for the Study of the Communist Party of the Soviet Union" (mimeograph; Washington, D.C.: State Department, 1961). Considerations of space restrict the footnotes below to primary sources and to major monographs. References to the enormous literature which touches peripherally on our subject will appear in my forthcoming book, Stalin's Battles with Communism, 1943-1948.

a "statist" line. In virtually every one of his public statements after the war, as during it, Stalin spoke of the possibility and desirability of peaceful coexistence between the Soviet state and the Western powers. In 1947, in a statement addressed clearly to Soviet Communists, Stalin declared that "outdated" views of Marx, Engels, and Lenin must be criticized and discarded.[1] A little later he called himself publicly a "businessman" as opposed to a "propagandist," openly distancing himself from the then highly vocal spokesmen of the Communist Party.[2]

Historians have ways of minimizing this paradox. Soviet writers for example, claim that there was never any difference between Stalin and the Party. By their account the Party built the state, the Party won the war, and the Party's overt leadership in national reconstruction after 1944 is clear evidence that the Party was in control all along. And, surprisingly, many outsiders have accepted this thesis. Until 1945, many outsiders tended to believe that Stalin actually had "left the Party behind" and that he was a businessman of their own ilk. But when it became evident after the war that Communism was very far from dead in Moscow, such outsiders felt cheated. They took it for granted that the Party revival, the single most conspicuous development in Soviet domestic politics between 1944 and 1948, was Stalin's work. They leapt to the conclusion that Stalin's pre-war and wartime statism was a trick designed to disarm them; that in reality he had all along been a Leninist out to conquer the world; and that there was no paradox in a self-styled businessman at the helm of a Soviet Party revival, but rather massive deceit.

The following chapter questions this conventional logic. It suggests there was paradox in what happened, and that the Party revival symptomized a domestic political trauma inside the Soviet Union during the years when the Cold War began. For reasons of space we shall be concerned largely with Soviet domestic events, and not document whether or how those events affected foreign policy. But we shall militate against oversimplification even there. If there is any single message, it is that the Soviet regime in Stalin's day was a tremendously complex organism ruling a vast society, about which historians must speak in carefully guarded terms.

THE WARTIME RELAXATION

As a first step towards understanding the Soviet Party's revival, one must recognize that the Soviet Union in 1945 was relaxed politically. For four years the entire energy of its peoples had been devoted to the single aim of repulsing the German invader. The struggle had led to the death of 20 million—one-tenth of the entire population—to the devastation of the country's most populous regions, to a vast mobilization of men into the armed forces, of women into wartime jobs, of workers and technical experts from the West to the Urals and Siberia. Hardly a citizen, young or old, had not suffered from privation and massive change in his way of life. The experience had been exhausting, and it had massively distracted people's minds from the domestic issues on which the prewar political tension had depended.

No doubt the bones of the prewar regime were still extant in 1945. The Party was still there, the secret police and the vast complex of camps were still there, Stalin was still there. We know the surviving power of the regime, not least of all from Solzhenitzyn, who was (as were countless others) clapped into prison in the spring of 1945 for having criticized Stalin in a private letter from the front.[3] But this very example suggests the relaxation in the political climate during the war: Solzhenitzyn would hardly have written such a letter in the years just after the great purges. Moreover, the regime itself had encouraged relaxation. Ilya Ehrenberg writes in his memoirs that during the war over Radio Moscow he used to broadcast promises to the Soviet peoples of a better future. As a regime spokesman, he urged them to fight hard for a world and a life which would be different (and better) than that of the prewar years.[4] And Boris Pasternak ended his great panoramic novel, Dr. Zhivago, with the words, "Although victory had not brought the relief and freedom which were expected at the end of the war, nevertheless, the portents of freedom filled the air throughout the postwar period, and they alone defined its historical significance."[5]

To recognize the extent of the political relaxation in the Soviet Union by the end of the war is to recognize that Stalin's regime faced limitations. It still ruled by fiat—that was its style. But presumably it had to wonder far more than before the war about how, and even whether, its dictation would be accepted. And from this it follows that historians should consider the measures the regime then took not as matters of unimpeded whim, but as matters considered necessary in the face of a revolution of popular expectations.

Even within the regime itself, the war had wrought changes of which the most important was a tremendous accretion of power to the armed forces. Before the war, as is known, the Soviet armed services had been subjected to very severe civilian controls. After the German attack in 1941, however, all that changed. First of all, the services grew immensely in size: by 1944 the Red Army's standing force was over 11 million, as opposed to 4 million in 1941.[6] This growth meant that the country's military leadership was then in effective administrative control of a considerable portion of the population. Further, the war brought to the army the temporary administration of vast territories; it made the army the demanding major consumer of much of Soviet economic production; and in 1944-45, it deeply involved the army in the governance of Eastern Europe and part of Germany—in other words in foreign affairs.

Beyond this, even before the Stalingrad campaign began in 1942, the regime specifically acknowledged—through Stalin's public speeches—its dependence on the military. After Stalingrad, Stalin and the other civilian leaders donned uniforms, and became marshals and generals; epaulettes and gold braid were restored for the first time since czarist days; and Russia's military and national past was rehabilitated.[7] Meanwhile, the regime increasingly dropped the old control system represented by political commanders and Party-directed cadre selection within the army;[8] and it tolerated, indeed encouraged the emergence of esprit de corps within the army. As outside observers, visiting foreign Communists, and insiders to the Soviet system alike report, a certain self-conscious arrogance existed by 1945 among the Soviet military commanders.[9] This arrogance was expressed even vis-a-vis Stalin himself and, like the revolution of popular expectations, must be considered a factor which limited his regime's freedom of operation.

Other major shifts in the wartime Soviet political system may be described in terms of a "withering" of Communist Party institutions. Before the war Stalin, for all his statism, held true to certain Party formalities. For example, the Party's Politburo remained the leading policy-making organ within the system. Further, after the great purges of 1936-38, Stalin reaffirmed the authority of the Party's ideology by publishing his own version of the Party's history and of dialectical materialism. And in Soviet administrative practice right up until the war, the Party played the role of a highly significant control apparatus separate from, and overseeing, the state bureaucracy.[10] Virtually from the day the war began, however, Stalin did break with such forms. In July, 1941, for example, the regime explicitly subordinated the Politburo, alongside the government and the military high command, to a state defense committee—the GOKO.[11] Even Soviet Party historians, who have a strong interest in proving that the Party was in command all through the war, acknowledge that Stalin after this did not use the Party as his forum of ultimate decision making again until late in 1945, and then did so sparingly.[12]

In general administrative practice the Party's fate during the war was hardly less drastic. There is no question that certain Party organs—most notably the Central Secretariat—played a vital role in the wartime governance of the Soviet Union. But it is indicative of the real situation that the Secretariat, run by G. M. Malenkov, ceased to be an organ distinct from the apparatus of state administration, but became an integral link in the bureaucracy, "substituting" itself for state organs.[13] Malenkov himself emerged in 1942, 1943, and 1944 not only as the head of the Party's secretarial arm, but simultaneously as a key leader of the state's war production bureaucracy, and as a representative of the economic ministries within the GOKO. A comparable mixing of Party and state functions was carried out by A. S. Shcherbakov. By 1943 he was head of the Party's Moscow organization, a member of the Central Secretariat, and in charge of the Chief Political Administration within the Red Army (before the war the only Soviet administrative apparatus where Party and state functions were merged); he was also a general who played a major role on the Moscow front, and chief of the Sovinformburo, an office technically subordinated to the Foreign Commissariat, which was the main source of news about the Soviet Union during the war.[14] Comparable empires—and comparable substitution of Party organs as wheels in the state bureaucracy—seem to have emerged in different ways throughout the Soviet administrative system during the war years.[15] Though outsiders may view all this as ultimate evidence that the party remained preeminent throughout the war, Party revivalists at the end of the war regarded "substitution" as anathema; so do Party historians who nowadays attempt to prove that the Party was responsible for the wartime victory.[16]

When the war broke out the all-union CP claimed 3,870,000 members and candidates.[17] A majority of them apparently were killed during the fighting, but wartime recruitment was so great that by May, 1945, the Party claimed 5,760,000 members. It now included about 3 percent of the entire Soviet population, and almost one-quarter of all personnel within the armed forces. This development was no more desirable to Party officials than the emergence of "substitution." At the time it seemed that the massive recruitment in the army led to the award of Party membership primarily for military valor. After 1945, Party spokesmen made it clear that membership growth resulted in a diluting of the Party's strength. Party historians today stress that cadre work during the war was very weak. On the home front, they indicate, the sheer scarcity of trained Party members, and massive fluctuation (that is, constant turnover) among those who remained, led in many places to a lapse of regular Party activities.[18] In the army, Party historians are scandalized to report, the Party's right to select cadres for promotion was expressly limited in November, 1943, not to be restored until mid-1946.[19] Further, it is a matter of record that the Party's network of cadre training schools broke down during the war. After 1944 even the regional Party high schools had to be reestablished.[20]

The wartime withering of the Party was more conspicuous in the ideological sphere than in any other. In 1941 Stalin compounded his prewar retreat from the value system of the revolution by invoking Russian national heroes from the past. Coincidentally, his regime rallied support of the war effort among the component nationalities of the USSR—even among the Jews—through the use of nationalistic symbols. In 1942, as the tide of official Russian nationalism increased, the regime instituted an "anti-sectarian campaign," which placed a pall of silence on aspects of Marxism-Leninism which might alienate the USSR's "imperialist" allies in the West.[21] One observer who spent the war in Moscow, reported that from 1942 until the spring of 1945 even joking criticisms of capitalism and imperialism were political sins within Soviet leadership circles.[22] A leading general noted that it was only in the late summer of 1944, when the Red Army was past the prewar Soviet frontiers, that the high command was permitted to talk of the possibility that revolution might now spread.[23] Meanwhile, it became permissible to speak with less regard for Party "correctness." Scientists and writers were less restrained by ideological considerations in 1945 than before the war.[24] As late as 1947, leading Soviet economists engaged in markedly free debate about the nature of the capitalist world, and a transcript of the debates was published on the very eve of the crisis year, 1948, in the controlled press.*

Herewith we can address directly the main question which any historian of the postwar period must face—not only the question of whether the power of the Soviet regime was limited at the end of the war, but also whether Stalin's own power was still intact. Often it is assumed that Stalin still had absolute power in 1945, because just as before 1941 and after 1948, his authority was uncircumscribed, all the elites acknowledged his leadership, and the Supreme Soviet in June, 1945, conferred upon him the title of Generalissimo. Yet power exists not merely in authority or competence—in other words in what outsiders and subordinates acknowledge—but also in actual control. And though Stalin's authority—indeed, his popularity—was surely as great (if not greater) in 1945 as it had been in 1941, we have just seen how probable it is that his control was more limited. With an undisciplined population, the arrogance of the military, and a drastically altered Party-state relationship within the huge governing bureaucracy, one may judge, indeed, that there must have been a major gap in 1945 between the competence of the *Vozhd*, unchanged since 1941, and his lessened control.

---

*This discussion concerned a book by E. Varga, published in 1946, which proposed that the major capitalist states had acquired some ability to plan their economies, and thus to survive. The debate was published as a supplement to the journal, (*Mirovaia Politika i Mirovoe Khoziaistvo*) in December, 1947.

Stalin himself told visitors in those relaxed days at the end of the war that he had to wrestle to impose the policies he wanted upon his colleagues.[25] Further, press and diplomatic reports from Moscow were filled, through the late war and postwar years, with tales of Stalin's impending retirement, ill health, and conflicts with his colleagues. These years were the heyday of the "prisoner of the Politburo" talk in the West.[26] It is common nowadays to deprecate such tales as symptomatic of that western naivete about Communism which in the 1930s had led Western reporters in Moscow to swallow as truth the great purge trials. But there is a difference. In the 1930s, the naivete of Western observers was sustained by the all-embracing totalitarian terror which limited their contacts in Moscow. In 1945, as we have seen, that terror was severely circumscribed; and what is more it was not the "naive" Joseph Davies who wrote home in 1945 that Stalin's power was limited, but the "hard-headed" experts.

Late that year, for example, just a few weeks before George Kennan composed the now famous "long telegram" warning the United States government not to trust the Russians, he wrote

> During the war Stalin has devoted a great deal of his own time to military matters. . . . The safety of his regime, and his own personal safety, appears to have lain largely in the hands of such men as Beria, Malenkov, and—until his death—Shcherbakov. These men . . . are among the few people . . . Stalin can at least trust. . . . This means [they] are very difficult indeed to replace . . . that they can sabotage with impunity the major directives of Soviet policy, knowing that . . . Stalin will always back them up in the end. . . . [27]

Kennan was not the only respected western authority to report in such terms that Stalin's personal control was weaker than before the war.[28] Consequently, when in the relaxed atmosphere of the day Stalin himself told visitors that he had to wrestle with his colleagues, it is not necessary for us to judge that he was just tricking outsiders. He was probably stating the obvious—something he felt could not be concealed.

THE PARTY'S REVIVAL

Many historians have recognized that the Soviet Party revival after 1944 was functional to the revolution of popular expectations described above, and to the powerful position the Soviet military leadership had won within the system during the war. Even in the

USSR there are numerous accounts of how Stalin himself launched the revival late in 1943 with public mention of the Party's "inspirational and organizational" virtues;[29] how in September 1944, the Central Committee ordered resumption of Party control over a wide range of cultural and propaganda affairs;[30] how in September 1945, the GOKO was replaced by the Politburo as the supreme political organ within the system; and how in 1946 and 1947 the Party's revivalist leader, A. A. Zhdanov, launched campaigns to eliminate "deviations" in cultural matters, "abuses" against the Collective Farm Statute, and "laxity" in the population's support of the five-year plan.[31] Soviet historians report in remarkable detail that as early as October 1944, the Central Committee attacked the problem of mass Party recruitment within the army, marking a turning point in civilian-military relations.[32] Moreover, early in 1946 the Politburo ordered a massive reorganization of the military high command, some of the more arrogant generals lost their high positions, and by 1948 the entire prewar apparatus of political controls over the armed forces was once again in place.[33]

Our objective here is not to repeat this familiar story, but to explain the fact that the revival took place in two major phases, which differed substantially from one another. The first proceeded under the general aegis of Shcherbakov who, as noted earlier, was one of the most powerful home-front figures in wartime Russia, and one of the outstanding bureaucratic "substituters." It was characteristic of this phase that an alleged Central Committee meeting of January, 1944, which launched the revival, also dropped the _Internationale_ as the official hymn of the Soviet state.[34] In cultural affairs, the Party's emphasis during this phase was not on more Marxism-Leninism, but on a more "Russian" science, on a more patriotic literature, and on the criticism of philosophical and other trends which could be considered noxious to the state because they were "foreign."[35] In organizational affairs in this phase, the Party fought not the laxity of Party "control" over the state administrative system, but the failure of Party units to hold meetings, the enormous fluctuation in Party office holding, and other failings which interfered with the Party's ability to help raise industrial production.[36] Generally speaking, in this phase of the revival, "substitution" was not considered a sin.

In the last weeks of 1944, however, Shcherbakov, afflicted with a fatal illness, retired from politics; Andrei Zhdanov, who had spent much of the war besieged in Leningrad (reportedly in political disgrace) assumed the leadership of the revival, and he radicalized it.*

---

*Zhdanov's return to Moscow was announced in _Pravda_, January 26, 1945, p. 2, though he had been released from his post in Leningrad some months earlier.

Shcherbakov's half-baked "Soviet Patriotism" now dropped out of sight in favor of a harsh partiinost reminiscent of the early 1930s. Party spokesmen now aggressively began to claim that it was the Party more than any other element within the Soviet system which had "inspired and organized" the victory, * and they called for outright Party supremacy, that is, an end to "substitution."

In the literature on the subject, and especially in Soviet literature, there is adequate acknowledgment of these two phases,[37] but the tendency is to explain them in terms of opportunity and sentiment. "As soon as the victory was gained," one generally reads, "the Party stepped up the campaigns to restore prewar normalcy." Practically no suspicion has been voiced that the second phase of the revival was more than a "continuation" of the first, or that the partiinost of the second phase was anything but "correct"—in other words, fully expected. In reality, however, the second phase began several months before the end of the war made it opportune; and the shift in emphases involved rather concrete political changes.

If there was a moment in which the radicalization of the Party revival occurred, it was at a great celebration held in Leningrad late in January, 1945.[38] Among those who spoke most ardently for it were men who had been associated during the war with Zhdanov in Leningrad, as well as regional leaders from those Russian republic and Ukrainian oblasty which had suffered German occupation; N. S. Khrushchev is an example. During the following three years, these leaders remained in the forefront of the Party's domestic policy offensive, far outshining leaders from Moscow and other regions which had been spared by the invader. For example, in the Zhdanovite journal, (Partiinaia Zhizn'), during 1947 there were full-length articles either written about Leningrad or authored by a prominent Leningrad leader in 10 out of the 24 issues; in contrast, only five articles related to Moscow, of which three followed an intervention in favor of Moscow by Stalin himself. Meanwhile one of the major accomplishments of the revival turned out to be demolition of the "substitutionist" managerial empires of the wartime home front.

This occurred with differing degrees of publicity and politesse. Regarding the secret police, for example, the only clear public sign of change was the removal of Beria from its direct command in January, 1946. Only in later years did the world learn about the beginnings

---

*The new line emerged clearly in the first issue, for example, of Voprosy Istorii, in 1945. Compare the trumpeting editorial in Pravda, May 16, 1945.

in 1946 and 1947 of the Stalinist struggle within the police sector.[39] The demolition of another major home-front "empire," that of Shcherbakov at Moscow, was disguised by the sudden death of Shcherbakov himself in May, 1945. Few observers thought twice about the fact that his major offices were all handed over to different nonentities and that for four years thereafter Moscow played no notable role in Soviet political life. The leadership of the Moscow organization passed to G. M. Popov. The Political Directorate in the Armed Forces passed to I. V. Skikin. Both fell in the purge of 1949, though neither was important enough to be executed. The Sovinformburo, Shcherbakov's third power-base, was apparently abolished at war's end. Other major home-front changes which took place during the Party revival were masked by the economic conversion of the country to peacetime production. But the facts are clear. Between late 1944 and mid-1946, the leadership of no less than 11 of the 17 "heavy-industry" oblasts between the Volga and Siberia was shaken up; much of the wartime economic command structure was simply abolished; and the key heavy-industrial commissariats were largely reorganized. Given the coincident Party attacks on "substitution," these changes amounted to a purge. And as the public could learn even at the time, G. K. Malenkov, the greatest "substituter" of all was also the greatest loser in the Zhdanovshchina, disappearing in October, 1946, even from the Party Secretariat.[40]

The Soviet Party revival after the war served to restrict popular expectations of change, and to restore civilian control over the armed services; it also strengthened the position of Party leaders in the country's western provinces. The "victory" of these regions poses a problem for the historian, because they were not in 1945 the seat of Soviet domestic political power and influence. On the contrary, they were underdog regions, provinces that had been cut off from the rest of the country, which from the point of view of "security" were contaminated by their exposure to facism, and which were physically ruined by the four years of battle fought on their soil.

Naturally one may specify some reasons why the Party leaders of these "liberated territories" should have been more eager to promote a Party revival than the leaders of the home front. In the postwar years, for example, the Soviet elites of the western lands had to start, as it were, from scratch, and quite naturally therefore could have regarded reconstruction of the Party, the original Bolshevik institution, as a necessary first stage in the reconstruction of the Soviet system as a whole.* On the home front, contrastingly, Soviet

---

*See Vedomosti Verkhovnogo Soveta, April 30, 1945,1: 4; and 2: 3 . It is relevant to note that the financial demands of the liberated

institutional control over the population had never been interrupted, and consequently such a general reconstruction was not in order. One may also suggest that Zhdanov and Khrushchev had a personal predilection for partiinost—even before the war Zhdanov had been a specialist in imposing Party supremacy on Soviet cultural activities—and that because of them, the wartime regional pride in the Leningrad and Ukrainian Party organizations focused on partiinost.[41] But these explanations do not account for the central fact that the second phase of the Party revival served the interests of these ravished, impuissant, contaminated regions of the Soviet Union to the very great detriment of such entrenched home-front bureaucratic empire builders as L. P. Beria and G. M. Malenkov.

A solution to this puzzle appears if one accepts our suggestion that Stalin's control over the home-front empire builders was severely reduced during the war. If that was the case, then evidently Stalin himself had a certain political interest in 1945 in precipitating an upheaval within the ruling bureaucracy. One may add that conditions were ripe for a massive political maneuver against the leading bureaucrats. The ruling bureaucracy would be shaken up in 1945 anyway, for the national economic machinery had to be converted from war to peacetime production, and enormous numbers of people had to be demobilized from the army and absorbed into the civilian job structure. From Stalin's point of view, therefore, it was entirely rational to take advantage of these shifts which would occur anyway, to replace the rulers of the wartime bureaucracy with people he could more easily control.

STALIN CHALLENGED?

As should already be evident, the Soviet political scene during 1945, when the Cold War began, was not static, but rather in the throes of major change. If our analysis is correct, the Party revival of that year symptomized not just an effort by the whole civilian regime to "normalize" its control over the population and the army, but also a complex manipulation by Stalin to restore his personal control over the home-front civilian elites. Moreover, another aspect of the Soviet

---

territories dominated the budget debate in the Supreme Soviet in April, 1945 to the virtual exclusion of the home-front regions which had dominated the debate of February, 1944.

domestic political struggle in 1945 heightens the impression that there was turmoil.

If one traces the later history of the postwar Soviet Party revival one comes upon a remarkable fact: the Party elites of the liberated territories, those same elites which seem to have been so useful to Stalin in 1945, later on paid for the Party revival. First in 1946 and 1947 Khrushchev and the Ukrainian Party endured a period of obvious difficulty. Then, in 1948, Zhdanov died, reputedly in disgrace. Early in 1949 the other Politburo-level leaders who had spoken for the revival in 1945 and 1946—Molotov, Mikoyan, Bulganin, and especially Voznesensky—were removed from power. Finally, the liberated territories as a whole came under fire. The purges in the Ukraine, first in 1947 and then in 1949, toppled 73 percent of the oblast Party first secretaries. On the home front, by way of contrast, the purging of 1949 took only 43 percent of the oblast first secretaries, and if one discounts those installed during the revival in 1945 and 1946, the home-front figure is under 36 percent (see Table 3.1).

Why did the liberated territories have to pay? We have seen the background and general inspiration of the Party revival, from which Stalin obviously gained a great deal. Why, then, all the carnage in 1949? This question suggests a further look into the sources, and an investigation of the practice of printsipnost', which was encouraged by the Party revivalists in 1945.

Printsipnost' may perhaps best be described as explicit citation of Marxist-Leninist doctrines to explain current events. Its spread marked the end of the great "anti-sectarian" campaign which had blanketed reference to those doctrines during the war. It is relevant here because in several respects it seemed antipathetic to Stalin.

In the first place it led to distortion of what Stalin himself was saying. One example: in November, 1944, Stalin declared in a speech that the war was leading to an "ideological" as well as a military victory.[42] Stalin did not mention Marxism-Leninism in the speech, and since he was addressing, inter alia, the Allies in the West, his omission of Marxism-Leninism presumably was intentional. But a leading Party journal, commenting on this passage in Stalin's speech, referred to the Party's leadership in the victory and to "Leninist-Stalinist internationalism"; then it asked its readers to look for "deep meanings".[43] Was this what Stalin had intended?

Another example: In May, 1945, Stalin, as is well known, delivered a highly nationalistic toast to the Russian people. In it there was no mention of either the Party or its ideology.[44] Yet the same Party journal commented on this toast with a long panegyric about how the Party had won the war almost single-handedly—and then, cleverly, the journal's chief editorialist wove in Stalin's praise of the Russians in such fashion as to make it seem that Stalin was a great Bolshevik

TABLE 3.1

Purge of Oblast First Secretaries
September 1948—December 1949

Region	Oblast First Secretaries Removed		Percent
War Zone			
26 Ukrainian obl.[b]	19[a]		73
18 occupied Russ. obl.	12		66
Home Front			
22 unoccupied European Russ. obl.	9		40
17 Volga-Ural-Siberian obl.	9[c]	Average	53
10 Far Eastern obl.	3	43%	30

[a](Includes 12 ousted in 1948-49 plus seven others removed in 1947.)

[b]The Byelorussian Party was purged in 1947 and a new First Secretary was appointed in 1949, but it did not suffer purging in 1949 on the provincial first-secretary level. The reason for this was probably the strong link between the wartime Byelorussian partisans (who provided the bulk of the postwar oblast first secretaries in the republic) and the NKVD.

[c]The nine first secretaries of Volga-Urals-Siberian oblasty who were removed in 1949 were in the main the new men who had been introduced into those oblasty in 1945 and 1946, during the Party revival.

Source: The raw material on which this chart is based is drawn from Pravda and other Party journals for the years in question, and will be published as an appendix to my forthcoming book, Stalin's Battles with Communism.

who felt that the Party had won the war.[45] Readers had to conclude that Stalin was backing the Party. But, again, was this what Stalin had intended?

A final example of the distortion which printsipnost' imposed upon Stalin's statements: In the winter of 1944-1945, the Party propagandists systematically went about digging out old quotations from Stalin which purveyed Party values. They then distributed these quotations with such injunctions as the following: Bolshevik printsipnost' means an irreconcilable rejection of every slightest deviation from Marxism-Leninism.[46] The reason they had to look for old quotations was that no recent ones were available. But with these quotations from 1920, the propagandists made it seem that Stalin wanted the Party workers to rely on abstract Marxism-Leninism in 1945.

Printsipnost', as practiced in 1945, seems in significant respects to have been a flat negation of all that Stalin attempted in his prewar struggles with the Party. Before the war, Stalin had gone to enormous lengths to limit the freedom with which Communists submitted to the ideological imperatives of Marxism-Leninism. In the expression of ideology Stalin remained Leninist. Indeed, he called himself no more than Lenin's "successor," never making himself "emperor" in name, as Napoleon had. But he compelled the followers of Marxism-Leninism to obey ideological imperatives only on the basis of a "correct" Stalinist interpretation. He forced such words as "Revolution," "Party," and "Marxist" into a rigid identification with the word "Stalin." And this obsession with "correctness" was of the essence of prewar Stalinism: this was the way he justified his violation in practice of virtually every accepted canon of Marxism-Leninism.

The new printsipnost' of 1945 negated prewar Stalinism in the sense that it encouraged free reference to the imperatives of Marx and Lenin. The Party journals which purveyed it urged Party workers at all levels to look back to "principles" of Marxism-Leninism which were allegedly "well-known." The message, put colloquially, was "open your eyes, see, and speak out."[47] And when they used old quotations from Stalin to support their imprecations, the effect was to reverse the process of the prewar system—the Party journals here expropriated from Stalin his own name, lending its "correct" authority back to the words "Marxist," "Party," and "Revolution" which Stalin had fought against.

There is yet another reason why the spreading printsipnost' of 1945 can be considered antipathetic to Stalin. Khrushchev in effect said so in his "secret speech" to the Party's 20th Congress. In the middle of that speech, Khrushchev declared that the "main role and the main credit for the victorious ending of the war belong to the Communist Party."[48] He noted this just after having complained that Stalin in 1945 had claimed for himself the sole responsibility for the victory. Khrushchev then stated that "it was precisely at this time [1945] that the so-called Leningrad affair was born—that is, that the purge of the liberated territories in 1949 was rooted in the controversies of 1945.[49] And, sure enough, if we look back at the documents we find clear evidence of Stalin's dislike of the Party's claim in 1945 that _it_ had won the war.

First,on May 25, 1945, as noted earlier, Stalin delivered his "Toast to the Russian People," in which he mentioned neither the Party nor its ideology. Next, in June, in a second widely publicized toast Stalin drank

> To the people who are often considered the cogs in the great machinery of the state, but without whom none of us marshals and front and army commanders are—to put it brutally—worth a cent.[50]

Seldom had Stalin had a more appropriate occasion than in this toast, suggesting the coming humiliation of the army, to praise the Party. But he did not mention the Party; he omitted it again. Then, in his third major public statement on the victory, Stalin became even more emphatic. On September 3, 1945, he declared

> The defeat of the Russian armies in 1904 . . . left a sad burden on the conscience of the nation. It left a dark spot of shame on our country. Our people, however, trusted and waited for the day when Japan would be defeated and the spot would be wiped away. We of the older generation have waited forty years for that day. And now that day has come.[51]

As Isaac Deutscher noted years ago, this was an insult to the Party, from whose point of view the defeats in 1904 had been a joyous event, making possible the revolution of 1905.[52]

In effect Stalin maintained a second political line during the summer of 1945, just after the Party's journals grew loud in support of printsipnost'. This was his own nationalist and "statist" line, clearly distinct from that of the Party. And, as indicated earlier, such a duality of political lines survived publicly until the Party revival ended in 1948-49. In view of this fact, it seems likely that by mid-1945 Stalin consciously felt the Party revival to be a serious challenge to him; the same conclusion is attested by the fearful purge and judicial murders of Party revivalists which occurred in 1948-49, after Zhdanov died and the Party revival abruptly stopped.[53]

How could the Party revival, which Stalin started, have become Stalin's rival? Khrushchev provided a partial answer in his "secret speech:" "After the conclusion of the Patriotic war the Soviet nation experienced a period of political enthusiasm."[54] Roy Medvedev refers to the political enthusiasm of the immediate postwar period and one can understand why enthusiasm was the order of the day.[55] 1945 was exciting, not just for the people of Moscow who demonstrated wildly in the streets. The Party elites also had reason for excitement, for they were to plan the future.

When one is excited and enthusiastic, one often says what one thinks. During the war, the Party elites had not said what they thought. For four long years they had labored under the great campaign against "sectarianism," which made them forswear Party cant, and even Marxist jokes against imperialists. Party cant was not for them (as might seem to us) "just jargon," but a political language of sorts. They could identify with it; it legitimized them; it was their language in the same mechanical fashion that the slogans of Enlightened Liberalism were the language of the 19th century European bourgeoisies. It follows that there were tensions between the Party traditions of the Soviet elites, and their enforced wartime "rationalism" and, correspondingly, release when in the spring of 1945, as witnesses have reported, jokes were again allowed.[56] Under such circumstances, it is likely that printsipnost' spread in the Soviet elites virtually spontaneously in the heady months of 1945, once the Party journals let down the bars. Stalin may have been faced with a prairie fire, which he himself, perhaps too sanguinely, had lit, but which he could not extinguish.

There is another, tougher, explanation of why Stalin turned against the revival. One of the revival's major features was its stress upon the integrity of the Party rules.* The evidence is clear that this formalism was not restricted to obliging members to pay dues. In December, 1945, the Party Politburo was allowed to resume its status as the Soviet Union's highest decision-making forum. The Politburo, for the first time in years, began to meet regularly and to keep minutes.[57] In the following months, moreover, it systematically debated and redefined its own functions, and those of the Secretariat and Orgburo. Meanwhile the Central Committee also met. There

---

*According to <u>Partinoe stzoitel'stvo,</u> no. 14, (1944), p. 28 , the study of the rules was to be a major theme at the newly established Party high school. <u>Partiinoe stzoitel'stvo,</u> no. 21, (1944), pp. 37ff., and no. 22, pp. 26ff, contain a long discussion of the rules, as do <u>Partiinaya Zhizn'</u>, no. 2, 1946, pp. 51ff, and no. 3, pp. 48ff.

was talk of holding a Party congress as the statutes demanded. Later on came talk of Stalin's resistance.*

Historians must be cautious in assessing such signs of direct "opposition" between Stalin and the Party revival in 1945. Into any construct of what happened must be inserted all the available facts. A most important fact is that no one who was there has told us in unvarnished terms that an open revolt against Stalin took place. Such a revolt is indeed improbable, given the well known sycophancy of Stalin's aides.

But we should remember that an open revolt may not be in question. On the one hand, Stalin was peculiar. He found threats, by many accounts, in little signs. So perhaps we may assume that in 1945, amidst the great tensions of the war and of the manipulations designed to restore his control of the bureaucracy, Stalin took fright against the Party revival, not over open opposition but over potentialities which suddenly at the moment of the victory appeared real to him.

On the other hand, we can usefully remember that there are blindspots in the Communist mentality. Some of these are familiar from the history of Titoism just after 1945. Few historians write any longer that Tito was precisely faithful to Stalin in 1945. There were conflicts between them, they were talked about, and they had consequences. But Tito _thought_ he was faithful—this is the important point—and the other Communist leaders of Eastern Europe also thought so, and all of them were mightily surprised in 1948 when it appeared to Stalin that Tito was a heretic.[58] Among these Communists, who were by no means naive, there was an innocence about the seriousness of inner-Party conflicts which historians cannot ignore. Milovan Djilas, a witness, explains this innocence in terms exactly reminiscent of the Soviet Party revival. Djilas writes:

> What actually happened to the Yugoslav Communists is what has happened to all, throughout the long history of man, who have subordinated their individual fate and the fate of mankind to one idea: unconsciously

---

*See Tito, _Prilozi za biografiju_ (Belgrade: Kultura, 1953), p. 446. According to V. Dedijer, Malenkov told the Cominform delegates in September, 1947, that there would shortly be a Soviet congress. According to an article in _Pravda_, April 28, 1964, the Politburo voted twice between 1944 and 1948 to hold a congress, but was overridden both times by Stalin.

> they described the Soviet Union and Stalin in terms required by their own struggle and by its justification.[59]

The Titoists, according to Djilas, expropriated Stalin's name at the end of the war, lending its "correct" authority back to their own cause, just as did the Party revivalists. Djilas says they did so unconsciously. A comparable configuration of Communist understandings may account for the opposition to Stalin among his sycophantic colleagues at home in 1945.

CONCLUSIONS

The first finding of this paper is that Stalin started the revival of the Communist Party of the USSR at the end of the war; not, as is often supposed, because he thought it somehow proper to rule through the Party, but because the war had sapped his control over the population, the army, and his own bureaucratic lieutenants. Our second finding is that, during the victorious spring months of 1945, the revival in its turn escaped his control, and that during the critical period when the cold war began, Stalin and his Party were locked in struggle with each other.

It seems clear, even without extensive analysis, that these findings are significant for the history of the cold war; for foreign policy was decided in those days by the same Soviet leaders who decided domestic policy. One promising area for reinterpretation, for example, may be the unity of motivation which is often attributed to the USSR and world Communism at the end of the war. If the Soviet leadership itself was not united, perhaps international Communism was less monolithic than is sometimes supposed. A second area which might stand reinterpretation is the sudden escalation of Soviet war aims during the early months of 1945. Perhaps one might associate this escalation with the domestic political trauma which was occurring at the same time. Thirdly, it may be reasonable in the light of our findings to regard J. V. Stalin more as a force of social order in the postwar world than is sometimes depicted. If he was in some sense "against" the Party at home, then perhaps his objectives abroad were less to spread revolution than to impose control over the forces of social movement in the zones of war.

NOTES

1. See R. H. McNeal, ed., I. V. Stalin, Sochineniya 3 vols. (Stanford, Calif.: The Hoover Institution, 1967) 16: 32. Letter to Razin.

2. Interview with H. Stassen, McNeal, op. cit., 16: 77-78.

3. Aleksandr I. Solzhenitsyn, The Gulag Archipelago (New York: Harper & Row, 1973), p. 19; see also p. 69, which suggests conditions in 1938.

4. Ilya Ehrenburg, The War (London: Macgibbon and Kee, 1964), pp. 74, 132-33.

5. Boris Pasternak, Dr. Zhivago (New York: Pantheon, 1958), p. 519.

6. Pravda, Jan. 15, 1960.

7. Alexander Werth, Russia at War (New York: Dutton, 1964), pp. 384ff, 674ff, for a picturesque eyewitness account.

8. See Yuril P. Petrov, Stroitel' stvo politorganov, partiinykh i komsomolskykh organizatsii armii i flote (Moscow: Voenizdat, 1961), p. 379 for striking hints about the wartime army's independence of political constraints; and his Partiinoe stroitel' stvo v sovetskoi armii i flote 1918-1961gg (Moscow: Voenizdat, 1964), esp. p. 451.

9. For example, Werth, op. cit., pp. 897ff; Milovan Djilas, Conversations with Stalin (New York: Harcourt, Brace, and World, 1962), p. 55; and K. K. Rokossovsky, Soldatskii Dolg (Moscow: Voenizdat, 1966), p. 92.

10. See Jerry F. Hough, The Soviet Prefects (Cambridge: Harvard University Press, 1969), pp. 108-09.

11. Pravda, July 1, 1941.

12. See Petrov, Stroitel' stvo Politorganov, p. 389.

13. See the essay by B. Nicolaevsky in Sotsial 'isticheskii Vestnik, no. 6, (1946), pp. 142-46; Boris Meissner, Sowjetrussland zwischen Revolution und Restauration (Cologne: Verlag fuer Politik und Wirtschaft, 1956), pp. 74-89; and the official Malenkov biography in Bol 'shaia Sovetskaia Entsiklopediia, 2d ed., vol. 26, pp. 145-46.

14. See the official Shcherbakov biography in Bol 'shaia Sovetskaia Entsiklopediia, 2d ed., vol. 48, pp. 262-63.

15. See M. I. Likhomanov, Organizatorskaia rabota partii v promyshlennosti v pervii period VOV (Leningrad; Leningrad University, 1969) for a fascinating account.

16. See, for example, the remarks by N. Patolichev in Partiinoe Stroitel 'stvo, no. 6, (1945), pp. 25ff; the striking editorial in the first issue of Partiiniaia Zhizn' (November 15, 1946), pp. 18ff; Pravda, (Feb. 13, 1948), which is cited in an American embassy report as "typical": United States Department of State, Foreign Relations of

the United States [cited henceforth as FRUS] 1948, vol. 4: 817; and such oblast Party histories as Kommunisty Sverdlovska (Sverdlovsk: S.U.K.I., 1967), pp. 254-55.

17. T. H. Rigby, Communist Party Membership in the USSR, 1917-1967 (Princeton, N.J.: Princeton University Press, 1968), pp. 241ff.

18. See, for example, A. A. Dobrodomov et al, eds., Ocherki Istorii Moskovskoi Organizatsii KPSS 1883-1965 (Moscow: Moskovskii Rabochii, 1966), pp. 601ff.

19. Petrov, Partiinoe stroitel 'stvo v sovetskoi armii i flote, p. 451.

20. See Partiinoe Stroitel 'stvo no. 3-4, (1944), p. 42; no. 10, (1944), p. 16; and no. 11-12, p. 48.

21. See Wolfgang Leonhard, Die Revolution entlaesst ihre Kinder (Cologne: Kiepenheuer und Witsch, 1959), pp. 234ff.

22. Ibid., p. 340.

23. See S. S. Biriuzov, Surovye gody (Moscow: Voennoe izdatel 'stvo, 1966), p. 362.

24. David Joravsky, comp., The Lysenko Affair (Cambridge: Harvard University Press, 1970), pp. 130ff.

25. See his remarks to Harriman in October, 1945; FRUS, 1945, vol. 4, pp. 373ff; and vol. 6, p. 712.

26. For references, see Adam Ulam, Stalin (New York: Viking, 1973), pp. 509, 588, 607, 609, 621.

27. Slavic Review vol. 27, no. 3 (Sept. 1968): 482-83.

28. Julian Towster, comp., Political Power in the USSR (New York: Oxford University Press, 1948), p. 392.

29. McNeal, op. cit., 15: 118, 142.

30. Partiinoe Stzoitel 'stvo, nos. 15-16, (1944), pp. 29-32.

31. The course of the revival may best be followed in such documentary collections as KPSS v rezoliutiakh i reshenyiakh, 8th ed. rev. (Moscow: Politizdat, 1971), 6; and KP v period VOV (Moscow: Vysh. P. Shkola, 1959, 1961, 1970).

32. See Petrov, Stroitel 'stvo politorganov, p. 379.

33. The record is put forth in English by Roman Kolkowicz, The Soviet Military and the Communist Party (Princeton, N.J.: Princeton University Press, 1967), pp. 71ff, 239ff.

34. Pravda, January 28, 1944.

35. See Bol 'shevik, nos. 7-8, (1944), pp. 15-19; and the follow-up essays by P. Fedoseev, M. Iovchuk, and M. Mitin in Bol 'shevik, nos. 9 and 11 of the same year.

36. See Shcherbakov's speeches in Partiinoe Stzoitel 'stvo no. 23, (1943), and nos. 2, 10, 11, and 21, (1944).

37. See for example the article by A. F. Vasil 'ev in Voprosy Istorii KPSS, no. 8, (1973), pp. 91-100.

38. Pravda, January 26-30, 1945, and February 1, 1945.

39. See B. Nicolaevsky, Power and the Soviet Elite (New York: Praeger, 1966), pp. 105ff.

40. R. Conquest, Power and Policy in the USSR, (London: Macmillan, 1961), ch. 4.

41. These varieties of Party pride have been inadequately researched, but see H. Salisbury, The 900 Days (New York: Harper and Row, 1969), ch. 50; and R. S. Sullivant, Soviet Politics and the Ukraine (New York: Columbia University Press, 1962), pp. 245ff.

42. McNeal, op. cit., 15: 163.

43. Partiinoe Stzoitel 'stvo no. 21, (1944), pp. 16ff.

44. McNeal, op. cit., 15: 203-04.

45. Partiinoe Stzoitel 'stvo no. 9-10, (1945), p. 3ff, esp. p. 13.

46. Partiinoe Stzoitel 'stvo no. 1, (1945), p. 41.

47. See for a clear example, Partiinoe Stzoitel 'stvo no. 4, (1946), pp. 24-25, which tells of "practical workers" who lack a Party perspective; "Comrade Stalin has compared such workers to oarsmen, who row honestly, spare no effort, flow through the water smoothly, following the current, but who neither know, nor care to know where it takes them . . . And the results? The results are clear. At the start these leaders cast a mold for themselves, then they become dullards, then they get sucked into the darkness of philistinism, and finally they get transformed into deluded philistines themselves."

48. B. Nicolaevsky, ed., The Crimes of the Stalin Era (New York: The New Leader, 1956), p. S44.

49. Ibid., pp. S42 and S46.

50. McNeal, op. cit., 15: 206.

51. Ibid., p. 214.

52. I. Deutscher, Stalin (New York: Vintage, 1960), pp. 528-29.

53. Roy Medvedev, Let History Judge (New York: Knopf, 1972), pp. 484ff, stresses Stalin's "jealousy" of Zhdanov just before the latter's death.

54. Nicolaevsky, op. cit., p. S45.

55. Medvedev, op. cit., pp. 480-81.

56. Leonhard, op. cit., p. 340.

57. Petrov, Stroitel 'stvo politorganov, p. 389. Petrov, the leading Soviet historian of Party-Army relations, claims to have seen the documents.

58. See the most recent and subtle version of Tito's "surprise" in V. Dedijer, The Battle Stalin Lost (New York: Viking, 1971), esp. ch. 5.

59. Milovan Djilas, op. cit., p. 12.

CHAPTER

4

AMERICAN FOREIGN AID AND YUGOSLAV FOREIGN POLICY

Stephen C. Markovich

Following its expulsion from the Cominform in 1948, Yugoslavia was able to survive the subsequent pressures from the USSR with the help of American aid. The primary objective of this aid, in both the American and Yugoslav view, was to help Yugoslavia maintain its independence; for the Americans, Yugoslav independence was important because of the many cold war advantages for the West that accompanied it, and for the Yugoslavs, independence had the highest priority because it was fundamental to their nation's internal development and foreign relations. Despite agreement on this objective, the two countries encountered considerable difficulties during the years that the United States extended aid to Yugoslavia; many of these difficulties arose when Yugoslavia found itself subject to pressures from the United States on questions of foreign policy and the status of its independence vis-a-vis the USSR. It is on these pressures that this chapter focuses.

Instances in which the United States did put pressure on Yugoslavia through foreign aid and the extent to which these pressures influenced Yugoslav decisions in foreign affairs are considered by reviewing and analyzing the 12 most important years, 1948-1960. Particular consideration is given to American-Yugoslav relations in the

---

Research for and preparation of this study were aided by a Faculty Research Grant, University of North Dakota and a Hill Family Foundation Grant.

context of foreign aid, focusing particularly on those instances in which pressures were applied and assessing American achievements in exerting them and Yugoslav successes in withstanding them.

AID AFTER THE EXPULSION

President Tito's strategy for more than a year after his country was expelled from the Cominform called for continued praise of the USSR and continued attacks on the United States and the West. But this strategy did not mean that the Yugoslav leader ruled out the possibility of receiving assistance from the West. On the contrary, his actions on the diplomatic level showed that he considered the West, particularly the United States, a means of escaping the consequences of the Cominform expulsion. Thus, a more conciliatory attitude on the part of Tito's diplomats brought a release of Yugoslav gold assets frozen in New York, a revision of America's trade policy with Yugoslavia, and loans from the World Bank and Export-Import Bank, all within a year of the expulsion. By the summer of 1949, Tito's criticisms of the West had begun to subside and Yugoslavia's relations with the West had gained a positive momentum.

While minor differences between the West and Yugoslavia sometimes jarred this momentum, two major issues—one concerning Greece and the other Vietnam—nearly brought it to a halt. Tito initially became disturbed with the Western reaction to his announcement in July, 1949, that Yugoslavia had closed its frontier to the Greek Communist rebels.[1] What aroused Tito was that some Western sources, the Italians in particular, interpreted his move as a concession made in return for American aid, and viewed it as a precedent for further concessions.[2] Although the available evidence suggested that Tito's main reason for closing the border was to protect Yugoslavia's southern flank from encirclement by Cominform supporters, Western persistence in interpreting it as a concession sparked Yugoslavia's latent suspicions of political pressure and drew a strong rebuke from the Yugoslav leader.

Tito reacted even more strongly when the United States departed from its policy of making no political demands and asked the Yugoslavs not to recognize the Vietnam rebel regime of Ho Chi Minh.[3] In this case Tito used a preelection speech to blast the Americans for pressuring the Yugoslavs and to remind them that his country was a dedicated socialist state which would not make any changes that would compromise its principles. Emphasizing Yugoslavia's independent foreign policy and referring indirectly to its recognition of Ho's regime, he declared

> We are not going to make any concessions with regard to our foreign policy. . . . Our foreign policy must be in harmony with our socialist, our communist principles. . . .
>
> If someone tells us that they will not trade with us and that we will not get some machines because we restored relations with this or that country, and we know that these relations are right in principle, then we do not want these machines. But we will recognize whatever state we think should be recognized, because this is in our interests, in the interests of socialism in our country.[4]

The United States dropped its request regarding Ho Chi Minh and tried to ease Yugoslav suspicions with statements reiterating American policy of strict noninterference in Yugoslav affairs. These statements were supported with two more loans from the Export-Import Bank, positive responses to Yugoslav requests for economic assistance in the summber of 1950, and the passing of the Yugoslav Emergency Relief Assistance Act toward the end of the year. And, in recommending the Emergency Relief Act to Congress, President Truman repeated that it was the policy of the United States to assist Yugoslavia in maintaining its independence.

Up to this point, the assistance that Yugoslavia had received from the United States was in the form of trade agreements, favorable loans, and a few grants. Each of these items was negotiated separately; that is, one of them came under a long-term arrangement or on a program basis. This relationship changed in 1951 when the United States together with Great Britain and France agreed to underwrite Yugoslavia's foreign payments deficit for the 1951/52 fiscal year. Under this tripartite arrangement, dominated by the United States, the American and Western policy of supporting Yugoslavia emerged from its first phase of stopgap assistance into one of a formal commitment to establish the Yugoslav economy on a sound basis. The significance of the tripartite grants was that the Western nations had committed themselves to assist in the construction of a Communist economy.

While this step to finance the Yugoslav economy appeared to concern the country's internal policy, for the Yugoslavs this support had significance for both their domestic and foreign policies. From their point of view, the rapid industrialization of Yugoslavia was the key to the nation's economic liberation and political independence. They had successfully led a revolution with industrialization as their goal. They had planned an ambitious five-year program for industrial development; they had stood up to Stalin when his actions threatened their program; and in the early negotiations for aid from the West as well as subsequent negotiations, they refused to do anything that would seriously delay the realization of this goal. The Yugoslavs persistently argued that the only way their country could maintain its political independence internationally was to establish a high degree of economic independence through a policy of accelerated internal development.[5]

The tripartite program underwrote a good portion of the Yugoslav payments deficits for four years, from July 1, 1951 to June 30, 1955, and for the most part enabled the Yugoslavs to continue their concentration on industrial development. Although some questions on Yugoslavia's internal development arose during the negotiations, at no time did these lead to any significant delays in the annual talks or to any major suspensions in aid deliveries. The donors, especially the United States, while they acquiesced to the Yugoslav position on the relationship of industrial development and international independence, were more interested in points directly related to Yugoslav foreign policy. Leo Mates, a principal representative for the Yugoslav government in the aid negotiations, maintained that foreign policy issues were certainly the crucial points on which the annual negotiations for tripartite and other aid nearly broke down. According to Mates, the Western powers tried to exert most pressure on issues regarding the Yugoslav army, specifically its possible amalgamation with NATO forces, and on issues regarding territorial disputes, particularly Trieste.[6] All of these issues were related. The question of military aid was closely connected to the question of Yugoslavia's joining NATO, whereas Tito's territorial and diplomatic disputes with his neighbors, especially Italy and Greece, were obvious obstacles to NATO membership. These points came up during the negotiations for tripartite aid, and also during American-Yugoslav bilateral negotiations for military assistance and additional economic aid.

Negotiations in 1951 for military assistance proved to be long and laborious. Over 10 months elapsed from Yugoslavia's initial request for arms aid in January, 1951, to the day the two countries signed an agreement the following November. These protracted talks were partially due to Tito's fear that quick acceptance of Western military assistance would lend confirmation to Soviet accusations that Yugloslavia had sold out to the capitalists and was now the advance guard of the West. At the same time he was genuinely afraid that the United States desired to validate the Soviet accusations by forcing the Yugoslavs into some type of alliance with the Western powers in return for military aid. Only after months of negotiations were these fears and some technical difficulties overcome, and the two countries signed a one-year bilateral agreement for mutual defense assistance.[7] The agreement required Yugoslavia to accept a U.S. military mission on its soil, to transfer certain raw materials to the United States, and to keep the public informed of operations under the agreement, but it did not contain any clauses imposing special military obligations on Yugoslavia.

Under the agreement, the Yugoslav government made frequent requests for heavy equipment such as artillery, tanks and aircraft. The American government usually fulfilled these requests despite some misgivings as to the effectiveness of heavy equipment in the hands of soldiers whose tradition and training had heretofore stressed guerrilla warfare. To be sure, the American government realized the importance of sending heavy equipment to Yugoslavia, for this equipment enabled the Yugoslav army to maintain a parity or margin over the satellite armies. At the same time, the United States had hopes that this equipment might act as a catalyst in enticing Yugoslavia to join a Western military alliance, preferably the North Atlantic Treaty Organization.

From the time American aid began flowing into Yugoslavia, President Tito stated that his country would not join any alliance "We cannot join the various pacts," said Tito, "because we occupy a special position and because we are a socialist country that does not believe in paper agreements but in realities."[8] Although he accepted the principle of collective security as stated in the United Nations Charter, he opposed the concept of pacts, alliances, or blocs because they tended to divide the world into two hostile camps. Yet when asked what America received in return for its military assistance, Tito answered: "The United States receives what it has been getting for years—an ally against aggression in this part of the world."[9]

Gradually the Yugoslav leader modified his view on blocs. In July, 1952, while once again rejecting the possibility of entering a pact, Tito nevertheless suggested that his government might consider a verbal agreement with Greece, Turkey, and Austria. A few months later, his vice president, Edvard Kardelj, stated that Yugoslavia would revise its opposition to regional pacts should war threaten and should the world situation continue to deteriorate. For Yugoslavia to consider such a pact, two essentials would have to be met: a guarantee of political equality for each member and a guarantee of noninterference in internal affairs.[10]

With Yugoslavia showing interest in a Balkan alliance, the United States increased its efforts to encourage the trend. A series of visits by high level U.S. military personnel produced statements in support of past arms aid and recommendations for further military support for Yugoslavia. Following these recommendations, the United States took additional steps to modernize the Yugoslav army and to standardize their equipment along the lines used by the Greek and Turkish forces.[11] The intensive American efforts together with the modifications of Yugoslav views on blocs brought results. On February 28,

1953, Yugoslavia signed a treaty of friendship with Greece and Turkey, and on August 9, 1954, the three countries signed a twenty-year pact pledging mutual aid and political cooperation.

Undoubtedly the efforts of American diplomatic and military officers played a role in effecting the Balkan entente. Yet it was also clear that President Tito saw other advantages in signing the pact apart from that of pleasing the United States as a payment for past aid or a quest for future assistance. "We did not join them" said Tito, "because they gave us aid. No, we did so because we maintained that it was in our own interest owing to the fact that we were exposed to pressure from the other side. . . . "[12] Moreover, Tito believed the pact protected not only his eastern flank but also his western flank. In effect, the pact put Italy on notice that the Balkans were for the Balkans, thereby squelching any latent ambitions in the minds of Italian irredentists still looking beyond Trieste down the Dalmation coast. Additionally, it served to undermine the strong Western support enjoyed by Italy in the Trieste question; within a month after the pact was signed, the Trieste question was settled.

Trieste had been an explosive issue since the end of the war. A political bombshell in the domestic politics of both Yugoslavia and Italy, the issue brought forth a profusion of statements, speeches, proposals, and counterproposals from both governments. Even the Western powers periodically entered the fray by issuing tripartite communiques favoring the Italian position. Not surprisingly, then, the question of Trieste frequently became entangled with the American policy of aiding Yugoslavia. During Yugoslav-American negotiations on foreign aid, the Italian government exerted constant pressure on the U.S. government to force a Yugoslav concession on Trieste. But the United States, while certainly making some attempts in this direction, was generally reluctant to assume an adamant position on such a volcanic point. When it did press the issue, as in the tripartite communique of October 8, 1953, Tito's reply was emphatic:

> Somebody in the West may say: 'Look how they are. And you are proffering them aid!' Well, we are thankful for the assistance, we said that hundreds of times, but we cannot sell our country for that aid, we cannot give our soil soaked with blood for that aid. We refuse aid if this is the situation.[13]

Robert Murphy, a key figure in the final stages of the Trieste negotiations, doubted that Tito would have surrendered on a matter of principle such as Trieste "for a shipment of wheat." Murphy made this statement to correct Sir Anthony Eden's suggestion that the Americans went to Belgrade, laid some wheat on the line, whereupon the

Yugoslavs grasped the pen and signed the Trieste agreement.[14] While Eden's statement probably overstated the case, Murphy's view tended to understate it. Murphy implied that there was no connection between a morning conversation he had with Tito on Trieste and an afternoon conversation he had with Svetozar Vukmanovic-Tempo on Yugoslavia's need for wheat. "When Vukmanovic-Tempo brought up this matter," wrote Murphy,

> I told him that perhaps the United States could be helpful, but that I had to come to Belgrade to ask for Yugoslav support on immediate settlement of the Trieste issue. Actually I was authorized to offer assistance if circumstances justified, and before departing for Rome, I informed Deputy Foreign Minister Bebler in the strictest confidence that the United States would be willing to deliver 400,000 tons to Yugoslavia.[15]

Murphy's colleague, Undersecretary Bedell Smith, was in a position to be more direct in a report he cabled to President Eisenhower. After explaining the complicated nature of the Trieste negotiations, Smith concluded "Both the wheat and the financial problem [financial debts] give us a certain leverage on the Yugoslavs, which we intend to employ in reaching a Trieste settlement."[16]

Robert Murphy was most likely correct in stating that the Yugoslavs would not exchange a principle for wheat. What bothered Murphy were the pushy attempts by the Yugoslavs to exact as much American aid as possible as their price for agreeing on a settlement on Trieste, a settlement with which they were apparently satisfied. On the other hand, Murphy was equally determined to get more than the agreement on Trieste for American assistance. Adamancy on both sides led to a statlemate in the negotiations. When the talks were resumed, Murphy still wanted the United States to hold out for more but Harold Stassen, now the chief American negotiator, decided to yield. The Yugoslav negotiator, wrote Murphy,

> continued to be offensively aggressive and at one point in the discussion, I slipped a note to Stassen saying: 'Now it's your turn to get tough!' But Stassen's scribbled reply was 'Let's get tough next year.' The Yugoslavs received everything they demanded, about $260 million worth, for which we never got a bit of satisfaction or benefit.[17]

Stassen's refusal to press Murphy's points suggested that with the settlement of the Trieste question the U.S. government was satisfied with the situation in southeastern Europe. After granting Yugoslavia $560 million in economic assistance and $590 million in military assistance over a five-year period, the American government could point to several successes: American-Yugoslav relations on the whole were better than ever in the postwar period; a communist nation on the East bloc's periphery was allied with two members of NATO; satellite Albania was more isolated than ever; the Trieste solution opened the door to an Italo-Yugoslav rapprochement; and economically Yugoslavia was tied to the West as over 75 percent of its trade and 100 percent of its aid was attributable to the United States and Western Europe. All in all, it seemed the once-belligerent satellite was becoming increasingly attached to the West.

Despite these gains, one black cloud loomed on the horizon. After the death of Stalin in March, 1953, the Yugoslav leaders had gradually but consistently diminished the barrage of invectives aimed at the USSR and its satellites. In the middle of June, they had resumed diplomatic relations with the USSR, at the request of the latter; and soon thereafter their relations with the satellite governments began to mend. Although the Yugoslavs responded cautiously to initial overtures made by the USSR, relations between the two Communist countries slowly improved. Finally, in May, 1955, a high-level Soviet delegation headed by Premier Nikolai A. Bulganin and First Secretary Nikita S. Khrushchev visited Yugoslavia. From the American point of view, a rapprochement between the USSR and Yugoslavia would not erase all of the gains made by U.S. aid policy but the basic reason for aiding Yugoslavia would disappear.

AID AFTER THE RAPPROCHEMENT

During the first six years of American aid to Yugoslavia, the United States had concentrated on drawing Yugoslavia closer to the Western nations through political, economic, and military ties. While there had been some attempts to limit Yugoslav relations with other Communist regimes, for example, North Vietnam, the United States did not push Yugoslavia heavily on such points. Now, however, the Yugoslavs were repairing their relations with the USSR and on this matter the American president tried to influence the Yugoslavs by suspending aid negotiations and stalling aid shipments in hopes of blocking or limiting the success of any rapprochement.

The United States began to employ dilatory tactics following Khrushchev's visit to Yugoslavia in 1955. Fearful lest Yugoslavia reenter the Communist bloc, the United States slowed down aid shipments and hinted that it would have to reexamine its aid policy should Yugoslavia declare "absolute neutrality."[18] These initial maneuvers appeared to have little effect on President Tito. Commenting on threats to cut off aid if Yugoslavia did, as Tito put it, sarcastically, "return to her family," he went on to say

> Aid was beneficial for us, but I have to tell you, comrades, that we will not give up our principles in international policies for aid, just as we did not nor will we renounce our ways in our internal social development. When it comes to aid, military or otherwise, we have not two but one alternative - not to accept with conditions attached.[19]

Although the Soviet-Yugoslav accord, wherein the USSR recognized Yugoslavia as an equal, was considered a diplomatic victory for Tito, the United States nevertheless wanted reassurance that Yugoslavia was in fact precluding a return to the Soviet bloc. Consequently, in the month of June, 1955, a series of diplomatic meetings initiated by American officials culminated in a conference in Belgrade of the Yugoslav undersecretary of state and the ambassadors of the United States, Great Britain, and France. In a joint communique issued on June 27, 1955, the four governments confirmed the existence of a wide measure of agreement in their approach to various international questions and expressed the conviction that a strong and independent Yugoslavia contributed to peace and stability.[20]

This episode was the first in a recurring pattern in which the Yugoslavs made moves toward a rapprochement with the USSR, and were then faced with suspensions in aid negotiations and deliveries which were resumed when the Yugoslavs publicly and/or privately reassured American officials that an improvement in Yugoslav-Soviet relations did not mean that Yugoslavia was giving up its independence. Throughout the remaining years of the aid program, aid suspensions came in connection with several points of Yugoslav policy but primarily on the Soviet-Yugoslav rapprochement and on foreign policy questions which, from the American point of view, were connected with the rapprochement.

No sooner had Tito given the United States assurances following Khrushchev's visit in mid-1955 when the United States again employed stalling tactics. During the fall of 1955, in the face of developing Soviet-Yugoslav ties, American aid shipments began to lag. Despite U.S. denials of any delays, the flow of aid, particularly military aid, was slowed down long enough to indicate that the delays were intentional. These delays, sporadic as they were, continued into 1956 and ultimately led to a sharp cutback by the United States in the spring of that year. In June, prior to two Belgrade-Moscow declarations on government and party ties, President Eisenhower, replying to a question on Yugoslav independence, said

> I would think that the Tito incident is not wholly and entirely a loss. However, I do agree that where we stand has to be re-evaluated. We have to take a look at where we stand with this individual now and what serves our best interests.[21]

Tito publicly denied that Yugoslavia was compromising its independence and its relations with the West:

> We are absolutely convinced that we are not losing our independence. Such talk is fabrication. The Soviet leaders never suggested that we should weaken our Western relations—economic, political, or cultural. We have been sorry to hear that in the U.S. there have been threats to cut off aid because of improvement in our relations with the Soviets. We are grateful for the aid, but we would never have accepted humiliating conditions for it that would tie our hands in domestic and foreign policy. All that was true in the past is true still and will remain so in the future.[22]

Nevertheless, President Eisenhower remained skeptical and aid shipments slowed increasingly through the summer months. When Eisenhower finally decided to resume the aid, he did so on a qualified basis. On the one hand, he resumed aid by permitting the State Department to begin negotiations for economic assistance and the Defense Department to continue small, long-planned deliveries of military supplies; on the other hand, he withheld the deliveries of jet planes and other items of heavy equipment "until the situation can be more accurately appraised." Furthermore, he placed the entire aid program on a short tether by directing that "those officers who conduct our day-to-day relations with Yugoslavia vigilantly apply the very helpful criteria established by Congress in section 143 [of the Mutual Security Act of 1956] to insure that the decision we have now made remains justified in future circumstances."[23]

The Yugoslav reaction was cool. In a statement issued by *Tanjug*, the official Yugoslav news agency, the Yugoslavs made known their objections to certain formulations in President Eisenhower's remarks. First, they found unacceptable his statement that the extension of partial economic aid was of indefinite duration subject to revision at any moment; since it was always possible, for one reason or another, to delay or cancel its further extension, this policy threatened the security of Yugoslavia by undermining the principles of independent and equal cooperation.[24] Second, they rejected his contention that American aid enabled Yugoslavia to preserve its independence: "We consider that there exists no threat to the independence of Yugoslavia on the part of the Soviet Union."[25]

This statement indicated two shifts in Yugoslav policy. First, it showed the Yugoslavs were ready to change the nature of American economic aid. In rejecting Eisenhower's "short-tether" policy, they proposed the adoption of a "new" type of economic cooperation that would enable Yugoslavia to purchase U.S. agricultural surpluses under long-term credits to be repaid in dollars or some other corresponding currency. Since this approach—credits in place of grants—was one the United States had also been advocating, the change was easily effected and most of the aid after 1956 came in the form of loans and credits.

The second and more notable shift came in the rejection of the U.S. statement on Yugoslav independence. Ever since the United States began aiding Yugoslavia in 1949, the Americans had justified this aid on the grounds that it enabled Yugoslavia to maintain its independence—an independence that served as an example to Soviet satellites. The Yugoslavs had frequently made public statements accepting this rationale. Witness, for instance, the statement made by Vice President Edvard Kardelj who, on pointing to the strikes and general unrest of workers in East Germany and Czechoslovakia, declared: "Five years ago we were alone and at present we have friends throughout the world. We have them also in the countries of the Soviet bloc. There is no doubt that the democratic socialist idea, which was victorious in our country, will one day be victorious in their country."[26]

At a meeting on Brioni Island in November, 1955, Secretary of State Dulles and President Tito agreed that the East European countries should be independent. "The final subject of our talk," said Dulles, "was the problem of the States of Eastern Europe. We reached common accord on recognizing the importance of independence for these States, non-interference from the outside in their internal affairs, and their right to develop their own social and economic order in ways of their own choice."[27] But the governments differed on the meaning of independence. For the United States, satellite independence meant the breakup of the Soviet bloc with a consequent establishment of anti-Communist regimes in these countries. For the Yugoslavs, independence meant that established Communist regimes would reduce their ties with the USSR and follow an independent road to socialism, a road similar to the one taken by Yugoslavia. Moreover, in the Yugoslav view, these regimes should be encouraged to turn from Moscow in anticipation of receiving aid from the West.[28]

The American interpretation of satellite independence made the Yugoslav leaders somewhat uneasy. If the United States hoped to use foreign aid to the satellite countries not only to assist them in asserting their independence but also to replace their Communist governments, then what was the ultimate American aim in extending aid to Yugoslavia? While the Yugoslav leaders realized the United States had no love for their political and economic system, they repeatedly made clear they would brook no interference. They assumed the same position with regard to satellite independence. A few days after the Dulles-Tito meeting, a Yugoslav spokesman announced that his country's attitude toward the East European countries remained unchanged. This attitude, he explained, was set forth in the joint declaration of June 2, 1955, by Tito and Bulganin wherein they called for noninterference, independence and freedom for each country to choose its own social system.[29]

The Yugoslav position on satellite independence required practical applications in October, 1956, when revolts in Poland and Hungary challenged Soviet domination in these countries. At first the Yugoslav leaders appeared stunned by the Soviet interventions, but inside of a week they broke their initial silence with public approbations of the new regimes in Poland and Hungary. The Yugoslavs were less concerned about the Polish than the Hungarian uprising. They likened the Polish move for independence to their own effort in 1948, that is, a move by one socialist country to achieve independence from another socialist country in order to choose its own road. (Twelve years later they took the same position in supporting Czechoslovakia.) In the Hungarian case, however, the Yugoslavs' reaction reflected anxiety over the possible development of an independent Communist movement into an anti-Communist movement. This anxiety was reflected in their accepting the second phase of Soviet intervention in Hungary after criticizing the first.

In retrospect, under either the American or Yugoslav interpretation of satellite independence, Yugoslavia's experience had definite limitations as a model for emulation by other East European countries. Its geographical position, strength of its army, loyalty of its party, and boldness of its leadership were some of the characteristics which distinguished the renegade country from most of the satellites, particularly in the 1950s. In addition, Stalin's successors moved quickly in using political pressure and military power to stem the revolts in Poland and Hungary in 1956 and Czechoslovakia in 1968. These distinctions and circumstances severely limited the opportunities of the satellites to widen their autonomy by following the Yugoslav example.

Although the satellites were not immediately successful in their attempts to effect changes, their attempts at any rate were attributed in part, by the superpowers and others, to the influence of Yugoslavia. Whatever the extent of this influence, Tito's regime consequently improved its standing with Washington, which credited the Yugoslav example. And as soon as the Soviet displeasure manifested itself in verbal attacks on Yugoslavia, American approval manifested itself in a reappraisal of certain suspensions and slowdowns that had been restricting American aid shipments for months. This reappraisal involving the international position of Yugoslavia and the degree of Tito's independence preceded a decision by Eisenhower regarding aid.

Eisenhower's task was made easier by Yugoslavia's critical responses to Soviet attacks and positive comments about the United States. In a speech before the Yugoslav Parliament, the Secretary of Foreign Affairs, Koca Popovic, warned Soviet leaders "to avoid all recurrence of Stalinism, which brought incomparably more harm to socialism than all imperialist plots put together."[30] A Borba editorial charged that the Kremlin was vilifying and isolating Yugoslavia through its campaign against the country—against its internal socialist system and against its independent foreign policies, particularly its policy toward the United States. On the last point, the editorial stated "Yet it [the USSR] is now ever more directly and acutely attacking Yugoslav-American cooperation, which is one of the very concrete and important achievements for the affirmation of active, peaceful co-existence in the world."[31]

The decision reached by President Eisenhower was favorable to the Yugoslavs. In early May, 1957, Deputy Undersecretary C. Douglas Dillon began negotiating with Ambassador Leo Mates on Yugoslavia's need for long-term aid. And on May 14, the United States announced the resumption of military aid, releasing about $100 million in equipment including 200 jet aircraft. In making the announcement, the State Department said a review had confirmed the president's belief that Yugoslavia was and firmly intended to remain independent.[32]

The Yugoslavs, pleased with the aid, now became critical of the rationale underlying U.S. aid resumption. "It is questionable," said a spokesman for the State Secretariat of Foreign Affairs, "whether a solution that makes arms deliveries dependent on the appraisal of our relations with third countries can be in accordance with our policy of independence."[33] A week later, President Tito expressed his annoyance when he said,"Nobody can force us to conduct a one-sided policy in our relations with other countries; we will never subscribe to such a policy because it is against our principles."[34] As if to prove his point, Tito permitted his defense minister, Ivan Gosnjak, to accept an invitation to visit the USSR. A few months later, on October 16, he made his point emphatically with the announcement that Yugoslavia would recognize East Germany.

On this occasion, as it had since 1955, the United States reacted strongly. As far as Washington was concerned, Tito's recognition of East Germany represented another link in a series of Yugoslav policy moves aligning Belgrade with Moscow. Just as other moves had led the United States to question the policy assumptions underlying American aid, so the recognition of East Germany provoked a similar response: "In the light of recent developments," declared a State Department official, "we are reappraising our program with Yugoslavia."[35] As a result, aid shipments were slowed down and negotiations for renewed economic assistance were postponed.

President Tito attempted to overcome this latest stall by clarifying Yugoslav policies in a meeting with U.S. Ambassador Riddleberger. In presenting his case, Tito argued that Yugoslavia made its own foreign policy decisions based on the merits of each particular situation and not on the basis of pleasing or displeasing the USSR. As proof of this he cited the refusal of the Yugoslav representatives to sign a 12-power declaration in Moscow because he declared the primacy of the Soviet Communist Party and because it contained some harsh anti-Western statements. Yugoslavia was and would remain independent, claimed Tito. During this meeting Tito also requested a termination of the military assistance program. Since the program was already near an end (no new shipments had been made for nearly a year and there was little chance of Congress appropriating any in the future), the two governments agreed to terminate with the understanding that promised commitments would be fulfilled and future purchases would be allowed.[36]

The Riddleberger-Tito meeting smoothed over mutual irritations which had strained American-Yugoslav relations since Khrushchev's visit to Yugoslavia in 1955. It also marked the beginning of a period stretching into 1960 which featured good relations between the two countries. Coinciding with this period of good relations was the end of the second Soviet-Yugoslav rapprochement and a renewal of their propaganda and ideological war.

Vice-president Vukmanovic-Tempo gave an indication of things to come in early January, 1958, when negotiations for economic assistance were renewed. Lauding the United States for giving aid without interfering in Yugoslavia's affairs, he pointed to the American-Yugoslav relationship as a model of cooperation "between a large developed country and a small underdeveloped country with a different social system."[37] President Tito picked up the theme in a speech delivered at the Seventh Party Congress in which he praised the United States for aiding Yugoslavia in its most difficult times and scorned the USSR for suggesting there were strings attached to the U.S. aid.[38] In a subsequent speech, in which he caustically rejected Khrushchev's charge that the United States was unloading "tainted goods" on Yugoslavia, Tito said "American wheat is not worse than Russian wheat.

The difference is that we get wheat from America and we do not get it from the Soviet Union. This helps us overcome our difficulties which, I am sad to say, are caused by the very people who should be helping us."[39]

With favorable relations between Yugoslavia and the United States and unfovorable relations between Yugoslavia and the USSR, negotiations for American economic assistance for 1958, 1959, and 1960, progressed relatively smoothly, with no lengthy postponements and no major delays. Even in 1960 when an improvement in Yugoslav-Soviet relations pointed toward a third rapprochement the Eisenhower Administration did not resort to delays in aid to try to block it. This apparent change in U.S. strategy can be explained in part by the increasing limitations on foreign aid as a means of exerting leverage in American-Yugoslav relations inasmuch as the bulk of the aid was now in the form of loans which resembled commercial transactions rather than bilateral grants. More important, however, it also reflected American recognition of Yugoslavia's status as a sovereign socialist state that was genuinely independent of the USSR.[40]

CONCLUSIONS

When the USSR threatened Yugoslavia's independence in 1948, the Yugoslavs met this threat by standing firm and then approaching the United States for assistance. The Yugoslavs also saw threats to their independence in dealing with the Americans but these were far more subtle in nature. Here they were not faced with an obvious, heavy-handed threat as in 1948 but with fending off minor encroachments which could have compromised their principles and limited their options. They met these encroachments by taking strong stands against them: on questions on which there was agreement between donor and recipient, the Yugoslavs invariably claimed they had other reasons apart from aid for making their decisions, and on questions on which there was disagreement they rejected the American positions outright. Moreover, in defending their positions, publicly and privately, the Yugoslavs were very often vociferously on the offensive; in fact, there were times when suspicion of pressure alone was enough to ignite forensic retorts from Yugoslav spokesmen, and other times when their grateful acceptance of aid was followed by an immediate attack on the American rationale. Overall, the Yugoslavs' defense was to meet any attempt, real or suspected, to use foreign aid to influence their foreign policy with an immediate, sharp attack against the pressure coming from the donor.

On foreign policy questions on which the donor and recipient agreed, the Yugoslavs dislcaimed the influence of aid. Thus, when the United States or another Western country suggested that foreign aid played a role in settling Yugoslavia's border disputes with Greece and Italy, in creating the Balkan pact, and in stimulating unrest in Europe, the Yugoslavs argued that there were other reasons that prompted the decisions and reactions of their government. To be sure, from Tito's point of view, closing the border to Greek Communists, settling the Trieste question, and signing a defense pact with Greece and Turkey strengthened Yugoslavia's position as well as that of the West. By closing the Greek border, the Yugoslavs removed pro-Soviet forces from their southern flank. By agreeing to a Trieste settlement, they took a first step in improving relations with a country that could help them in West Europe generally. And by signing the Balkan Pact, they indirectly used the power of NATO to check any military threat from the East. Finally, any fragmentation of the Communist bloc stemming from movements for independence by satellite regimes benefited the Yugoslavs as well as the West since a softening of the Soviet position tended to increase Yugoslavia's security and prestige.

The reason that the Americans could attribute a role to foreign aid in effecting these Yugoslav policies and that the Yugoslavs could claim that they would have followed these policies with or without aid, was that their respective countries were in agreement on these matters. There were in fact advantages for both donor and recipient. As long as the goals of the United States and Yugoslavia were similar, then foreign aid could be a catalyst in achieving them. The prospect of aid made some decisions easier for the Yugoslavs by providing them with additional incentive to adopt policies which already promised them benefits. This was the situation in the early years of the aid program, the years between Yugoslavia's expulsion from the Cominform in 1948 and Khrushchev's visit to Yugoslavia in 1955. During this period there were few differences between donor and recipient on the major reason for giving aid, namely to maintain Yugoslavia's independence. Agreement on this point enabled the United States and Yugoslavia to work towards additional goals of mutual interest.

At no time, however, could the Americans persuade Tito to yield on questions on which there was sharp disagreement, that is, on any issue or principle which the Yugoslav leader viewed as fundamental to his Communist identity. Any suggestions that his country join NATO or refuse to recognize Ho Chi Minh's regime were rejected by Tito. His ability to stand firm on issues of this nature, and the American caution in pressing him on such matters, limited the degree to which U.S. aid could influence Yugoslav policies. Since the United States did not wish or was unable to influence Yugoslavia on such decisions when the very independence of the country was threatened, then its possibilities of influencing Tito's regime greatly diminished when the pressure from the East lifted.

Before the Khrushchev visit in 1955 Yugoslav independence of the Communist bloc was clear-cut. After the visit a fundamental difference arose between the United States and Yugoslavia on the meaning of independence. The Yugoslavs felt that as long as they made their own policies they were fulfilling their pledge to remain independent; the fact that their policies sometimes agreed with Soviet policies was beside the point. But the Americans thought otherwise; they viewed any coincidence in Yugoslav and Soviet policies as an indication of Belgrade's submission to Moscow's leadership. Yugoslav independence, the basic objective of American aid policy, had become blurred.

Although President Eisenhower continued to state publicly that all the United States wanted was that Yugoslavia remain independent, his directives on distribution and negotiating of aid indicated he was more concerned with the day-to-day development of Tito's foreign policy. Whenever a Yugoslav policy took a pro-Soviet turn, the American president made known his displeasure by suspending aid deliveries or postponing aid negotiations. Following the Khrushchev-Tito meeting in 1955 and when Belgrade supported Kremlin positions on some international issues, Eisenhower suspended aid deliverieis and suggested a reexamination of the program itself.

These dilatory tactics placed only modest limits on Tito's maneuverability. At most they limited the enthusiasm of his support for Soviet positions and the tone of his criticisms of the United States. Thus, whenever Tito moved too close to the Kremlin to suit the United States, Washington reacted with a delay in aid. Each delay resulted in Tito's making some public statement or gesture toward the United States to reaffirm his independence of the Kremlin. Yet the conciliatory responses which these delays elicited from Tito did not cause him to change any major policy decision. Eisenhower could not dissuade him from recognizing East Germany, either with threats before recognition or delays in aid shipments afterwards. In summation, when Yugoslav and American goals or interpretations differed, the United States had little success in using aid to restrain Yugoslavia from following a policy opposed by the United States.

NOTES

1. Borba, July 11, 1949.
2. New York Times, July 12, 1949, p. 8.
3. Hamilton Fish Armstrong, Tito and Goliath (New York: Macmillan, 1951), pp. 274-75. Confirmed in personal interview with

former Ambassador George V. Allen, Washington, D.C., August 18, 1964.

4. Borba, February 19, 1950.

5. Slobodan Brankovic, "Impact of Foreign Aid on the Postwar Development of Yugoslavia" Yugoslav Institute of International Politics and Economics Belgrade: 1961), p. 41.

6. Personal interview with Leo Mates, participant in the early aid negotiations and Ambassador to the United States, 1954-58, Belgrade, spring, 1965. See also Tito's speech in Borba, January 13, 1951.

7. See U.S., Department of State, United States Treaties and Other International Agreements, vol. 2, pp. 2254-61, for the text.

8. Josip Broz Tito, Govori i Clanci (Speeches and Articles) (Zagreb: Naprijed, 1959), 7: 48-49.

9. Ibid., 6: 236.

10. New York Times, November 5, 1952, p. 6 and February 24, 1953, p. 1; and Tito, op. cit., 7: 113-14, 291-93.

11. New York Times, September 29, 1952, p. 4; November 16, 1952, p. 3; and December 5, 1952, p. 6.

12. Borba, October 11, 1953.

13. Borba, October 11, 1953.

14. Robert Murphy, Diplomat Among Warriors (Garden City, New York: Doubleday, 1964), pp. 422-25.

15. Murphy, op. cit., p. 422.

16. Dwight D. Eisenhower, Mandate for Change 1953-56 (Garden City, New York: Doubleday, 1963), p. 419.

17. Murphy, op. cit., pp. 426-27. For a Yugoslav view of these negotiations, see Svetozar Vukmanovic-Tempo's description in his Revolucija Koja Tece: Memoari, (Beograd: Kommunist, 1971), 2: 211-21.

18. New York Times, May 15, 1955, p. 1.

19. Tito, op. cit., 10: 177.

20. U.S. Department of State Bulletin, 33, July 11, 1955, pp. 49-50.

21. New York Times, June 7, 1956, p. 10.

22. Tito, op. cit., 11: 146-47.

23. U.S. Congressional Record, 85th Cong., 1st Sess., 1957, 103, Part I, 48.

24. Tanjug, October 17, 1956.

25. Borba, October 19, 1956.

26. Borba, June 28, 1953.

27. U.S. Department of State Bulletin, 33 (November 21, 1955). p. 856.

28. Borba, November 6, 7, 8, and 9, 1955.

29. New York Times, November 12, 1955, p. 3.

30. Borba, March 11, 1957.

31. Borba, March 10, 1957.

32. U.S. Department of State Bulletin, 36 (June 10, 1957), pp. 939-40.

33. Borba, May 18, 1957.

34. Politika, May 24, 1957.

35. New York Times, October 24, 1957, p. 5.

36. U.S. Department of State Bulletin, 39 (July 14, 1958), p. 84 and New York Times, March 26, 1958, p. 8.

37. Borba, January 11, 1958.

38. Tito, op. cit., 13: 162-63.

39. Ibid., p. 261.

40. See Milorad M. Drachkovitch, United States Aid to Yugoslavia and Poland (Washington: American Enterprise Institute, 1963), for a discussion of the various views held by Americans on U.S. aid to Yugoslavia. Some of the general studies which deal with foreign aid as an instrument of foreign policy are David A. Baldwin, Foreign Aid and American Foreign Policy (New York: Praeger, 1966); Herbert Feis, Foreign Aid and Foreign Policy (New York: St. Martin's Press, 1964); George Liska, The New Statecraft: Foreign Aid in American Foreign Policy (Chicago: University of Chicago Press, 1960); Joan M. Nelson, Aid, Influence, and Foreign Policy (New York: Macmillan, 1968); and Andrew F. Westwood, Foreign Aid in a Foreign Policy Framework (Washington: Brookings Institution, 1966).

PART II

SPECULATIONS ABOUT DETENTE

CHAPTER

5

DETENTE "MYTHS" AND SOVIET FOREIGN POLICY

Robert C. Horn

It hardly needs to be stated that there exist great differences of opinion on the matter of the current detente between the United States and the USSR. Controversy abounds as to just what detente means, what it ought to mean, and where it is leading the two superpowers specifically and world politics in general. This is as it should be. Those of us concerned with the nature of Soviet foreign policy, for instance, are struggling to decipher Soviet intentions and perceptions and the overall Soviet reality. Many of us are also seeking to define what the optimum realizable relationship between Washington and Moscow might be and how both sides could best arrive there. The many-sided discussion by government officials, academics, newspaper columnists, and others serves the purposes—or ought to—of raising and clarifying the issues involved in these questions. Nevertheless (and not surprisingly), there are some pervasive arguments and/or assumptions, particularly in the literature, but also in public statements, that seem to this writer to raise points that are misleading in their emphases. These frequently tend to obfuscate rather than clarify the current status of U.S.-Soviet relations which we have come to call detente. No one analyst or political figure necessarily embraces all of these and, fortunately from my point of view, many do not fall victim to any. Yet, due to their wide acceptance, often implicit presentation, and significance in the current debate, five such contentions—there may be others as well—warrant examination and qualification. These five are admittedly interpretations of Soviet foreign policy and Soviet-American relations that differ from my own. Moreover, they deal with aspects that are clearly controversial, with questions for which no conclusive answers exist. It is in the interest of convenience of labeling, therefore, rather than out of arrogance or self-righteousness that herein lie all the answers, that I have chosen the term "myth" to designate those arguments or assumptions with which I take issue. The purpose of this paper is to examine these myths and offer contrary interpretations of the points they raise. The emphasis is on these alternative understandings rather than on the derivations, roots, and adherents of the myths. Moreover, the thrust of this study is to attempt to gauge Soviet perceptions of these issues as this is essential to a balanced view of the nature of detente. This author's hope is that this brief analysis will provide the rudiments of a framework for viewing detente and will thereby contribute toward clarifying our understanding both of detente and of contemporary Soviet foreign policy.

MYTH I: DETENTE PRECLUDES CONFLICT OR COMPETITION

For the USSR detente is an offshoot of peaceful coexistence, the general line of Soviet foreign policy. As such, as the British analyst Walter Laqueur, among others, has rightly recognized, it does not preclude struggle but is indeed a form of continued struggle or competition with the West.[1] It is the continued pursuit of Soviet interests vis-a-vis the West by all means available short of the use of force or the direct application of military power. It is difficult to see why the USSR's pursuit of its perceived interests should be surprising to students of the USSR and international politics. This is the nature of the beast, that is, of all states. Nor should it be surprising that in many cases Soviet interests may be seen from Moscow (and/or Washington) to clash with American perceived interests. What is surprising is that in many quarters it is argued, or more often implied, that there cannot be a true detente while such competition or conflict between the two superpowers continues.[2] Justification for such skepticism regarding detente is most commonly found in the Kremlin's activities in the Middle East,[3] but also in the Soviet strategic buildup, activities during the India-Pakistan war, and expansion of the Soviet navy.[4]

In large part these differences among observers of contemporary world politics can be explained by the lack of a common understanding of the term detente. Is it a state or a process? What are its minimal requirements or attributes? What is the proper time frame by which to evaluate it? An aspect of our problem, as Marshall Shulman has written, derives from the fact that "For those who live by words or phrases that sum up the entire situation at a glance, there is no simple substitute for the term 'cold war'."[5] Given the convenience of employing catch-words that symbolize a mass of details and interrelationships, however, the use of some word or phrase is likely. Taken in its fundamental meaning, the relaxation of strains or tensions, detente would seem to be usefully applicable to contemporary Soviet-American relations. Certainly in this context it is more accurate than "normalization" as relations between Moscow and Washington have "normally" been strained. Herein also lies the central flaw in Myth (or Implicit Argument) I: What is there in the history of U.S.-USSR relations that would lead us to expect the complete disappearance of differences and clashes of interest? Two superpowers with perceptions of their role in international politics and their own interest are bound to have differences and Soviet-American differences—real, imagined, perceptual—have been evident since 1917. This historical legacy is of such duration and such intensity that it ought to be apparent that only substantial efforts and changes over time will diminish its force. Thus, it is even less realistic to expect the creation of an instant and totally cooperative relationship between the two. If detente is to be anything significant in these circumstances, it must be a slow and gradual identification of areas of common interest—arms control, for example—and the working out of ways to deal with these and other issues on which interest may diverge. In Professor Shulman's words,

> That we will continue to be rivals for a considerable time seems dictated by our situations. But that rivalry can be less dangerous to the world and less overcast with hostility if it operates within commonly accepted rules of the game, and in time it may be diminished by a recognition of our growing common needs.[6]

A tense and hostile relationship provides little opportunity to establish rules of the game and identify common interests. The detente process we have witnessed since 1969 (to the extent a particular year can be specified) has already had the beneficial impact of providing increased opportunity. Soviet-American relations are less emotional and more relaxed and increased discussions and contacts have allowed enough of a common perception to develop to enable the two sides to sign numerous agreements pledging a variety of forms of mutual cooperation. Whether common norms of behavior are being established is not yet clear. (While the 1973 Middle East war may have indicated the negative, the more recent Cyprus crisis may serve as a positive indicator.) "Unrealistic idealism" as to the depth and speed of change of Soviet-American relations, as former President Nixon recently and accurately stated, "could tempt us to forego results that were good because we insisted upon results that were perfect."[7] There has to be a beginning point and progress may well not be in a straight line.

A recent State Department publication summarized the situation in the following terms:

> However the dimensions of detente are perceived, both sides, it seems, agree that detente is necessary because of the danger posed by the accumulation of nuclear weapons; that detente is necessary not because we do not have opposing interests in many parts of the world or because our systems are not totally different—but precisely because these conditions do prevail; and that while occasional conflicts of interest will occur, detente makes possible a more rapid settlement and insures a certain restraint. And, finally, both sides seem to agree that detente is necessary because there simply is no other rational alternative.[8]

Detente thus far has meant an improved international atmosphere and has seen significant change in both Soviet and American foreign policy. This is meaningful progress and to expect more at this time is hardly realistic.* How much further Washington and Moscow can go in this relationship remains to be seen.

---

*There is an extreme variant of this myth that asserts that true detente (or rapprochement) will not come about until the USSR changes its internal system. Something of this has been expressed by Senator Henry Jackson (see summary of the problem in Congressional Quarterly Almanac 29, 1973, p. 794, and 30, 1974, pp. 514-15), Soviet dissident writer Andrei Amalrik rather eloquently in Will the Soviet Union Survive Until 1984? (New York: Harper and Row, 1970), pp. 57-58 , and Soviet dissident physicist Andrei Sakharov (Washington Post, September 19, 1973) as well as implied by some of the articles cited in Footnote 2. Effective rebuttal has been expressed by President Nixon: "What is our capability to change the domestic structure of other nations? Would a slowdown or reversal of detente help or hurt the positive evolution of other social systems?" (See Footnote 7), Secretary of State Kissinger, Marshall Shulman (see Footnote 5), and Soviet dissident historian Roy Medvedev (New York Times: November 9, 1973). Basically, this "requirement" of detente seems far less realistic to me even than the unrealistic expectation or demand that the USSR discontinue competing with the West and drop all interests that differ from ours.

MYTH II: THE SOVIET REGIME AND ITS POLICIES ARE MONOLITHIC AND SINGLE-MINDED

There has been a distinct trend in the West in the recent past toward greater sensitivity to the crucial role of internal divisions within the USSR, particularly within its decision-making circles, and to its input into foreign policy. Although we still are aware of only the crude outlines of internal differences and their impact on Soviet external behavior, we have developed a wealth of evidence of such differences. Put in oversimplified form, we know that in many cases conservative elements of the Party apparatus align with the military and secret police forces (the heads of the last two were elevated to Politburo status in April 1973) in opposition to government ministries, the technocrats, and more liberal CPSU leaders. The interrelationships are likely very complex: divisions may exist on a number of criteria and the line-up of the two or more sides may not be consistent from issue to issue. At the basis of the differences is the allocation of economic resources. Major and related differences also exist on the perception of external threats. Substantial debates, usually implicit and veiled from the Western view, have taken place in the USSR on these and other issues. Soviet foreign policy is intricately interwoven with these internal divisions. As Wolfgang Leonhard has observed, the change to greater moderation in Soviet foreign policy in 1969 came as the "result of a serious tug-of-war between various factions of the top leadership."[9]

Notwithstanding the above, Myth II seems to continue to exist all too pervasively. It seems to be too little remembered, kept in the forefront, and acted upon in the West. That is, for example, on the basis of hard-line statements or acts, we often seem eager to jump to the conclusion that <u>this</u> is Soviet policy. In the heat of the moment there is too great a tendency to forget that the statement or action may represent posturing in the internal debate, an action allowed as part of a compromise, or a testing of the waters by one contestant, rather than the policy of the regime. (Even so, of course, these naturally will have an impact on the West and the Soviet leadership should be aware of that.) What is called for on our part, then, is extreme cautiousness in instant analysis, a well-honed sensitivity to attempting to place all developments into the context of Soviet internal politics, and an equally sharp awareness that each step (or statement) by the United States will likely have an impact on Moscow's internal debate (although predicting precisely the nature of that impact is something altogether different). This problem can perhaps be further explicated in terms of its relationship to Myth III.

MYTH III: HARD-LINE IDEOLOGICAL STATEMENTS REVEAL THE TRUE NATURE OF SOVIET FOREIGN POLICY

Probably nothing has given Western analysts of Soviet foreign policy more difficulty than identifying the role of ideology in that policy. Countless articles and introductions to texts have been devoted to weighing the relative weights of national interests and ideology in Soviet behavior. Although it seems that Western scholarship long ago saw the merits of examining the Soviet record, rather than Soviet rhetoric (not necessarily eliminating the question of the ideological element of Soviet perceptions), certain aspects of Soviet behavior in this period of detente seem to have kept the issue on a front burner. A basic aspect of what Leopold Labedz has cited as "creeping Newspeak" is that "*detente* is a matter of 'peaceful coexistence' in which the attacks on 'imperialism' are to be permitted as 'ideological struggle,' while criticism of Soviet actions is to be banished as 'a return to the spirit of the cold war'."[10] And, as Marshall Shulman has argued,

> There is a fundamental contradiction in the Soviet position that 'peaceful coexistence between states with different social systems is possible,' but that it is consistent with, and even intensifies, the 'ideological struggle.' . . . From the point of view of the United States, a campaign of 'ideological struggle' against the 'imperialist enemy' perpetuates attitudes of implacable hostility and sets narrow limits on the relaxation of tension, and there is a strange inconsistency between this Soviet stance and its attacks on foreign radio broadcasts as contravening the spirit of 'peaceful coexistence'.[11]

While I must agree with Labedz and Shulman that this current "ideological struggle" campaign pursued by the Soviet Union contradicts much of its actual detente policy, there is a clear danger, I think, in dealing with this ideological element at face value.[12] That is, the real questions are: 1) What lies behind the intensified ideological campaign, and 2) How significant is it in helping us to understand Soviet policy? The answers that I see are based on the fact that this campaign is related almost exclusively to internal needs and situations and has exceedingly little to do with Soviet international behavior (beyond being one more attempt to insure the continuing solidarity of the socialist camp, particularly in Eastern Europe).

The ideological offensive functions internally in two ways: First, it has been adopted by the regime as the necessary domestic counterpoise to an external policy of relaxed relations with class enemies. (It is thus actually an ideological <u>de</u>fensive.) It has been accompanied by an increasingly repressive policy of internal control. As Wolfgang Leonhard has summarized,

> . . . the moderation and flexibility which have characterized Soviet foreign policy since 1969 have had no echo in domestic affairs. The harsh internal policy which has affected all decisive aspects of Soviet society since Khrushchev's downfall has become even harsher in the last few years. This contrast between a more flexible and more moderate foreign policy vis-a-vis the West on the one hand, and a harsh internal policy on the other, has become a distinctive trait of the present Soviet system.[13]

The Soviet regime clearly feats the penetration of outside influences into Soviet society and the erosion of the CPSU's control. As long as foreign relations dealt with the United States and West Germany as still-dangerous aggressors, this internal danger was not seen as acute. It has been aggravated, however, by detente, by new agreements, summits, and the obvious cooperation between the USSR and such antagonists. Thus, for Moscow detente represents a calculated gamble vis-a-vis the Soviet political system (as well as Eastern Europe) and every effort must be made to maintain vigilance (that is, the monopoly of political power must remain in the hands of the Party leadership).

It has been suggested that in order to deal with economic needs and problems the Soviet regime was faced with the choice of undertaking large-scale internal reforms or going abroad for assistance.[14] Quite obviously, the Russian leaders have opted for the latter in order to avoid the former. It has also been suggested that in the internal political struggle the ideological struggle was a trade-off for peaceful coexistence. Again according to Marshall Shulman,

> The net result of thse conflicting domestric pressures has been that Brezhnev has won a free hand to implement his policy of 'peaceful coexistence' abroad, while the apparatus of orthodoxy and control has been given a free hand to tighten the lines of ideological vigilance at home, and to prosecute the 'ideological struggle' between capitalism and socialism with renewed vigor.[15]

In any case, this sensitivity of the Soviet regime to outside attempts to erode its control, surprising only in its degree, makes the extreme variant of Myth I—that the Soviet system should be changed in return for U.S. trade and real detente—all the more incredible. Not only does such an approach overestimate the power of foreign influence but it is likely to work to the advantage of the hard-line elements in the Soviet leadership who have warned that detente with the United States will mean threats to the Soviet system. While private pressure may be useful, governmental interference (such as Senator Jackson's amendment) in what the Soviets see as an internal affair will hardly serve the cause of detente.[16]

Second, it must be kept in mind that, as mentioned in the discussion of Myth II, the ideological offensive may also only be functioning as an instrument in the domestic debate. Indeed, there exist a great number of Soviet documents, articles, and editorials that have argued the various sides of the detente issues. Perhaps the most prolific spokesman for the need for detente has been Georgy Arbatov, the reputedly influential head of the Institute of the U.S.A. His article in the institute's journal,[17] seems to be a typical example of one aspect of his approach. It is a relatively straightforward argument that there exist "problems whose solution would be in the interest of the Soviet Union and the U.S.A. and at the same time would not be contrary to the legitimate interests of other countries and peoples." He warns of the danger of continued tensions in Soviet-American relations, the destabilizing factor of the arms race, the need for increased economic and other cooperation, and the need to deal with these aspects, keeping in mind "a correct understanding of the interests of both sides, including the interests of the United States. . . ."

At other times, however, Arbatov apparently has seen the need to adopt a less direct approach. In these cases he has utilized a rather militant-sounding ideological analysis to argue basically the same pro-detente points. It may well be that cloaking arguments in ideological-struggle terms and double meanings is seen at times as a more effective—or necessary—means of joining the domestic debate. Take for example, a reprinted translation of an Arbatov article which appeared in 1971.[18] Here the Soviet specialist on American affairs seems to be making two points concerning the reasons for the current improvement in Soviet-American relations. One is that it is due to diminished U.S. power and the bankruptcy of past American foreign policy. Second, it is due to "the strength of the resistance of its ["imperialism's"] adversaries." Where a hard-line or orthodox approach would undoubtedly emphasize the second aspect as being more crucial, Arbatov focuses at great length on the first and deals only fleetingly with the second. Still, on the surface, his condemnation of U.S. foreign policy seems heavily ideological in tone and rather hostile. When read more closely, however, many key passages seem to point to the likelihood that they were intended to say something else even more important. For example, when Arbatov criticizes American "reliance upon military might" and "position of strength" policy, he seems to be warning Moscow's "hawks" (an extremely oversimplified yet convenient designation, as it is in the American context) that such approaches would be equally counterproductive for the USSR. "There is no way" of gaining from such policies, he says.

> The threat of thermonuclear war today lies not only in that some lunatic may 'press the button'; it is in the very policy of 'local' military adventures, nuclear blackmail, an unrestrained arms race, and high-handed intervention in the affairs of other countries.
>
> This policy is itself capable of directing the development of international relations into a channel in which it will no longer be possible to retain control over events.
>
> In this sense there can no longer be any purely "local" conflicts and wars in today's world; they all have far-reaching consequences. This is testified to by the experience of the U.S. adventure in Vietnam, which frustrated the relaxation of tension then under way, complicated the international situation, whipped up the arms race, and produced growing instability in the world arena.
>
> The principal consequence of the 1960s for the United States consisted in the fact that its policy not only did not help it advance in the struggle for the strategic goals set by Washington, but actually undermined the country's international position and complicated the situation at home.[19]

Arbatov seems to be urging that the USSR avoid a repetition of policies that led the United States into difficulties. He goes on to acknowledge "the extravagance of the arms race" and the fact that it and foreign policy adventures can exacerbate internal problems. It does not seem that these points could have been missed by those involved in the debate in the Kremlin. When he states that "even so rich a country as the United States could not simultaneously have both 'guns' and 'butter'," what is he implying for the USSR, an economy with a gross national product (GNP) which is less than one-half that of the United States? In closing, Arbatov quotes "the German military theorist Clausewitz" to the effect that it is impossible to deal with new conditions and relationships if one thinks "in terms of a purely military understanding of events." His message for Soviet military leaders, a group seen as generally skeptical of detente, seems clear. If this interpretation of Arbatov's arguments is at all accurate, then it would seem to represent one more aspect of the proper perspective into which Moscow's current "ideological struggle" campaign ought to be placed. We must continue to read between the lines.

MYTH IV: DETENTE HAS BEEN AND IS BEING PURSUED BY THE USSR OUT OF OFFENSIVE MOTIVES

It seems reasonable to assume that virtually all foreign policies of any state have both offensive and defensive components. This might be seen in a minimum/maximum concept in terms of expectations or in a short-range/long-range time approach (or a combination of the two). Nevertheless, it would also seem that a determination of the greater motiviation—offensive or defensive—could be made for a state's policy with the yardstick (still vague, of course) of reasonable expectations in a near-future time frame. An example would be the case of the obvious motivating factor in contemporary Soviet foreign policy of the policies and postures of the People's Republic of China (PRP). Surely one could say that the Russians have offensive motivations vis-a-vis China—to eliminate China as a competitor power. Yet, as the 1969 Russian talk of a "pre-emptive nuclear strike" has subsided, it has seemed clear that the actual defeat or elimination of China was such a long-range motivation or goal as to be nonoperational. That is, it is much more probable that Soviet policy has been motivated defensively vis-a-vis China—to reduce the direct threat to the USSR and to counter the indirect one to various Soviet interests.

The same can be said for the economic motivation in recent Soviet policies. It can be said that this was offensive in the sense that the USSR seeks to build itself into a greater economic power than the United States and thus outstrip and bury capitalism. This, however, is exceedingly long-range and the economic motivation can be more reasonably seen as a defensive one, as seeking outside assistance in order to deal with serious internal difficulties and popular dissatisfactions. The point of all this is that, to the extent the terms offensive and defensive can be usefully employed to describe Soviet motivations, there seems to be a rather widespread myth that these motivations are offensive, such as nuclear superiority over the United States, expansion of Soviet power in Europe, the emasculation of the United States and NATO, the further consolidation of Soviet control of Eastern Europe, and so on. If an observer is persuaded of these offensive motives, he accepts a particular picture of the Soviet perception of detente and the policies the West should pursue toward the USSR. It seems to me, however, that in the mix of offensive and defensive threads in the motivations for contemporary Soviet foreign policy, the defensive ones have clearly predominated. If true, this would be an insight into the nature of detente as the Soviets see it and would paint an entirely different picture of Soviet behavior and how the West might deal with Moscow. Although this is impossible to prove, some informed speculation is in order.

While there certainly is no single-factor explanation for the changes in Soviet foregin policy begun in 1969, the China factor stands out as among the most significant of the various Soviet motivations. The border clashes that began on the Ussuri River in March drove Sino-Soviet relations to a new nadir. Intermittent fighting continued throughout the summer and relations did not begin even to stabilize until the talks between Premiers Kosygin and Chou En-lai in September. Moreover, China was also beginning to present a significant diplomatic challenge to the USSR as well, particularly with the first "straws in the wind" of a normalization of relations between Peking and Washington. As Vernon Aspaturian has written, China was now challenging the USSR (in addition to physical clashes along the border) in both of Moscow's worlds—in the Communist system and in the global arena.[20] As early as February, the Russians were calling attention to feelers—particularly by China toward the U.S.*—hinting at a Sino-American rapprochement.[21] Moscow also saw possibilities of Chinese ties with West Germany or Western Europe; indeed, Mao had linked the region potentially (along with Japan and Canada) to China for several years in his concept of a "second intermediate zone."[22] Judging from Soviet commentary at the time it seems clear that the USSR perceived a multilevel threat from an assertive and diplomatically active China†

---

*It is unlikely also that the Soviets were not sensitive to the implications of change in U.S. relations with China indicated in Richard Nixon's October 1967 article in Foreign Affairs or that they long remained unaware of Nixon's approach to Charles de Gaulle for assistance in improving relations with the PRC.

†Vladimir Reisky de Dubnic argues that the "China peril theme" was used by the Soviets to camouflage their own "hegemonic aspirations." While not denying the internal and external "usefulness" of the Chinese "threat," I obviously disagree and believe Moscow perceived a real threat from Peking. See de Dubnic "The 'China Peril' Theme

and quickly sought policies to counter this. Soviet dissident historian Andrei Amalrik wrote in the first half of 1969 that the conflict with China would present the successive dangers of Washington siding with Peking or at least not aiding Moscow, West Germany and Japan perhaps doing the same, Eastern Europe becoming de-Sovietized, and Communist authority collapsing within the Soviet Union.[23] Apparently the Russian leaders shared at least some of these perceptions with Amalrik, for Soviet policy began to move during 1969 in precisely these directions: detente with the United States was begun, the decision was reached again (as it had been in 1968, only to be rendered meaningless by the invasion of Czechoslovakia and the Western reaction) to enter into the Strategic Arms Limitation Talks (SALT), detente was begun in Europe, feelers were extended to West Germany and Japan, calls for guaranteeing the status quo in (particularly Eastern) Europe were issued, and internal controls were strengthened.* Concrete gestures by the Nixon administration toward China (easing of trade and travel restrictions were initiated in July 1969) and increasing Sino-West European contacts led to accelerated Soviet efforts.[24] On perhaps three occasions, beginning in 1969 or 1970, the USSR reportedly (the Russians deny it) sought tacit American support in some sort of immediate action against China.[25] In any case, it is apparent that Moscow felt compelled to take significant initiatives in international politics in the face of an increased challenge from China that symbolized a changing international order.[26]

Additional motivations (all interrelated with one another) combined with the defensive one of the China factor to encourage the Soviet leadership to these initiatives. One of the most significant of these had to do with the state of the Soviet economy. Again, this was primarily a defensive motive. By 1968, serious economic problems which had existed toward the end of Khrushchev's rule began to reemerge. The growth rate began to decline again and the competition for resources sharpened. This loss of economic momentum became more pronounced during 1969 as the performance goals for 1970 were cut back and there were repeated delays in publishing the outlines for the ninth Five Year Plan (1971-75).[27] The lag in the USSR's adaptation of its industrial

---

in Soviet Global Strategy," Bulletin of the Institute for the Study of the USSR 18, no. 6 (June 1971): 3-19 .

*Many of these themes found their first clear-cut emphasis in Foreign Minister Gromyko's address to the Supreme Soviet, July 10, 1969; see Pravda, July 11, 1969.

system to the scientific and technological revolution became increasingly apparent and increasingly an obstacle to economic growth. Agricultural difficulties continued unabated. As indicated earlier, the Soviet leadership, by refusing to undertake substantial internal economic reforms, had only one alternative—to seek the necessary trade, technology, and capital from abroad. This could come primarily from the United States, West Germany, and/or Japan. "The realization of these expectations" of massive economic assistance from the West, as Marshall Shulman has pointed out, "manifestly requires an international climate of reduced tensions,"[28] that is, detente. (Moreover, a detente situation can justify the reallocation of resources away from the military and thus leave a larger slice of the pie for internal economic needs. This was a crucial aspect of Khrushchev's approach and is still an important theme in the Soviet internal debate.)

In light of the above, another Soviet motivation for detente, that of improving its position in Western Europe, may be seen as something more than an offensive one of simply reducing American influence in Europe (and weakening NATO) and replacing it with some kind of Soviet hegemony perhaps akin to Soviet power vis-a-vis Finland.[29] Here may be an area of "mini-max" in terms of Soviet motivations and goals. That is, the USSR may well have in mind the offensive maximum of pushing the United States out of Europe and establishing itself as the predominant power there. But that is a longer-range goal. A more immediate explanation for Soviet detente policy in Europe would be the need for the minimum: the keeping quiet of its western front in a time of conflicts on the eastern, the prevention of diplomatic and economic inroads by China in Western and Eastern Europe, and the possibilities of Western economic resources to aid the ailing Soviet economy. Beyond these very definite defensive goals and much vaguer offensive ones, the Russians probably do not have a very detailed blueprint for what they would like to see in Europe. As Robert Legvold has remarked,

> Soviet leaders doubtless have some vague sense of what would be an ideal state of security in Europe. It may not be—indeed quite probably is not—a full and articulate vision, much less a clear design motivating day-to-day policy.[30]

Moscow is even more clearly on the defensive in Eastern Europe. One of its motivations for its more moderate foreign policy is to gain Western acquiescence—and East European resignation—to Soviet hegemony in that region. I strongly agree with Adam Ulam who has pointed to the "tendency in the West to overlook the dilemmas and anxieties that the USSR's system of alliances . . . produces for Moscow."[31]

Social and economic problems in those states combining often with political rigidities and the still important forces of nationalism create feelings of vulnerability in Moscow's part. Yet next to the preservation of its own power within the USSR the maintenance of Soviet political control in Eastern Europe continues to be the Soviet leadership's most vital interest. The Russians are acutely aware of the dangers that detente represents to their control over Eastern Europe—increasing penetration by the West, possible "Finlandization" of the region (the obverse of the normal Western notion)—and consequently spare no effort in calling for vigilance and unity within the socialist community.[32] (Here is an example of the external usefulness of the ideological struggle campaign.) The Kremlin evidently hopes, in a period when the (partially manipulated) fear of "German revanchism" had already lost much of its rallying force, to utilize detente to bring about and insure the recognition of the status quo in Europe. In the medium- to long-run this would be a stable way to confirm Soviet control in Eastern Europe.

The achievement of rough nuclear parity with the United States by the USSR in 1969 (indeed the Soviets moved ahead of the United States in land-based ICBMs at that time) has been a major motivating force in Moscow's policy of detente. It was only with the attainment of such parity that Moscow felt it could negotiate with Washington; that is, it would not be bargaining from a position of weakness (which is the only remaining role if one power insists on maintaining a position of strength). The problem in weighing Soviet defensive (the above economic and political factors) and offensive (detente and arms negotiations as stalling tactics while moving to strategic superiority) motivations is that, as in the case of Western Europe, the Kremlin may not have a concrete goal or plan in mind for its strategic power. The author, for one, is inclined to agree with the view of RAND's Thomas Wolfe that "the Soviet leaders probably embarked on the buildup without a fixed blueprint for the future and without having settled among themselves precisely what sort of strategic posture vis-a-vis the United States would prove satisfactory to Soviet policy needs during the next decade."[33] That is, the leadership could agree on the fundamental goal of equality with the United States at least and on opening preliminary arms limitation talks. (The latter was pursued with varying degrees of energy from June 1968 on, although the internal debate on the substance of the negotiations and agreements has continued throughout the period. Gromyko's July 1969 speech to the Supreme Soviet seemed to reveal significant progress in the emergence of a pro-SALT consensus.) Until that was achieved, no further decisions were required. What stage the internal debate is in, now that parity has been attained, is not clear, but it is obviously of critical importance to the future of detente. Thus, the precise mix of offensive and defensive threads cannot now be determined.

Finally, Moscow has been motivated to pursue detente because of changes in American foreign policy. Former President Nixon's offer of an "era of negotiation" was one indication of this and did a great deal to lessen Moscow's skepticism regarding U.S. policy in the Nixon administration. Also, Moscow's assessment—as in the above-quoted Arbatov article—that Washington's power is in the decline due to objective factors internally and externally might represent an offensive motivation: pursuit of the opportunity to improve the USSR's overall power position relative to that of the United States.[34] The realization, however, that Moscow's detente policy began when the United States was still heavily involved in Indochina and was pursued at the first summit in Moscow during a major American escalation in Vietnam ought to give pause. That is, it can be argued that Moscow was seeking detente despite continued American power and certain American policies and that the defensive motives suggested above may be more explanatory. There would again seem to be an important mix of defensive threads interwoven with the offensive ones in this motivation, too.

MYTH V: RESULTS OF DETENTE HAVE BEEN ASYMMETRICALLY FAVORABLE TO THE USSR

Detente is necessarily a long-term process and the results therefore cannot yet be in. Nevertheless, there do seem to be sound reasons that ought to encourage us to question the rather popular myth that the results thus far have been heavily favorable to the USSR and basically detrimental to the United States. (Since world politics is no longer—if it ever was—a zero sum game, gains for one side are not necessarily translated into commensurate losses for the other and vice versa. Arbatov, for one, certainly recognizes this.) By examining briefly the developments in each of the areas of Soviet motivations for detente discussed above, perhaps some qualifications of this myth can be suggested. What seems to be useful here is not to compile or quote extensively from the various agreements reached, but rather, as in the case of Soviet motivations, to try to analyze Soviet perceptions. It is the Soviet view that we must try to gauge.

The threat from China in its various manifestations is clearly still present for the Soviets. Tension has been decreased but no agreement has been reached in the border talks; while war does not seem likely, the build-up of troops and materiel on both sides has continued. Washington has continued the improvement of relations with Peking (if slowly). Moreover, the United States not only rejected Soviet enticements to take action against China (or to refrain from any involvement if the Soviets did) but worked into the agreement on the prevention of nuclear war signed at the 1973 summit two principles that would make a Sino-Soviet conflict even less likely: that (Article 2) the United States and the USSR would refrain from the threat or use of force against each other or other countries and that (Article 4) they would enter into consultations should there develop a risk of war between them or involving other countries.[35] Diplomatically, the challenge from the PRC has increased. Peking has clearly accelerated its drive for ties with Western states—as evidenced by its admittance to and participation in the United Nations, former President Nixon's visit to China, increasing intergovernmental and economic exchanges with Western European countries[36]—and has accompanied these efforts with constant warnings about the intentions of Soviet foreign policy. Moscow's sensitivity to Peking's efforts toward Washington and West European capitals has been expressed in great quantity and with great vehemence.[37] In essence, Moscow laments that "the facts show that the Chinese leadership is not content with a natural normalization of relations with capitalist states but is doing everything possible to inject into this process anti-Soviet, anti-socialist tendencies."[38]

Economically there has been some movement, but from Moscow's point of view it must be far short of expectations. Trade has grown from $200 million in 1971 to $1.5 billion in 1973. This is still a small amount given the size of the two economies and, from Moscow's perspective, even that has been accomplished only with great difficulties. The latest of several political obstacles to increased economic ties has been the successful effort initiated by Senator Henry Jackson and others to refuse most-favored-nation status to trade with the USSR until Moscow allows free and open emigration and also to restrict the size of export-import bank credits. Given their great sensitivity to threats to their internal control, these obstacles are likely to outweigh the gains from the infamous wheat deal in the minds of Soviet leaders. As stated in the Soviet journal International Affairs,

> The attempts by some circles in the West to impose on the Soviet Union various "preliminary terms," to demand ideological "concessions" or to use peaceful coexistence to promote ideological penetration of socialist countries are totally intolerable and have nothing in common with the expansion of mutually beneficial cooperation.[39]

Indeed, it seems hardly surprising that the attempt at "internal interference" coupled with the relatively meager gains offered in terms of credits moved the Soviet leadership to reject the trade pact with the United States.

It would seem the Soviets have done only marginally better in the area of Western Europe. They have become a more important political voice in that region and may have aided in what may be further declining American influence there. Relations have been normalized with the Federal Republic of Germany and economic contacts increased. West European integration seems stalled and the Soviet-urged Conference on Security and Cooperation in Europe may be contributing to these and other developments more or less favorable to the USSR. On the other side of the ledger, however, it must be kept in mind that all in Europe is in flux and trends are difficult to discern with any degree of certainty. Moreover, as mentioned, China's diplomatic activities and West European travels to and ties with Peking have increased. The four-power agreement on West Berlin may represent a plus for the West—not necessarily a minus for the Soviets—by increasing that city's security and affirming its links to West Germany. Brezhnev himself seems unsure enough of the USSR's own role in Western Europe to have assisted the Nixon administration in defeating the Mansfield amendment to pull U.S. troops out of Europe.[40] Thus, it is not clear where the USSR stands relative to five years ago.

Soviet security in Eastern Europe seems, at least for the immediate future, to have increased. The 1968 invasion of Czechoslovakia has had its intended quieting effect and the West has yet to attempt to exploit detente by seeking to loosen the Soviet political grip in the region. Growing international acceptance and recognition of East Germany has fulfilled a long-sought Soviet goal. In this sense, detente has not meant so much an increase in Soviet power and control as often perceived in the West but rather a confirmation and recognition of reality. Furthermore, from the Soviets' point of view, given their long-standing (and justified) feeling of vulnerability in Eastern Europe, the degree of quiet in the region may well be a temporary phenomenon.

To the extent that Moscow's motivation in SALT has been to establish the recognition of Soviet nuclear strength and parity with the United States, this has been accomplished by the SALT I accords. If Moscow's motivation is more offensive, to delay any thorough and permanent agreement until achieving superiority, the groundwork may have been laid also. Nevertheless, it is still an open and fluid situation and there is nothing in the Interim Agreement of 1972 that consigns the United States to permanent inferiority. Clearly it is the Soviet perception that is the key to future Soviet moves on the strategic level. All indications are that the Soviets are not likely to be strategically content until they, like the United States, have deployed MIRVs (which they have recently begun to test). And this issue of perception is made exceedingly complex by the fact that the strategic question is probably the most debated and most divisive foreign policy-related issue faced by the Soviet leadership. Secretary of State Kissinger's assessment of the 1974 summit referred directly to this: "My impression from what I have observed is that both sides have to convince their military establishments of the benefits of restraint and that is not a thought that comes naturally to military people on either side."[41] An extremely important unanswered question is how the leadership will finally come to perceive the utility of superiority (and this will depend greatly on the perceptions of the utility to United States policy of the former American predominance);[42] we have already referred to Arbatov's approach and can infer the outlook of more conservative elements. These differences are not dissimilar from those in the United States as seen in the above statement by Kissinger and other recent ones by Senator Fulbright (amidst the accusations that it is the Russians who are blocking further agreements). The difficulty of arriving at any comprehensive accord is necessarily going to be enormous, since it affects both sides' basic perceptions of security. The lack of a permanent agreement at the 1974 summit ought not to allow us to overlook this and the fact that several not insignificant agreements have been reached at each of the three summit meetings. In Kissinger's mind, and we would agree, it is the next 18 to 24 months that will indicate the future status of the arms race, not the last such period.

Lastly, it can be said that the USSR has improved its overall power position vis-a-vis the United States. That is, more countries now view the USSR as a global superpower. Still, how much of this is attributable to what we call detente? Largely it is a recognition of the reality of Soviet power. The real question has been what form this improved power status would take operationally. Moscow has improved its ties in South Asia, for example, but has recently been accorded something of a setback even there with India's detonation of a nuclear device. In Southeast Asia, the Soviets allowed the United States to bomb and mine and blockade North Vietnam and its ports and are currently having difficulty in the region competing with China and Japan.[43] In the Middle East, Moscow's mixture of opportunism and restraint did little and Washington's stock has risen dramatically there.* These developments, or in some cases nondevelopments from

---

*Richard Ullman is quoted in Time (July 1, 1974) as being surprised at the extent to which the Soviets were willing to jeopardize relations with the United States in the Middle East conflict. Wilfred Burchett, "The Superpower Show that Flopped," Far Eastern Economic Review (November 5, 1973): 29-30, on the other hand, cites evidence of Soviet restraint and the positive influence of detente during the crisis.

the Soviet view, combined with more of the same as discussed earlier in this section,provide us once again with a mixed picture as to results for the USSR.

CONCLUSION: DETENTE REVISITED

There would seem to be little point in rehashing these five myths and my qualifications of them in this conclusion. What may be useful would be to pull togehter some of the threads of the arguments and assumptions that structure this writer's understanding of the nature and meaning of detente.

The first point concerns the nature of Soviet foreign policy. Soviet international behavior has changed greatly since Stalin's time. Khrushchev moved in fits and starts toward a detente with the West; his successors have gone a great deal further and since 1969 have introduced more moderation and flexibility into Soviet policy. Given the motivations I believe are behind this change, as disaussed earlier, this new Soviet policy is likely to be pursued for longer than just the immediate short run. That is, the problems of China (even when Mao dies China will still be a major power which shares conflicting interests and an extensive border with the USSR), economic shortcomings, security in Eastern Europe, as well as relations with West Europe and the United States,would not seem to be susceptible to any immediate solution. To the extent that this is so and despite Brezhnev's personal and signficant role in Soviet detente policy, this general foreign policy course is likely to be continued even should the General Secretary be forced to leave his post due to illness or advanced age. This is not to deny that there are differences within the Kremlin regarding the meaning and effect of detente; and undoubtedly Brezhnev and his closer supporters have to defend the benefits of detente to more skeptical colleagues. Nevertheless, it is my feeling that barring a substantial shake-up in the Soviet leadership (which cannot be ruled out totally and could clearly be impacted by Soviet perceptions of Western efforts to use detente to gain benefits at the expense of the USSR), the same internal and external problems will continue to exist and will continue to suggest the same or similar approaches to their solution.

Second, detente seems to me to be necessarily a long-term process in another sense. The past differences between the United States and the USSR are too great to be resolved in short order.

Third, detente is a necessary process. The alternative is a spiraling arms race, growing domestic discontent in both states, increased tension in world politics, increased possibility of misperception and misassessment of one another and consequently, the increased likelihood of dangerous confrontations between the superpowers.

Fourth, atmospherics such as the trappings of summit meetings as well as the so-called functional agreements concluded on peripheral matters are indeed significant. These aid in removing the legacy of the cold war—mutual misperceptions, distrust, hostility, stereotypes, nonunderstanding—and that is the critical and necessary first step toward more stable and less tense relations. Former President Nixon has been cited in this regard (see Note 7) and so should General Secretary Brezhnev: An "everything-or-nothing principle is of no use in world politics. One should always strive for moving forward, using every opportunity."[44]

Finally, from the point of view of Western policy, there are dangers of lessening of will in the West, "detente euphoria,"[45] of going astray in the pursuit of a worthwhile goal,* and in the slackening of allied cooperation and consultation—for real differences can and will remain between the two states.† Yet these dangers are no greater than those of being unresponsive to Soviet gestures and insensitive to Soviet interests and motivations. These must be balanced. It will be a difficult period for the West—and no less for the Russians—to deal with, for we—like the Soviets—are used to having, and seem to find necessary, relatively unmixed relations with allies and adversaries. We, as well as the Soviets, will need sophistication to live with a mixed relationship of conflict and restraint, competition and cooperation.

NOTES

1. Walter Laqueur, "Detente: Western and Soviet Interpretations," _Survey_ 19, no. 3 (Summer 1973): 74-87.

---

*The Senate subcommittee investigating the 1972 grain transaction reached that conclusion in its report of July, 1974.

†Georgy Arbatov concurs: "Since they embody two opposing social systems and are the most economically and militarily powerful representatives of these systems in the world arena, these two states are separated not only by profound differences but also by serious contradictions in many important fields. One cannot expect that relations between the U.S.S.R. and the U.S.A. will suddenly enter an era of tranquil harmony. Such things do not happen in real life;" translated in the _Current Digest of the Soviet Press_ 23, no. 51 (January 18, 1972): 1-4.

2. For various degrees of skepticism, see, for example, ibid.; Elliot R. Goodman, "Disparities in East-West Relations," Survey, 19, no. 3 (Summer 1973): 88-96; Leopold Labedz, "The Soviet Union and Western Europe," ibid., pp. 12-29; William R. Kintner, "The US and the USSR: Conflict and Cooperation, Orbis, 17, no. 3 (Fall 1973): 691-719; Pierre Hassner, "Europe: Old Conflicts and New Rules," ibid., pp. 895-911; Richard Pipes, "America, Russia and Europe in the Light of the Nixon Doctrine," Survey 19, no. 3 (Summer 1973): 30-40; and The United States and the Demands of Detente Diplomacy (A Conference Report, Foreign Policy Research Institute, May 1973).

3. Uri Ra'anan has perhaps raised the most provocative questions regarding recent Soviet policy in the Middle East in terms of its implication for broader questions of Soviet foreign policy and U.S.-Soviet relations; see his, "The USSR and the Middle East: Some Reflections on the Soviet Decision-Making Process," Orbis, 17, no. 3 (Fall 1973): 946-77. Certain contrary evidence is presented by Wilfred Burchett, "The Superpower Show that Flopped," Far Eastern Economic Review, (November 5, 1973): 29-30.

4. A valuable assessment of the developing Soviet navy can be found in Barry M. Blechman, The Changing Soviet Navy (Washington: Brookings Institution Staff Paper, 1973).

5. Marshall D. Shulman, "Toward a Western Philosophy of Coexistence," Foreign Affairs 52, no. 1 (October 1973): 35-58.

6. Ibid., p. 50.

7. Richard M. Nixon, address to Commencement Ceremony of U.S. Naval Academy, June 5, 1974.

8. Department of State, The Meaning of Detente (June 1974), p. 3.

9. Wolfgang Leonhard, "The Domestic Politics of the New Soviet Foreign Policy," Foreign Affairs 52, no. 1 (October 1973): 69. Other discussions of this theme in contemporary Soviet policy and politics abound. Some particularly interesting ones include Thomas W. Wolfe, Soviet Interests in SALT: Political, Economic, Bureaucratic and Strategic Contributions and Impediments to Arms Control (RAND Corporation, September 1971); and Shulman, op. cit., p. 48. One wonders about the applicability to the Soviet system of the idea expressed by some that for the United States the greater task is the reaching of agreement within the American decision-making apparatus rather than with the Russians. For an excellent analysis of this process in the United States, see John Newhouse, Cold Dawn. The Story of SALT (New York: Holt, Rinehart & Winston, 1973).

10. Labedz, op. cit., p. 20.

11. Shulman, op. cit., pp. 56-57.

12. One such example may be Lothar Metzl, "The Ideological Struggle: A Case of Soviet Linkage," Orbis 17, no. 2 (Summer 1973): 364-84.

13. Leonhard, op. cit., p. 59.

14. Ibid., p. 70.

15. Shulman, op. cit., p. 48.

16. See Nils H. Wessel, "The Political and International Implications of Soviet Dissent," Orbis 17, no. 3 (Fall 1973): 793-802.

17. See Georgy Arbatov, "U.S.A.: Economics, Politics, Ideology," S.Sh.A.: Ekonomica, Politika, Ideologiia (November 1971), translated in the Current Digest of the Soviet Press 23, no. 51 (January 18, 1972): 1-4.

18. "American Foreign Policy on the Threshold of the 1970s," Orbis 15, no. 1 (Spring 1971): 134-53.

19. Ibid.

20. Vernon V. Aspaturian, "Moscow's Options in a Changing World," Problems of Communism 21, no. 4 (July-August 1972): 1-20.

21. See for example, Radio Moscow, Domestic Service in Russian, February 17; TASS, International Service in English, April 1; and Radio Peace and Progress, in Mandarin to China, May 20, 1969.

22. See Radio Moscow, Domestic Service in Russian, January 3, 1969, for the first of many that seemed to reach a height with the border clashes in March. Since these coincided with a "Berlin crisis," it is perhaps understandable that Moscow may have feared anti-Soviet collusion on its eastern and western fronts.

23. See Andrei Amalrik, Will the Soviet Union Survive Until 1984? (New York: Harper and Row, 1970), pp. 52-62.

24. See Giovanni Bressi, "China and Western Europe," Asian Survey 12, no. 10 (October 1972): 819-45.

25. Among others, see Shulman, op. cit., p. 45, and Joseph Alsop in the Los Angeles Times, 18 January 1973.

26. The significance of the Chinese threat particularly in terms of the potential of Sino-U.S. relations is also argued in Ian Clark, "Sino-American Relations in Soviet Perspective," Orbis 17, no. 2 (Summer 1973): 480-92; and Thomas W. Robinson, "Soviet Policy in East Asia," Problems of Communism 22, no. 6 (November-December 1973): 32-50.

27. See Thomas W. Wolfe, "Impact of Economic and Technological Issues on the Soviet Approach to SALT," RAND Corporation (June 1970).

28. Shulman, op. cit., p. 44.

29. See James E. Dougherty, "The Soviet Union and Arms Control," Orbis 17, no. 3 (Fall 1973): 766-74; and The United States and the Demands of Detente Diplomacy, op. cit.

30. Robert Legvold, "The Problem of European Security," Problems of Communism 23, no. 1 (January-February 1974): 16.

31. Adam B. Ulam, "The Destiny of Eastern Europe," ibid., p. 2.

32. For example, see Brezhnev's address to the International Meeting of Communist and Workers' Parties in Moscow, June 7, 1969, in International Affairs, no. 7, (July 1969); and Boris Pyadyshev, "Strengthening the Positions of Peace and Socialism," New Times nos. 18-19 (May 1974): 10-12.

33. Wolfe, op. cit., p. 21.

34. See Aspaturian, op. cit., p. 4, concerning the offensive factor in this Soviet motivation.

35. All of the documentation from the 1973 Summit can be found in Department of State, The Washington Summit: General Secretary Brezhnev's Visit to the United States, June 18-25, 1973.

36. See Bressi, op. cit., and de Dubnic, "Europe and the U.S. Policy Toward China," Orbis 16, no. 1 (Spring 1972): 85-103.

37. For example, see Y. Agranov, "Peking's Great-Power Policy and Western Europe," International Affairs, no. 4 (April 1974): 23-27, 34; and I. Alexeyev, "Manoeuvres of the Peking Diplomacy," International Affairs, no. 2 (February 1974): 26-33.

38. Alexeyev, op. cit., p. 33.

39. Y. Molchanov, "The Leninist Policy of Peace," International Affairs, no. 2 (February 1974): 7.

40. See Labedz, op. cit., p. 12.

41. Press Conference in Moscow, July 3, 1974.

42. For an interesting reference to this, see Thomas W. Wolfe, Soviet Interests in SALT: Political, Economic, Bureaucratic and Strategic Contributions and Impediments to Arms Control, op. cit., p. 37n.

43. For a discussion, see Robert C. Horn, "Changing Soviet Policies and Sino-Soviet Competition in Southeast Asia," Orbis 17, no. 2 (Summer 1973): 493-526.

44. Pravda, September 25, 1973.

45. See Goodman, op. cit., p. 93.

CHAPTER

6

SOVIET POSTWAR FOREIGN TRADE POLICY: STABILITY AND METAMORPHOSIS

Steven Rosefielde

INTRODUCTION

The emerging reality of Soviet-American detente increasingly demands the resolution of several enduring problems which have prevented Western scholars from fully comprehending Soviet behavior in international affairs. One of the thornier issues of this sort involves determining the principles upon which Soviet foreign trade policy is predicated. Particularly vexing in this regard is not so much global strategy, but the practical rules which govern the commodity composition of Soviet international trade. With the aid of revealed preference techniques and the proper valuation of Soviet traded goods, this study attempts to uncover empirically the long-run policy goals that determine the observed postwar pattern of Soviet-COMECON commodity

---

The author wishes to express his gratitude to J. M. Montias for his many helpful criticisms and TEMPO for its research support. See John Michael Montias, Economic Development in Communist Rumania (Cambridge: Massachusetts Institute of Technology, 1967), 135-85. Montias has recently extended this approach with techniques similar to those developed in this paper. See "The Structure of Comecon Trade and the Prospects for East West Exchange," Economic Growth Center, Yale University, Discussion paper no. 201, April 1974; Also "Notes on Socialist Industrialization, the Commodity Composition of CMEA Trade, and Prospects for East-West Exchange." (Unpublished paper.)

exchange. The insights gleaned from revealed policy preference analysis are then utilized in conjunction with other evidence on the state of the Soviet domestic economy to forecast the probable course of Soviet-COMECON trade relations in the 1970s. As the subtitle of this essay ('Stability and Metamorphosis') suggests, our econometric findings point to a radical transformation in Soviet international trade policy over the near term. Since the persuasiveness of this conclusion hinges on a set of detailed technical economic arguments, we begin by reviewing the basic theory of commodity specialization before proceeding to to considerations of a statistical nature.

SPECIALIZATION

The concept of specialization is central to any empirical study of commodity composition, representing as it does the limiting case where import and export goods are classified into mutually exclusive sets. Specialization, however, is also a matter of degree varying continuously with the proportion in which specific commodity groups are represented in imports and exports. Although these two concepts are obviously related, relative specialization poses specific problems of measurement, which must be clarified before the policy implications of any observed pattern of commodity trade can be assessed.

Conventional economic analysis deals primarily with real goods and services as the basic arguments of utility and social welfare functions. A priori judgments about desirable mixes of goods and services are never presupposed because they depend in a complex way on the community distribution of income and wealth, as well as the shape of individual preference surfaces.

The analysis of commodity structure necessarily goes beyond the conventional utility function specification by tacitly assuming that the pattern of traded goods is significant in itself. Whether the commodity composition of traded goods expresses the level of industrialization or serves as a covert measure of comparative advantage without prespecifying the functional relationship linking planners' or society's preferences with the structure of traded goods, it is impossible to evaluate unequivocally the degree of specialization exclusively in physical, current, or constant value terms. If physical goods are used as the relevant choice criteria, two difficulties obtrude. First, individual commodities may be so highly differentiated that complete specialization becomes a tautology, since by convention differentiated goods will be mutually exclusive. Second, aggregation of heterogenous goods cannot be validly performed without the interjection of value weights in one form or another. As a consequence of these problems, measurement of specialization in physical terms lacks the sanction of theory.

Moreover, insofar as constant price valuation is merely a proxy for the study of commodity specialization in physical terms weighted by imputed planners' preferences at a discrete point in time, it cannot be justified in terms of 'production potential standard' precisely because the objective of specialization analysis is to discern in detail the changing pattern of commodity trade, not the capacity of an economy to trade a prespecified bundle of goods in varying volumes. By the process of elimination, specialization, if it can be assessed at all, must be expressed in current values, reflecting current planners' preferences. This means that specialization research must necessarily focus on the shifting composition of tradable goods aggregated into homogenous categories at prices which correspond with variable rather than constant planners' preferences.

So long as these intricacies are clearly understood, empirical measures of specialization can be interpreted as a reflection of the changing policy objectives of foreign trade planners without necessarily prejudging the deeper conformity of realized ex post trade with the doctrine of comparative advantage theory.

NOMENCLATURE AND SPECIALIZATION POLICY

Pure theory suggests that if transaction costs are positive it is irrational for two nations to exchange identical products, since both countries could increase social welfare merely by substituting the domestically produced good for the foreign one, saving service costs without foregoing consumption. If perverse behavior is excluded by assumption, along with the problem of reexports, the logic of Pareto efficient exchange compels us to reject the idea that goods of the same type can be simultaneously imported and exported by a given country. Commodity specialization, therefore, is not an empirical matter, it is a logical tautology, and any specialization study which assumes this difficulty away must rest on very shaky grounds.

Valid specialization analysis begins with the recognition that its objective is the evaluation not of specific commodities, but of large commodity categories which possess inherent policy interest. Since the determination of such groups is necessarily arbitrary, various commodity classification schemes can be employed. The nomenclature used in this study was selected through the process of elimination.

The unified 1962 foreign trade COMECON nomenclature, valid until 1971, contains 6,238 identifiable commodities.[1] This establishes the upper feasible limit for empirical measurement of Soviet foreign trade specialization. Practical policy decisions, however, can hardly be supposed to be consistent at this level of detail, making it inappropriate for our purposes. Consideration can also be given to the 71 sector classification scheme of the reconstructed Soviet producers' price input-output table. The statistical comparability of the foreign trade data contains the enigmatic category 'complete plants' with no obvious 1-0 correlative. In addition bilateral Soviet foreign trade commodity statistics are typically incomplete in the sense that identified imports and exports classified by detailed commodity groupings do not sum to the value totals given in the foreign trade handbooks. Allocation of this unknown commodity residual to specific 1-0 sector must necessarily entail highly arbitrary judments. To overcome these debilities an eight-sector classification scheme has been chosen which truncates and adjusts the one digit CTN nomenclature by aggregating categories 3 (chemicals, fertilizers, and rubber) and 5 (organic raw materials) into an organic raw material grouping; categories 6 (live animals) and 7 (raw materials and food stuffs) into an agricultural classification, and by treating the residual as a separate sector. The resulting nomenclature is set forth below:

1. Machinery and equipment (CTN 1)
2. Fuels, metals, and mineral raw materials (CTN 2)
3. Organic raw materials (CTN 3, 5)
4. Building materials (CTN 4)
5. Agriculture (CTN 6, 7)
6. Food (CTN 8)
7. Industrial consumer goods (CTN 9)
8. Residual

This scheme possesses several interesting analytic properties. It is neither too aggregated to bear on the real concerns of practical foreign trade planning, nor is it so disaggregated that it exceeds the ability of sophisticated planners to impose a consistent set of norms on the composition of traded goods. In addition, it is compatible with input-output nomenclature permitting us to transform foreign trade ruble values into domestic adjusted factor costs.

ADJUSTED FACTOR COSTS

Previous studies of the commodity composition of Soviet traded goods have invariably been based on foreign trade ruble prices, which purportedly serve as a reasonable surrogate for world prices. In the absence of alternative computationally feasible standards of valuation this rationale is compelling. But it should always be remembered that comparative advantage necessitates a comparison of domestic with foreign prices. World prices in themselves cannot be used to elaborate a rational commodity specialization strategy because they neither reflect planners' preferences nor domestic production cost. Commodity specialization, measured in foreign trade ruble prices, more than likely reflects the consequences of policy refracted through alien prices as distinct from the desired structure of tradable goods itself.

Converting official trade statistics into the domestic production cost form employed in the foreign trade planning process, however, is no easy matter. Soviet literature abounds with formulas which seek to transform domestic (sebestoimost') values into one or another opportunity cost, scarcity price variant. To cut through the morass of alternative domestic price adjustment formulas, it is helpful to assume that whatever price formula is actually employed by the Soviet Ministry of Foreign Trade in computing domestic production cost, the resulting prices bear some resemblance to properly computed adjusted factor-cost prices. This assumption makes it possible to utilize factor-cost prices derived from input-output analysis to approximate the foreign trade planners' conception of domestic production cost, while simultaneously serving in its own right as an independent estimate of domestic Soviet opportunity cost.

The adjusted factor-cost values employed in this study are derived in the following manner: Direct turnover taxes, and the indirect price (sebestoimost') distortion which results from levying turnover tax on intermediate goods, are iteratively removed from official Soviet input-output flows with the aid of input-output techniques. This transforms domestic production in purchasers' prices to a pure prime-cost form that is further adjusted by imputing capital services to each commodity by sector of delivery. More specifically, the capital stock by sector of origin is transformed to a sector-of-delivery basis by premultiplying the 1966 Soviet tax distortion deflated producers' price (I-A) inverse, by the aggregate capital vector, which has the effect of summing direct-plus-indirect capital for each jth intermediate input required to sustain a unit delivery of the ith good to final demand. Multiplying the resulting capital stock vector by an imputed capital service rate (here 12 percent), yields capital service value added which is then allocated by sector to final consumption.[2]

DOMESTIC COST CONVERSION COEFFICIENTS

Because Soviet foreign trade statistics are not reported in domestic purchasers' prices, sector specific conversion coefficients derived from I-O sources linking domestic and foreign trade prices have been used in computing Soviet trade flows in adjusted factor costs. Equation 1 expresses this transformation algebraically.

$$(1) \quad \pi_{AFC,j} = \pi_{F,j}(\pi_{P,j}/\pi_{F,j})(\pi_{AFC,j}/\pi_{P,j})$$

where

AFC = adjusted factor cost
F = foreign price of either a homogeneous import or export
P = the domestic purchaser price
j = the jth commodity j = j (1, . . ., 8)

Since input-output analysis is predicated on the assumption of homogenous sectoring, exports and imports of the same type should have identical prices. This convention enables us to convert exports to adjusted factor costs with the same equation employed for imports.[3]

THE SPECIALIZATION INDEX

Specialization indices have been computed by applied practitioners of economic analysis since Folke Hilgert developed his measure of bilateralism in the 1920s. Michael Michaely, Bela Balassa, C. H. McMillan, and most recently John M. Montias have adapted the general concept to their special needs.[4] Because theory is an imperfect guide to practice, every specialization measure exhibits peculiarities of its own. A central perplexity surrounding the formation of any specialization index is the proper handling of export commodity surpluses or import deficits. Suppose for example that a country imports and exports the same sets of goods in the same proportions, but runs an export surplus twice the market value of its imports. If no correction is made for the trade surplus, commodity specialization measured in value terms could be high, when on a proportioned basis it is zero. This difficulty is compounded in the Soviet case by the omission of sizable volumes of imports and exports which are observable only as a residual between aggregate exchange and enumerated commodities. The appropriate allocation of the residual among commodity groups cannot be achieved in a neutral way because even a proportional distribution could easily bias the true composition of traded goods. Adjustment for these encumbrances cannot be perfect. The solution adopted here is twofold: First, imports and exports are proportioned to negate the influence of aggregate trade imbalances. This implies the arbitrary judgment that trade surpluses or deficits are separable functions of commodity composition. Second, rather than allocating the residual on some conventional basis to the various commodity groups, the residual is treated as a homogenous activity. In accordance with Kostinsky's recent speculations this homogenous activity may well be military hardware.[5]

Subject to all the qualification above, equation 1 represents the statistic upon which all the ensuing computations are based

$$(2) \quad \psi_j = \sum_{i=1}^{8} \left| \frac{X_{ij}}{\sum_{i=1}^{8} X_{ij}} - \frac{M_{ij}}{\sum_{i=1}^{8} M_{ij}} \right| \Big/ 2$$

where

ψ_j = the specialization statistic generated in Soviet trade with the jth country

X_{ij} = the ith commodity export from the USSR to the jth country

M_{ij} = the ith commodity import of the USSR from the jth country

As equation 2 stands, the term enclosed in the absolute value brackets has a range from zero to two, which is normalized from zero to one by the devisor. This means that complete specialization is represented by one, perfect nonspecialization by zero.

EMPIRICAL FINDINGS

The patterns and trends in Soviet-COMECON commodity composition measured by the specialization statistics which follow shed significant light on the revealed policy priorities of Soviet foreign trade planners. Specifically they demonstrate the following:

1. A secular trend toward increased commodity specialization in Soviet trade with the COMECON as a bloc, 1955-68.
2. This trend is highly correlated with relative domestic growth rates of the machinery and equipment, fuels and metals, light industry (excluding food), and agriculture sectors.
3. Commodity specialization trends in Soviet trade with individual COMECON nations are diverse and compatible with the bloc patterns only when valued in adjusted factor costs.

4. Differences in the intensity of commodity specialization between the USSR and individual COMECON members have substantially diminished.
5. By rearranging commodity flows with individual bloc nations, increasing specialization in some, decreasing it in others, the Soviets have been able to intensify their specialization of the aggregate bloc mix, while simultaneously imposing a more unified policy of equal commodity specialization intensity with each member of the bloc individually.

These results are best assessed sequentially. Table 6.1 presents specialization statistics computed for Soviet-COMECON trade both in foreign trade ruble and 12 percent domestic adjusted factor-cost prices. In the first few years after the political consolidation that followed Stalin's death, the commodity composition of Soviet-COMECON trade was relatively unspecialized. If 0.50 is taken as the boundary separating specialized and nonspecialized trade patterns, an average figure of 0.35 unmistakably indicates the tendency toward nonspecialization. However, despite some fluctuations, chiefly in the foreign trade ruble measure, Soviet-COMECON trade grows increasingly specialized during the Khrushchev and early Brezhnev years. Moreover, evaluated in adjusted factor costs, the standard most consistent with domestic planning practice, the commodity composition of Soviet trade with the bloc becomes specialization intensive as early as 1960, reaching 0.57 in 1968.[6] The trend is nearly monotonic and conveys as forcefully as statistics of this kind can convey, a revealed planners' policy preference in favor of commodity specialization. Although the Soviets have always emphasized the virtue of the international division of labor, the evidence contained in Table 6.1 suggests that they may adhere to this principle more faithfully than could be surmised on the basis of causal analysis.

Ideology however, even in the forms of Smithian division-of-labor theory may be flagrantly in opposition to rational economic behavior. In order to evaluate whether the specialization policy described above corresponds with changing domestic economic conditions, the underlying import and export commodity patterns must be scrutinized. As Tables 6.2 and 6.3 reveal, all eight commodity categories are neither equidynamic or of equivalent importance. Most of the variation in the specialization pattern over time can be traced to four groups: fuels and metals, machinery and equipment, agriculture, and light industry. A linear regression of the form

$$(3) \qquad \Gamma = \alpha \left| \frac{y_j}{\sum_{j=1}^{n} y_j/n} \right| + \epsilon$$

TABLE 6.1

Soviet-COMECON Commodity Specialization 1955-68

	Foreign Trade Ruble Prices	12 Percent Domestic Adjusted Factor Cost
1955	34	32
1956	35	38
1957	44	45
1958	43	47
1959	45	50
1960	48	53
1961	48	53
1962	49	55
1963	47	55
1964	50	57
1965	50	57
1966	47	56
1967	46	56
1968	48	57

Sources: All foreign trade statistics underlying the specialization indices above are taken from Paul Marer, Soviet and East European Foreign Trade, 1946-1969 (Bloomington, Ind.: Indiana University Press, 1972). Foreign trade ruble conversion coefficients are found in Treml et al., The Structure of the Soviet Economy (New York: Praeger, 1972), pp. 159-69. Adjusted factor cost conversions are explained in Rosefielde, "The Complete Producers' Price Soviet Input-Output Table for 1966," Duke University-University of North Carolina Occasional Papers on Soviet Input-Output Analysis, June 1974, and The Effect of Adjusted Factor Cost Valuation on the Interindustry Structure of Soviet National Product, U.S./USSR Studies Working Papers (Santa Barbara, Calif.: TEMPO, 1974.)

was employed to assess the relationship between normalized net exports (r) by commodity group and a normalized index of relative domestic production ($|y_j/\Sigma_{j=1}^{n} y_j/n|$) on the supposition that sectors exhibiting rapid growth will be export biased, while those expanding more slowly than average will be import prone. This conjecture is borne out statistically using 12 percent adjusted factor-cost valuation. The r = 0.8594 is significant at the 0.999 level explaining 73.9 percent of the coefficient of determination our regression is buttressed by input-output computations of per-worker

TABLE 6.2

Net Soviet-COMECON Exports
(Foreign Trade Ruble Prices)

	Machinery and equipment	Fuels and metals	Organic raw materials	Construction materials	Agriculture	Food	Light industry	Residuals
1955	-0.2761	-0.0009	0.1178	-0.0038	0.1164	-0.0325	-0.0313	0.1104
1956	-0.2437	0.0797	0.1384	-0.0063	0.0633	0.0100	-0.0989	0.0576
1957	-0.2932	0.1509	0.0913	-0.0052	0.1751	0.0192	-0.1028	-0.0353
1958	-0.2955	0.2159	0.1159	-0.0081	0.1030	-0.0099	-0.1190	-0.0024
1959	-0.2966	0.1896	0.0788	-0.0071	0.1213	0.0256	-0.1480	0.0362
1960	-0.3057	0.2377	0.0970	-0.0048	0.1105	-0.0137	-0.1586	0.0377
1961	-0.2767	0.2552	0.0936	-0.0048	0.0741	-0.0310	-0.1677	0.0574
1962	-0.2995	0.2703	0.0797	-0.0040	0.0888	-0.0146	-0.1767	0.0561
1963	-0.2717	0.2934	0.0739	-0.0046	0.0639	-0.0037	-0.1930	0.0418
1964	-0.2801	0.3252	0.0734	-0.0026	0.0438	-0.0350	-0.1797	0.0551
1965	-0.2796	0.3203	0.0909	-0.0015	0.0435	-0.0454	-0.1723	0.0441
1966	-0.2271	0.3133	0.0941	-0.0010	0.0374	-0.0338	-0.2060	0.0232
1967	-0.2107	0.3160	0.0808	-0.0002	0.0534	-0.0360	-0.2180	0.0146
1968	-0.2263	0.3115	0.0812	0.0009	0.0503	-0.0386	-0.2168	0.0379

Source: S. Rosefielde, Transformation of 1966 Soviet Input Output Table From Producers to Adjusted Factor Cost Values, no. GE 75TMP-47 (Santa Barbara, Calif.: TEMPO, August 1975).

TABLE 6.3

Net Soviet-COMECON Exports
(12 Percent AFC Prices)

	Machinery and equipment	Fuels and metals	Organic raw materials	Construction materials	Agriculture	Food	Light industry	Residuals
1955	-0.2014	-0.0014	0.1319	-0.0049	0.1119	-0.0289	-0.0802	0.0729
1956	-0.1531	0.1168	0.1547	-0.0069	0.0591	0.0106	-0.2230	0.0418
1957	-0.1915	0.1821	0.0971	-0.0058	0.1565	0.0165	-0.2359	-0.0190
1958	-0.1860	0.2535	0.1203	-0.0089	0.0903	-0.0067	-0.2638	0.0012
1959	-0.1765	0.2447	0.0912	-0.0075	0.1112	0.0254	-0.3173	0.0290
1960	-0.1805	0.2951	0.1078	-0.0050	0.0999	-0.0072	-0.3383	0.0282
1961	-0.1583	0.3188	0.1061	-0.0049	0.0683	-0.0194	-0.3518	0.0412
1962	-0.1703	0.3379	0.0922	-0.0039	0.0814	-0.0064	-0.3717	0.0409
1963	-0.1466	0.3675	0.0873	-0.0044	0.0600	0.0029	-0.3999	0.0332
1964	-0.1596	0.4033	0.0866	-0.0025	0.0407	-0.0240	-0.3859	0.0414
1965	-0.1633	0.3946	0.1029	-0.0012	0.0404	-0.0322	-0.3750	0.0339
1966	-0.1150	0.3918	0.1099	-0.0003	0.0355	-0.0196	-0.4255	0.0233
1967	-0.0997	0.3956	0.0970	-0.0009	0.0501	-0.0200	-0.4427	0.0189
1968	-0.1089	0.3922	0.0978	-0.0022	0.0473	-0.0227	-0.4419	0.0340

Source: S. Rosefielde, Transformation of 1966 Soviet Input Output Table From Producers to Adjusted Factor Cost Values, no. GE 75TMP-47 (Santa Barbara, Calif.: TEMPO, August 1975).

variation in the independent variable.* From the viewpoint of foreign trade policy making, equation 3 suggests that achieved differential rates of domestic industrial growth do not entirely accord with planners' preferences, and that international trade provides a convenient mechanism for altering perceived domestic imbalances. Since a policy of this sort is consistent with both short-run and intermediate-term planning, the validation of the hypothesis embedded in equation 3 reveals that the pattern of Soviet-COMECON commodity specialization is sensible at a realistic level of foreign trade policy formation, although this of course does not prejudge the ultimate rationality or lack of it, on general equilibrium-welfare grounds. (The evidence of our regression is buttressed by input-output computations of per-worker capital productivity which corresponds on a sectoral basis with domestic GVO trends.)

The simplicity of the commodity specialization pattern which characterizes Soviet-COMECON trade is thrown into even starker relief when contrasted with the divergent trends exhibited in Soviet

---

*It is important to understand the precise nature of the null hypothesis tested above. Conceptually, our concern is for the weak assertion that domestic commodity groups growing faster than average will be correlated with increased net export intensity, or decreased net import intensity. Likewise, slower growing domestic sectors will be associated with increased net import or decreased net export intensity. The validity of this null hypothesis in no way depends on the properties of continuity and differentiability, or more concretely, net exports are not specified to vary continuously and proportionally with the rate of growth. As a consequence of this weak specification we have conventionally designated the slower growing sectors by a negative sign, and normalized the net export variable so that diminishing net exports are scaled proportionately with increasing net imports, implying that the direction of specialization change, and not the direction of specialization per se is the relevant variable. Where appropriate analogous normalization techniques are applied to the growth variable, which is scaled positive-negative to indicate divergence from the sector growth rate average, measured as the midpoint between the least rapidly, and least slowly expanding sectors. Because the data series entail so many complex transformations to reflect consistently our weak null hypothesis, our statistical results should be treated as approximations, subject to some modest variation where the scaling conventions are altered.

TABLE 6.4

Specialization Ratios for Soviet Trade
with Selected COMECON Nations
(Foreign Trade Ruble Prices)

	East Germany	Czechoslovakia	Hungary	Poland	Bulgaria	Rumania
1955	0.78	0.46	0.71	0.51	0.53	0.27
1956	0.68	0.38	0.72	0.46	0.56	0.15
1957	0.72	0.38	0.80	0.44	0.42	0.20
1958	0.74	0.45	0.73	0.29	0.49	0.12
1959	0.71	0.54	0.60	0.31	0.47	0.15
1960	0.75	0.59	0.60	0.36	0.49	0.16
1961	0.71	0.58	0.70	0.34	0.55	0.27
1962	0.71	0.60	0.66	0.38	0.46	0.26
1963	0.73	0.58	0.70	0.35	0.47	0.36
1964	0.72	0.57	0.61	0.36	0.49	0.33
1965	0.71	0.57	0.57	0.34	0.52	0.36
1966	0.73	0.54	0.61	0.36	0.53	0.42
1967	0.67	0.57	0.57	0.40	0.52	0.42
1968	0.64	0.58	0.62	0.42	0.50	0.43

Source: S. Rosefielde, Transformation of 1966 Soviet Input Output Table From Producers to Adjusted Factor Cost Values, no. GE 75TMP-47 (Santa Barbara, Calif.: TEMPO, August 1975).

TABLE 6.5

Specialization Ratios for Soviet Trade
with Selected COMECON Nations
(12 Percent AFC Prices)

	East Germany	Czechoslovakia	Hungary	Poland	Bulgaria	Rumania
1955	0.70	0.45	0.72	0.52	0.46	0.26
1956	0.68	0.44	0.72	0.43	0.57	0.14
1957	0.74	0.40	0.77	0.41	0.37	0.19
1958	0.77	0.48	0.75	0.24	0.45	0.13
1959	0.75	0.60	0.69	0.28	0.41	0.18
1960	0.77	0.64	0.68	0.40	0.51	0.18
1961	0.74	0.63	0.76	0.38	0.56	0.28
1962	0.76	0.63	0.74	0.43	0.51	0.30
1963	0.79	0.63	0.77	0.42	0.50	0.38
1964	0.79	0.64	0.69	0.43	0.55	0.39
1965	0.77	0.61	0.68	0.40	0.61	0.43
1966	0.80	0.61	0.70	0.47	0.63	0.47
1967	0.75	0.63	0.66	0.51	0.62	0.49
1968	0.72	0.64	0.70	0.53	0.58	0.54

Source: S. Rosefielde, Transformation of 1966 Soviet Input Output Table From Producers to Adjusted Factor Cost Values, no. GE 75TMP-47 (Santa Barbara, Calif.: TEMPO, August 1975).

trade with individual members of COMECON. Tables 6.4 and 6.5 present specialization statistics representing the net commodity composition of Soviet trade with East Germany, Czechoslovakia, Hungary, Poland, Bulgaria, and Rumania. Valued in foreign trade ruble prices, Soviet commodity specialization declines with East Germany, Hungary, and Poland, increases with Czechoslovakia and Rumania, and remains constant with Bulgaria. Although the pattern is more regular in domestic adjusted factor prices with commodity specialization increasing in Soviet trade with Czechoslovakia and the two less industrialized COMECON states, Bulgaria and Rumania, remaining static for the others, it is nonetheless evident that aggregate Soviet-COMECON specialization is no simple reflection of underlying nation-by-nation trends. In fact Tables 6.4 and 6.5 in somewhat different ways both suggest a policy objective ostensibly at variance with the Smithian division-of-labor principle. Compare the dispersion of specialization values in Tables 6.4 and 6.5 between 1955 and 1968, summarized in Table 6.6.

In 1955 the dispersion of the commodity specialization statistics around the mean reached more than 20 points in either direction, which by 1968 was reduced to less than 10 points. This narrowing of dispersion indicates that Soviet foreign trade policy makers are endeavoring

TABLE 6.6

Dispersion of Commodity Specialization in Soviet Trade with COMECON Member States

	1955	1968
Foreign Trade Ruble Prices		
low	27	42
mean	54	53
high	78	64
Domestic 12 percent Adjusted Factor Cost Prices		
low	26	53
mean	52	62
high	72	72

Source: Tables 6.4 and 6.5.

to establish more unified norms of specialization across the bloc. Implicit here, of course, is the further political decision to afford equal treatment to bloc members insofar as basic economic conditions allow.

At this point it may well be asked how the Soviets can satisfy two well-known policy objectives, specialization and leveling the economic consequences of unequal development, with only one policy instrument. If the revealed preference approach accurately reflects planners' policy intentions, Soviet foreign tradeplanners adopted a clever strategem. They intensified specialization in light industrial imports and fuel exports with all COMECON nations, but switched the pattern of machinery and equipment trade, so that countries with relatively low specialization levels like Czechoslovakia became more specialized at the expense of East Germany whose net machinery and equipment exports to the USSR fell from 0.77 in 1955 to 0.43 in 1968. Needless to say, the specific commodities involved in each bilateral country comparison differ from the Czechoslovakian-East German example, but in the main the Soviets appear to have augmented commodity specialization with the bloc as a whole, while narrowing the dispersion in specialization levels among COMECON members by rearranging the commodity composition of a few groups of trade goods between COMECON members. Thus it seems that the Soviets, faced with the tricky task of satisfying disparate ideological objectives without grossly compromising their own material interests, have succeeded in discovering and implementing a foreign trade policy which not only reconciles the ideological imperative, but also reflects changing relative product scarcity in the domestic economy.[7]

This achievement needs to be appreciated in the broad perspective. Soviet economic planning, even after the advent of the computer, is still a primitive process. Mathematical simulation of optimal general equilibrium-welfare production solutions to the rational allocation of scarce resources is not yet feasible. This means that practical planners must rely on "reasonable" economic and political guidelines, conditioned by available statistics and accounting practices in formulating their operational economic objectives. The commodity specialization measure developed in this paper seeks to identify the policy goals of Soviet foreign trade planners as revealed by the realized pattern of post-Stalin Soviet trade with the COMECON. It cannot and does not bear on the economic rationality of Soviet foreign trade at a deeper theoretical level. Yet, even if we recognize that revealed preference analysis can convey only an incomplete impression of Soviet policy formation to the extent that realized statistical evidence represents planners' intentions, the strong pattern and plausibility of the behavior implied by our findings suggests that the revealed preference approach effectively expresses salient aspects of Soviet foreign trade policy formation. More exactly, our results demonstrate that Soviet foreign trade policy, in lieu of optimal planning, is guided by two considerations of a political-economic nature, a crude Smithian division-of-labor principle, and the implicit welfare judgment that economic relations between the USSR and individual COMECON members should be predicated on uniform economic standards that ignore differences in relative levels of economic development. This, of course, does not mean that Soviet foreign trade policy is altruistic. It merely suggests that the Soviets have found it politically expedient to pursue a policy which statistically substantiates a fundamental impartiality in the treatment of developed and less developed COMECON states. That these divergent objectives could be achieved, without obviously violating Soviet material interests as our regression results have shown, is a tribute to the ingenuity of Soviet foreign trade planning.*

METAMORPHOSIS: SOVIET-COMECON TRADE POLICY IN THE 1970S

Sustaining these achievements in the 1970s, however, may prove to be a formidable task. The material interests of the COMECON countries during the last decade were remarkably compatible. For their part, the Soviets desired to augment domestic stocks of consumer goods to satisfy burgeoning domestic demand, purchasing these goods with their relatively abundant supplies of natural resources and rela-

---

*J. M. Montias has arrived at conclusions which differ from our results employing a similar methodology. Interpreting COMECON trading practices in the context of the World Market, Montias finds a positive correlation between "hard goods" surpluses and COMECON trade with the West in the postwar period. This implies that Soviet foreign trade planners are at least in part guided by a different set of policy objectives than the rest of COMECON, a point Montias himself advances. Those interested in sorting out the differences between Soviet and COMECON foreign trade policy are directed to Montias' excellent study. See J. M. Montias, "The Structure of Comecon Trade and the Prospects for East-West Exchanges," Economic Growth Center, Yale University, April 1974. See also, van Brabant, Bilateralism and Structural Bilateralism (Rotterdam: Rotterdam University Press, 1973).

tively inexpensive machinery and equipment. Although the particular material needs of each COMECON nation varied, in the main the Soviets judiciously adjusted the commodity mix of traded goods with their partners so that the more industrialized countries found outlets for their machinery and equipment in return for the natural resources they required, while the less developed members of the bloc provided processed foods and light industrial products in exchange for the capital goods needed to speed their industrialization.

New economic factors are eroding this harmony of interest. The Soviets are less anxious to export natural resources than they had been in the past, and as we shall demonstrate,the domestic imperative for importing consumer goods is increasing. This means that the Russians are likely to push machinery and equipment exports to pay for the consumer goods they require. In the process however, they may well impinge upon the material interests of the East Europeans. On the one hand the Soviets could easily press the COMECON countries to increase their consumer goods exports beyond the point of desirability, forcing the developed member of the bloc to curtail (proportionately) its own machinery and equipment exports, while on the other hand restraining the rate of increase in machinery and equipment exports from the developing COMECON nations.

The tensions generated by this impending conflict of interest will be further exacerbated by the economics of detente. Soviet material interests in the 1970s impel them to increase their imports of capital goods from the West, not—as often thought—to augment their internal rate of technological progress,[8] but to overcome a severe domestic labor shortage. Since it is unlikely that the Soviets can pay for these imports through the direct sale of their machinery and equipment, they will have to divert their exports of natural resources from the East to the West. A policy of this sort will necessarily generate considerable intra-COMECON friction, and intensify the centrifugal forces at work countervailing the goal of East European economic and political integration.

To understand the roots of the emerging new tendencies of Soviet-COMECON relations,let us consider some fundamental quantitative evidence. It has been shown, using adjusted factor-cost data, that Soviet postwar growth is best explained by the constant elasticity of substitution (CES) specification of aggregate industrial production.[9] The parameters which characterize this specification in the Soviet case provide us with three essential pieces of information:

1. Technological growth in the Soviet economy is occurring at the respectable rate of 2.8 percent per year.
2. The elasticity of factor substitution is extremely low, less than 0.50.
3. Capital utilization intensity is unusually high.

These findings imply that the widely discussed slowdown in the rate of aggregate Soviet economic growth, which manifested itself in the 1960s, hinges less on inferior rates of neutral technical change than deeper problems of capital design and relative rates of new factor formation. During the postwar period the growth of Soviet manpower has subsided, while the capital stock has continued to grow at an annual rate of 9 percent. This has meant that labor has increasingly become the scarce factor or binding constraint retarding the growth of industrial output. Soviet technology, however, has persisently exhibited a capital saving bias, coupled with an inflexible design which limits the range of permissible factor substitution. Given a choice between designing adaptable capital goods that economize capital or labor and allow easy factor substitution, the Soviets have opted for capital saving innovation with limited substitution possibilities. This preference has resulted in a situation in which relatively large quantities of labor are required in the production process, that if not forthcoming cause the marginal productivity of capital to decline precipitously.

As the growth of the labor force dwindled in the 1960s without an offsetting improvement in the rational allocation of the existing labor force, the consequences of the Soviet pattern of capital accumulation impressed themselves on aggregate economic performance, most noticeably in the retardation of economic growth. Since Soviet planners are understandably loath to accept secularly declining rates of national product growth, they have come under increasing pressure to reverse this trend. Several alternatives are available, but they are not equally promising. An input-output analysis of the sectoral structure of Soviet productivity using adjusted factor-cost data reveals that while the capital productivity of the machinery and equipment, light industrial, and food processing sectors are similar, their respective labor productivity ratios diverge dramatically.[10] Light industrial and food processing activities are subtantially more labor intensive than machine building. This means that should Soviet planners desire to augment consumer-oriented production in the 1970s, their efforts will be circumscribed by the binding labor constraint. Capital will have to be diverted from the capital intensive sectors to the labor intensive sectors of the economy which inescapably means that the growth of the national product must fall faster than before.[11] Confronted with this dilemma, the Soviets will certainly endeavor to foster labor-saving innovation while trying to procure consumer goods from alternative sources. Since the quickest way to acquire labor-saving capital goods is through trade with the West, it can be anticipated that the Soviets will increasingly use the opportunity afforded by detente to purchase equipment that may eventually allow them to reattain the rapid rates of economic growth that characterized the Stalinist model in the past. Although the

Soviets could easily purchase consumer goods as well from the West, allowing them to concentrate on the production of goods for which their capital saving technology is best suited, Soviet foreign trade planners will undoubtedly prefer to conserve their scarce foreign exchange by importing light industrial consumer goods from the COMECON countries. Thus a profound change in the material interests of the USSR is pressing toward a pattern of East-West commodity specialization inimical to COMECON integration and solidarity.

CONCLUSION

During the next decade Soviet material interest will become increasingly incompatible with the national economic objectives of its COMECON partners, as the economy's low aggregate substitution elasticity and high capital intensity increasingly retard national product growth in a labor-scarce environment. In devising a foreign trade policy which relieves the pressure on scarce domestic labor resources, Soviet planners will be tempted by opportunities for borrowing labor saving technology from the West afforded by detente. While this strategy may well assist the USSR in improving its aggregate economic performance, Soviet-COMECON relations which were so adroitly managed in the 1950s and 1960s are likely to deteriorate under the strain as the structure of East-West trade is rearranged to the detriment of East Europe. This tendency, moreover, could conceivably be exacerbated if increased Soviet economic dependence on the West ramifies into the political domain. In any event, past problems of COMECON integration are likely to pale in the wake of the changing material interests of the bloc. (Complete tables of Soviet imports and exports by country and commodity in adjusted factor-cost prices, as well as a bibliography, are available from the author upon request.)

NOTES

1. Barry Kostinsky, <u>Soviet Foreign Trade Statistics</u> (Foreign Demographic Analysis Division, Bureau of Economic Analysis, Social and Economic Statistics Administration, U.S. Department of Commerce, February 1974), p. 25.

2. See Steven Rosefielde, "The Complete Producers' Price Soviet Input-Output Table for 1966," Duke University, University of North Carolina Occasional Papers on Soviet Input-Output Analysis, June 1974; also <u>The Effect of Adjusted Factor Cost Valuation on the</u>

Interindustry Structure of Soviet National Product, U.S./USSR Studies Working Papers (Santa Barbara, Calif.: TEMPO, 1974).

3. Conversion coefficients are derived from Treml, et al., The Structure of the Soviet Economy (New York: Praeger, 1972), pp. 159-69. Kostinsky has informed me that new coefficients currently being compiled will not differ critically from previous values. Treml has cautioned that the Soviets' price differentiate by COMECON trading partner. Insofar as discrimination of this sort reflects valid differences in quality no distortion need be implied. But if economic factors do not account for preferential pricing, the reliability of our statistics is commensurately impaired, and this possibility should not be overlooked. In a similar vein Bill Lee has pointed out that the Soviets apply special price coefficients in valuing imports not produced in the USSR. This may imply that price discrimination has a valid economic justification.

4. Michael Michaely, Concentration in International Trade (Amsterdam: North Holland, 1967); Bela Balassa, "Tariff Reductions and Trade in Manufactures among Industrial Countries," AER 56 (June 1966): 466-73; H. G. Grubel, "Intra-industry Specialization and the Pattern of Trade," Canadian Journal of Economics and Political Science 33, no. 3 (August 1967): 374-88; C. H. McMillan, "Soviet Specialization and Trade in Manufactures," Soviet Studies 24, no. 4, (April 1973): 522-32; J. M. Montias, "The Structure of Comecon Trade and the Prospects for East West Echanges," Economic Growth Center, Yale University, Discussion paper no. 21, April 1974.

5. Kostinsky, op. cit., 99-113.

6. In a recent article Franklyn Holzman shows how Soviet accounting transforms nominally balanced imports and exports into a national income surplus, revealing in the process that domestic costs constitute the economy-wide standard of commodity valuation and decision making. See Franklyn Holzman, "Foreign Trade in the Balance of Payments and GNP Accounts of Centrally Planned Economies," University Center for International Studies, University of Pittsburgh, 1973.

7. Those concerned with the relationship between these results and general equilibrium theory should consult Rosefielde, Soviet International Trade in Heckscher-Ohlin Perspective (Lexington, Mass.: Heath Lexington, 1973).

8. Raymond Vernon, "Apparatchiks and Entrepreneurs: U.S.-Soviet Economic Relations," Foreign Affairs 52, no. 2, (January 1974): 253-54.

9. Steven Rosefielde and Knox Lovell, "The Impact of Adjusted Factor Cost Valuation on the CES Interpretation of Postwar Soviet Economic Growth," unpublished, 1974. Also see Martin L. Weitzman, "Soviet Postwar Economic Growth and Capital Labor Substitution,"

AER 60 (September 1970); and T. Krishna and Ephraim Asher, "Soviet Postwar Economic Growth and Capital Labor Substitution: Comment," AER 64 (March 1974).

10. Rosefielde, The Effect of Adjusted Factor Cost Valuation on the Interindustry Structure of Soviet National Product, U.S./USSR Studies Working Papers, op. cit.

11. For the Soviet view see A. I. Notkin, ed., Sotzialisticheskoe Nakoplenie: Voprosy Teorii i Planirovaniia Nauka (Moscow, 1973). In particular see K. B. Leikina, "Zameshchenie Faktorov Obshchestvennovo Proizvodstva i Povyshenie Effektivnosti Nakopleniia," ibid., pp. 205-18.

CHAPTER

7

TOWARD A COMPARATIVE FOREIGN POLICY OF EASTERN EUROPE

Zvi Gitelman

It is widely agreed that the relationship between the USSR and Eastern Europe has undergone significant change in the last 20 years and that this relationship is still very much in flux, with many of the actors redefining their roles periodically and seeking a stable set of principles upon which to base the relationship. In the Stalinist era the Soviet-East European relationship was essentially an imperial one. Eastern Europe was completely subordinate to the USSR in many ways and through several instruments. Policy and personnel decisions were made in Moscow or with Moscow's approval. The USSR exploited the economies of the East European countries for its own gain; thousands of Soviet "advisers" and other personnel served as the eyes and ears of the imperial center; and East European countries were forced to adopt Soviet models in politics, economics, and even culture.[1] With the East European countries seen as satrapies of the larger empire, rather than as truly sovereign states, it made little sense to study their foreign policies. It was patently obvious that they took their cues in foreign policy, even more than in domestic policy, from the USSR and so it was Soviet foreign policy that mattered. The one exception was, of course, Yugoslavia, and because of her deviation from orthodoxy and her formulation of a new political program and foreign policy doctrine, much more attention was paid by Western scholarship to Yugoslav domestic and foreign policy than was devoted to other East European countries.

The inclination to study the obviously deviant case continued after Stalin's death and after Soviet and East European leaders joined in changing both the theory and the practice of international relations among socialist states. Albania and Rumania differed in their respective ways from the general foreign policy line followed by the other states and so they became the focus of scholarly attention. Though there is wide agreement on the idea that East European states are no longer mere satrapies of a Soviet empire and that they have gained the ability to bargain and negotiate within the Soviet alliance in order to promote and defend their own positions, Western scholarship has not yet paid much attention to the behavior of the individual East European states either in the international arena or within the socialist bloc. It is as if we have acknowledged the individuality of the actors in principle, but have not yet engaged in studies of the individual actors.

Instead, a substantial effort has been devoted to describing and analyzing the overall nature of the Soviet-East European relationship. It is clear that "the old communist dream of one united communist state"[2] has collapsed and that, increasingly, international relations among Communist states take on the features of relations among nation-states generally, despite the assertion that Communist international relations are "international relations of a new type."[3] East European states are now participants rather than pawns in the decision-making process on bloc programs and policies. "No doubt, the Soviet Union remains much more equal than any of the East European countries in the decision-making councils of the bloc, but the latter have gained the ability, individually and collectively, to advance or protect their own national interests against those of the Soviet Union and other bloc countries."[4] Bargaining, rather than commanding, has become the method by which issues are resolved, though in extreme cases the USSR is both willing and able to return to command and coercion in order to get its way.[5]

Coercion has diminished in importance as a cement binding the Soviet-East European alliance, and ideology—or more precisely, shared values and outlooks—has probably become more important. Organizations and formal institutions, such as COMECON and the Warsaw Pact, play a much more important part than they did in Stalin's time when informal and personal ties connecting Stalin with the East European satrapies were the chief means of Soviet-East European coordination. Moreover, whereas Stalin attempted to keep bilateral ties among the East European states to a minimum so that each unit of the empire would have ties of dependency only with the imperial center itself, today there are all kinds of meaningful multilateral ties among the East European states. Even subnational groups, such as professional associations, that had been isolated and sealed off from their counterparts in other Eastern and Western countries under Stalin, have now built firm links to each other. R. V. Burks has pointed out that there have been changes in at least three types of linkages between the USSR and Eastern Europe: 1) The Soviet Union no longer appoints and removes the leadership in Eastern Europe, though it may retain influence and even veto-power over major appointments; 2) policy formulation and implementation is now largely a national responsibility, whereas it once was the exclusive privilege of Moscow; 3) ideology had become more important as a cohesive force holding the USSR and Eastern Europe together.[6] Finally, "we can characterize the changes that have come about in the post-Stalin era as changes in the mix of prescriptive and restrictive messages emanating from the Soviet Union and transmitted to Eastern Europe, and as changes from consensual relations to some approximation of cooperative ones. The Soviet Union has ceased to issue . . . directly or by implication, detailed directives on domestic and foreign policy to its East European allies, but it continues to define the limits withi-in which policy choices can be made, those limits having been broadened considerably since 1953."[7]

While we are able to describe the changes that have taken place in the Soviet-East European relationship, we are less sure of what those changes add up to. In other words, no clear, stable picture has emerged of the Soviet-East European relationship. As Thomas Wolfe notes, "It is difficult to find a label that properly describes the evolving alliance system in Eastern Europe."[8] There may be several reasons for this. One is that Soviet-East European relations have been in almost constant flux since 1953 and they have presented a rapidly moving target to those who would try to pin them down. Both under Khrushchev as well as under the present Soviet regime the USSR has alternated between trying to gain greater control over the other socialist states and relazing that control; between punishing deviation and tolerating it, between approving "multiple paths to socialism" and preventing socialist states from exploring one or another of these paths. Thus, the rules of the Soviet-East European game are always changing and are at times unknown, forcing the players to play in a situation of uncertainty and high risk and leaving the spectators confused about the nature of the game itself and uncertain about the positions and abilities of the players. Secondly, the Soviet-East European relationship is different from more familiar types of alliances and coalitions. Shared ideology and forms of government make it different from other inter-state alliances which might be based on mutual interest alone, or on a common cultural area, or on the need to repel a common enemy. This is no longer an empire, but it is hard to accept the idea that it has evolved into a "socialist commonwealth." George Modelski has suggested that the difficulties presented to the analyst by the present state of Soviet East European relations are part of a larger phenomenon. "The pyramidal structure of authority ('with one great power wielding all legitimate authority') clearly evident in 1960 is under heavy attack, but no clear substitute for it has either been evolved or even proposed. But we might note that in this particular respect the Communist system is experiencing the same type of structural problem as is the entire international system: the traditional authority structure of Great Power control is undergoing serious questioning without a clear-cut alternative either at hand or in sight."[9]

Lacking a clear conception of any sort of steady state of Soviet-East European relations, scholars have tried to clarify the picture by finding out at least how much has changed, what (or who) has changed, and in what direction this change has gone. These questions are by no means settled and there have been many kinds of attempts to provide answers to them. However, it seems that whatever the method employed, the same fundamental question underlies almost all of the research: how much cohesion—unity or integration are other terms used—is there between the USSR and Eastern Europe? Almost all of the literature on the foreign policy of East European states has explicitly or implicitly addressed itself to the question of whether the particular state or states are becoming more or less independent of the USSR. When Soviet-East European relations are regarded from the Soviet perspective the question becomes whether the USSR is losing control or reasserting it over other socialist countries. Thus, we have studies on "unity and conflict," "conflict and cohesion," indicators of political "integration," "distance" between the USSR and various socialist states, and so forth.[10] There are still attempts made to conceptualize the Soviet-East European relationship in a broader way—whether as a bloc, an alliance, a "hierarchical regional system," an international system or subsystem, and so on[11]—but much of the literature has been addressed to the question of cohesion within the entity, however the entity might be conceived.

While this is an important question and efforts to answer it are worthwhile, it does have its limitations. Focusing on cohesion and conflict can seriously distort our vision of the aims of East Europe foreign policies. For example, the recent efforts of several socialist states to develop and expand relations with members of the NATO alliance can legitimately be viewed in the perspective of cohesion or disunity in the Soviet-East European alliance, but they should not be viewed exclusively in this light. Herbert Dinerstein has argued that "The main purpose of cross-alliance relationships between secondary alliance members is to gain leverage as against the alliance hegemony, often on issues which are of secondary importance to the hegemonic power but of primary importance to the weaker power. . . . The countries of Eastern Europe want to improve their bargaining position with the Soviet Union by establishing better relations with France and especially West Germany."[12] While the achievement of greater autonomy vis-a-vis the USSR may be part of the East European country's calculus, the major purpose of seeking better relations with a Western country is often to improve the economic or security position of the East European country itself. This aim would be pursued even if such a policy would not in any way increase autonomy from the USSR. As we shall try to demonstrate, the Polish reconciliation with the Federal Republic of Germany was not motivated by a desire to move away from the USSR but by a long-standing wish to solve, or at least alleviate, what the Poles see as their most pressing foreign policy problem.

An exclusive concentration on cohesion and disunity also neglects foreign policies which have no direct impact on the relationship with the USSR and by implication assigns lesser importance to such policies. From the perspective of the East European country itself these policies may be very important indeed. Finally, if we take seriously the notion that the East European states do enjoy some autonomy in policy making and implementation, it would seem that East European policies and behaviors ought to be examined for their intrinsic interest and importance, not merely as factors which are conducive to greater or lesser cohesion with the USSR.

Another way of ascertaining and measuring the changes that have taken place in the Soviet-East European relationship is to study those institutions—most prominently, COMECON and the Warsaw Pact—which are the formal expressions of the alliance. By studying the interaction of the USSR and its allies within these institutions, and by examining the development of the institutions themselves we can learn a good deal about the overall relations within the Soviet alliance. Thus, it is the studies of these institutions which have documented the ability of East European states to pursue their individual interests, to bargain with other socialist states, including the USSR, and, within limits, to dissent from the prevailing line.[13]

Studies of "integration" in Eastern Europe are another genre wherein the Soviet-East European relationship is examined. Borrowing from the various theories of regional integration that have been developed largely out of the West European case,[14] attempts are made to apply notions of regional integration to Eastern Europe, once again largely in order to answer the question of whether the Soviet bloc is moving toward more or less integration. This literature is not yet very extensive—Roger Kanet lists nine articles which apply some form of integration theory to Eastern Europe—and there is no consensus on how best to apply this approch to the area.[15] Integration theory may be too closely tied to the realities of Western Europe. Moreover, as Cal Clark reminds us, "The nature of bloc bargaining processes by which supranational decisions are made still remains obscure. . . . This leaves us a long way from a model of East European integrative activity. Such a model would have to include the goals, strategies, and bargaining sources of the different actors; and these can only be hazarded in rather general and vague terms . . . our ability to estimate the level and scope of Soviet bloc integration may be much more advanced than our causal theories about the process of integration."[16]

As Clark implies, studies of East European integration may allow us to discern major trends over longer periods of time, but they are not very helpful in illuminating the details of the Soviet-East European relationship: what are the motivations, goals, calculations, and tactics of the individual actors? What are the instruments of control and coordination and how effective are they? What are the rules of the game which govern the relationship, how do those rules change and why do they do so? A refined and improved integration approach may serve to show us the general contours of the forest, but it will do little to illuminate the individual trees. If we take seriously our assertions that the different trees in the forest have indeed assumed their own shapes and characteristics, then it should follow that they are worth examination. In fact, in order to study integration or cohesion in a concrete and detailed way, we should begin paying more attention to individual countries, particular issues, and specific interactions among countries and other actors. This could achieve two purposes: we might be able to learn more about foreign policies of individual states and their determination and implementation, and we might also be in a position to make more informed judgments on general tendencies within the East European area as a whole. We could refine our notions of "integration" and "alliance" by specifying on what kinds of issues which states agree or disagree, and why they do so. It is true, as James Rosenau points out, that "Only by identifying similarities and differences in the external behavior of more than one national actor can analysis move beyond the particular case to higher levels of generalization."[17] In the Communist sub field, however, we seem to be proceeding from the top down—we have focused most of our attention on generalizations and have yet to examine in detail the particular cases which could support—or undermine—those generalizations.

In short, our understanding of Soviet-East European interaction, among other problems, would be enhanced by comparative study of the foreign policies of socialist states. Clearly "It has . . . become relevant to examine the foreign policies of the communist East European countries as something more than Moscow-developed manifestations of what Stalin used to call the monolithic socialist camp."[18] Not only do these policies differ, and thus complicate the question of integration and cohesion, but even when policies are similar, motivations and consequences may be different. Poland and Czechoslovakia may follow a similar policy line toward West Germany, but their priorities and motivations are different, with the result that eventually their behavior toward Germany may vary and even cause conflict among socialist states. It is obvious that the USSR does not relate to all socialist countries, even those still within the Soviet alliance, in the same way. It may be necessary to build a more complicated and differentiated model of Soviet-East European relations, taking into account the reality that Soviet-East German relations are on a different footing than, say, Soviet-Hungarian relations. In recent years subgroups within the alliance have appeared. In the early and mid-1960s the "Northern Tier" countries—Poland, Czechoslovakia, and the German Democratic Republic (GDR)—displayed a different attitude toward West Germany from that of Rumania, Bulgaria, or Hungary (and the attitude of each one differed somewhat as well). In the course of the "Prague Spring" a revived "Little Entente" of Czechoslovakia, Rumania, and Yugoslavia seemed to be in formation. These kinds of developments complicate—and make more interesting—international relations in Eastern Europe and make it imperative to examine details and particulars of those relations. This has been done, of course, by scholars, analysts, journalists, and others. Yet, what seems to be missing is the effort to link the details of individual sets of events or of particular countries' foreign policies to the broader questions of integration or of the evolving nature of the Soviet-East European relationship. Even those interested in the alliance institutions cannot ignore the policies of individual states, for it is they and not the organs of COMECON and the Warsaw Pact that determine the postures and behaviors of alliance members within the regional bodies. Somehow, the complexity of interactions among members of the alliance must be taken into account in any effort to build a broad model of the Soviet-East European relationship.

EAST EUROPEAN FOREIGN POLICY: THE CASE OF POLAND AND THE FEDERAL REPUBLIC OF GERMANY

The evolution of East European relations with the Federal Republic of Germany can serve as an example of the complexity and variety which are possible in Soviet-East European relations and in relations between Eastern Europe and countries or alliances outside that area. It is no surprise to find Rumania breaking ranks with the others and establishing diplomatic relations with the FRG in 1967. After all, we expect such behavior from a "maverick" in the bloc. But it is instructive to look at the relations of the FRG with the more orthodox members of the alliance because there we will find diversity of outlook and action and an interplay between the USSR and other socialist countries which confirms concretely the notion of bargaining and coalition building within the alliance. Though we do not pretend to cover this issue comprehensively, even a bare outline will illustrate the point.

The "German issue" means different things to different countries. To the German Democratic Republic it means the resolution of the question of its own legitimacy; to the Poles it means the recognition of the territorial integrity of post-1945 Poland and the settlement of World War II in a psychological and material sense; to the Czechoslovaks, as to the Poles, it means the acceptance by the FRG of the consequences of World War II and the renunciation of the Munich agreement; to the Hungarians, Rumanians and Bulgarians—as well as to the Yugoslavs—it is not so much a question of security as it is a matter of economic, and perhaps political, opportunity. For the USSR, which alone plays the roles of a regional and global power, the German issue has to be seen in the broader context of East-West relationships and Soviet interests in Europe. At times, the varying interests enumerated here coincided, at times they conflicted; the USSR was able to achieve coordination of policies toward Germany at certain juctures and not at others.* This means that intensive and extensive negotiations had to take place among the East European states and between them and the USSR. Certainly the question of cohesion or conflict within the alliance is relevant here, but greater cohesion or greater diversity was not the goal of the international activity surrounding the German issue, though it may well be a product of it. In other words, each socialist state at some point was pursuing its national interest, not in disregard of alliance interests or of the constraints imposed on its activity by membership in the alliance, but in the realization that this was an issue central to the national interest and that it cannot totally ignore that interest and be guided solely by considerations of the alliance. On peripheral issues which do not directly affect the immediate interests of an East European state it can afford to follow the Soviet lead almost automatically. Thus, on the Arab-Israeli issue where the USSR is involved by virtue of its role as a world power but where most of the East European states are not deeply affected, the East Europeans can follow the Soviet lead at little cost. (The Rumanians do not do so

---

*Lawrence Whetten offers the interesting thesis that the Warsaw Pact countries consciously divided the labor among them on the German question. " . . . Warsaw's slice of the concerted action contained the issues of recognizing territorial borders. It is now apparent that Hungary was responsible for conducting the Pact's campaign to convene a European security conference . . . This apportionment of selected issues to individual members left the Soviet Union a freer hand in dealing with the more crucial matters affecting European security . . . " Germany's Ostpolitik: Relations Between the Federal Republic and the Warsaw Pact Countries (London; New York: Oxford University Press for the Royal Institute of International Affairs, 1971), pp. 120-22.

because for them an important principle is involved—the maintenance of relations with all sides in international disputes). But with regard to an issue such as the German one, alliance solidarity can be considered as only one among several important considerations, not the least of which is the national interest as it is perceived by the decision makers.

For Poland the German question has been the paramount foreign policy issue since the end of World War II. Historically, Poland has had to choose among four options: 1) to ally with either Russia or Germany; 2) to attempt to isolate herself and be totally independent of European conflicts (this was the strategy pursued by interwar Poland); 3) to rely on a third, outside force such as France or Great Britain; or 4) "to instigate a general and permanent European settlement, a security system, in which Poland's situation between Russia and Germany becomes a mere fact rather than a liability. This is the option which Poland has pursued, with interruptions, since the publication of the first version of the Rapacki Plan in February 1958."[19]

Recent Polish-West German relations may be divided into three phases. Between 1956 and 1958 Poland made several offers to the FRG in an attempt to begin "normalizing" relations between them. These overtures met a hostile reception in the Adenauer government which was committed to the Hallstein Doctrine and which saw these Polish overtures as a Soviet-inspired move to tempt the FRG into abandoning that doctrine. In the following years several attempts to improve relations and tentative explorations, such as Berthold Beitz's visit to Warsaw (1961), bore no fruit, except for the signing in 1963 of a three-year trade agreement and the establishment of a West German trade mission in Warsaw. This mission did not have consular powers and there was no progress made toward the establishment of diplomatic relations. In 1964, rebuffed by the West Germans, the Poles, who had hitherto been willing to overlook the interests of the German Democratic Republic for the sake of improving relations with the Federal Republic of Germany (FRG), aligned themselves with the GDR against the FRG. Poland now set three conditions for normal relations with the FRG: 1) above all, recognition by the FRG of the Oder-Neisse line as the permanent boundary of Poland; 2) recognition of the GDR by the FRG; 3) a full renunciation of nuclear weapons by the FRG. Poland became the staunchest defender of the GDR's stance on the German question and was a key element of the "Northern Tier" alliance—Poland, the GDR, Czechoslovakia, and the USSR—against West Germany.[20] Some have argued that Polish German policy was "under the thumb of East German interests for almost five years"[21] and that the GDR "impose[d] its will on Poland,"[22] but it is not clear how the GDR was able to do so or why Poland would agree to subordinating its own interest to that of the GDR. The hardening of the Polish line toward the FRG is explicable in terms of the FRG's rebuffs of Polish overtures, gestures which were not easy for the Polish government—any Polish government—to make or for the Polish population to accept. Moreover, Poland was highly sensitive to any Soviet-FRG rapprochement since that might eventually result in an overall European settlement which would not be fully satisfactory to Polish interests. The old nightmare of a German-Soviet deal at the expense of Poland might have forced Poland into an alliance with the most militant and unyielding foe of the FRG. That nightmare might have appeared when, at the very end of his political career, Khrushchev dispatched his son-in-law to Bonn to test the possibilities of an improvement in Soviet-German relations. Later on, the USSR took no decisive action when Rumania and the FRG established diplomatic relations. The Polish leadership chose to back the GDR in part in order to forestall a Soviet-FRG rapprochement. Finally, the 1960s were a period of internal upheaval and instability within the Polish party. The specter of West German revanchism may have been useful to the leadership in its attempts—which were ultimately unsuccessful—to keep the lid on both population and party. By 1968 Poland had added to its conditions for rapprochement with Germany two more stipulations: that the FRG renounce the 1938 Munich agreement ab initio and that the separate status of West Berlin be acknowledged by the West Germans. But the Poles had taken the view, in contrast and, indeed, in opposition, to the East Germans, that the entry of the Social Democrats into the FRG government was a positive development and that some changes in the FRG attitudes were possible.

In March 1969, the Budapest conference of the Warsaw Pact proposed a European security conference and softened the standard harsh attacks of the FRG. "Using the conference proposal as a cover, the leaders in Budapest, Bucharest and Warsaw attempted to reassert their specific national interests in the new atmosphere of decreased tension."[23] In March and April 1969 there appeared in the Polish press several revised views of West Germany and a debate on the nature and intentions of the FRG reflected the fact that the Poles were rethinking their position.[24]

The climax to these developments came in a speech by Wladyslaw Gomulka on May 17, 1969. He suggested the conclusion of a border agreement with the German Federal Republic (GFR), dropped the conditions concerning the Munich settlement and the renunciation of nuclear weapons, and did not insist on recognition of the GDR. Clearly, Polish interests were being placed ahead of all other considerations. Recognition of the Oder-Neisse line, said Gomulka, would make the Polish government welcome the establishment of diplomatic relations with the Federal Republic. The tone of the speech was also in marked contrast to the usually harsh terms in which Polish leaders spoke of the FRG. Ross Johnson suggests several reasons for this turnabout in Polish policy. Poland was disappointed in the failure of the GDR to assist in a large way in the modernization of Polish industry. Softer West German expressions on the Polish issue may have encouraged the Poles to believe that the Germans were amenable to changing their position. Within the Polish party there were pressures, especially from Moczar's "Partisan" group, to pursue a more assertive and autonomous foreign policy. The Budapest Appeal had signaled to the East Europeans that the cultivation of relations with the West was now to be alliance policy. At the same time it may have aroused the Poles once again to a vision of Soviet-West German reconciliation. The Poles felt they had to take an initiative of their own to ensure that their interests, as they perceived them, would be protected.[25] Johnson later observed that "The shift in Poland's policy towards West Germany . . . was only the most striking manifestation of a larger shift in Polish foreign policy toward greater national self-assertiveness—a shift that the European security campaign helped sanction."[26] Neil Ascherson explains Gomulka's initiative as a "dramatic return to a forward foreign policy." He suggests that

> Pessimism plays an evident part: West Germany cannot now be kept from nuclear potential, Strauss may still come to power one day; the Soviet Union is preoccupied with China. Without abandoning her fears of West Germany or her fundamental reliance on Soviet defence, Poland is looking after her own intersts. . . . Reliance on one neighbour is certainly still in force. But it is being reassessed today on the basis of a more realistic view of Soviet interests in the modern world; after a long break Poland is again conducting her own German policy.[27]

It may also be that, having been disappointed in the economic aid that East Germany was providing, the Poles decided to explore the possibilities of increased West German economic aid.

The victory of the Sozialistische Partei Deutschlands (SPD) and Willy Brandt's assumption of the chancellership meant that the German government would be prepared to change its Eastern policy, on the one hand, and that the Polish government could be more sanguine about German intentions, on the other. Brandt enjoyed more trust by the Poles than any other German leader and they were convinced of the sincerity of his desire to come to an agreement with Poland and with other East European countries. German policy now shifted from seeking accommodation through unification to seeking detente through "normalization." Negotiations between Poland and the FRG began in February 1970, and the list of issues to be taken up lengthened as both sides realized that the other attached great importance to the proceedings and was committed to a serious attempt to resolve outstanding issues. Five rounds of negotiations had not yielded an agreement, when in August the USSR and the FRG signed a treaty. This probably surprised the Poles and undoubtedly provided an incentive to conclude their own negotiations with the FRG for fear that a Soviet-FRG rapprochement might not take due account of Poland's interests. At the same time, the GDR was making known in no uncertain terms its displeasure with Poland's actions. The East Germans were afraid that Polish actions would betray their interests, while the Poles were uneasy about Soviet actions which might jeopardize Polish interests. Each party was acting in what it saw as its own national interest. On December 7, 1970, after both the FRG and Poland had committed their national prestige to reaching a successful agreement, and after each side had made concessions, a normalization treaty was agreed upon. In five articles the treaty provides not for the de jure recognition of the Polish frontiers but for agreement of the two parties that the existing Oder-Niesse line "shall constitute the western frontier of Poland." This followed the Zgorzelec formula of 1950 wherein the GDR and Poland had agreed on Poland's western frontier. The treaty expressed the intention of both sides to proceed with the normalization of relations and to expand economic and cultural contacts. It also expressly subordinated this agreement to the Potsdam and Paris agreements so that Allied rights and prerogatives were not superseded by the the Polish-FRG treaty. Both sides had agreed to deal separately with other issues that existed between them, and so the Poles sent a message to the FRG regarding the repatriation of ethnic Germans living in Poland, and Brandt declared that the treaty was not a substitute for a peace treaty, that the Poles had committed themselves to take up diplomatic relations with the FRG when the treaty would come into force, and that normalization with Poland and Eastern Europe could not be considered complete until some agreement was reached on the situation in and around Berlin.[28]

Because of internal political considerations in the FRG, and because of lingering distrust and hesitancy on the part of the Poles, the latter did not ratify the treaty until May 1972. It is fair to say that the hopes aroused by the treaty have not been fulfilled very rapidly. Economic relations have not developed as rapidly or as extensively as the Poles had hoped and the repatriation issue has become a bone of contention. The Poles continue to be irritated by the statements of German politicians who oppose normalization. The resignation of Willy Brandt, whose precipitant was the discovery of an East German spy in his immediate circle, has disappointed those who expected that normalization would be more rapid and more far reaching. Mieczyslaw Rakowski, the prestigious editor of <u>Polityka</u>, recently expressed his feelings. " . . . During the period which followed the signing of the treaty there were many signs in the FRG's political life of the existence, to say the least, of unfriendliness toward Poland and many examples which gave irrefutable proof of the fact that practices contrary to the rules and spirit of the treaty were only reluctantly abandoned." Rakowski noted "a strengthening of certain unrealistic attitudes toward the Polish People's Republic (PPR) which is contrary to the spirit of the treaty" and denied that Poland had not fulfilled its obligations on the question of repatriation, accusing Bonn of constantly escalating its demands on this issue.[29]

Whatever the present state of Polish-West German relations, the implications of the normalization treaty are great, not only for the roles of Poland and the FRG in Europe and for East-West relations generally, but also for the relations between Poland and the USSR and perhaps between the USSR and its East European allies generally. After all, as many Polish and foreign observers have pointed out for years, Poland's alliance with the USSR rested to a significant extent on the latter's being the only guarantor of Poland's territorial integrity and of her security. Now that the German threat has been substantially minimized, will Poland be more free to act in the international arena? Will her political dependence on the USSR diminish? The USSR's role in the Polish-FRG agreement should not be minimized. The USSR set limits on Polish behavior, directly affected the ability of both Poland and the Federal Republic to negotiate and agree with each other, and certainly influenced—perhaps even determined—the timing of that agreement. But the USSR did not determine the basic Polish outlook nor did it set the Polish agenda in regard to the Federal Republic. There was—and is—a coincidence of Polish and Soviet interests, but there was no dictation of Polish policy and the various shifts it has undergone. Earlier, the USSR had followed a strategy of multilateralism in its dealings with the West, but having itself engaged in bilateral negotiations it had been forced to allow bilateral relations to develop between the East Europeans and the West Germans. "Further, by accepting something less than what the Czechoslovaks, Poles, and East Germans regarded as non-negotiable terms, the Soviet Union will no longer be able to pose as the absolute guarantor of East European interests, as she did before August, 1970. . . . The East Europeans could only conclude that they had been left to their own resources; an important beginning had been made in transforming the processes of conflict resolution and political detente from international or national preferences."[30] Whether or not this is the beginning of a long-term trend remains to be seen; too often we have seized upon particular developments in Soviet-East European relations as marking the beginning of long-range and perhaps irreversible tendencies.* But however the matter turns out, the fact is that on the German issue, one which is vital to several of the East European states, they pursued essentially nationally determined interests. Poland consciously refused to accept the formula of "unreserved respect" for her borders, which the Soviets were satisfied with in their agreement with the FRG, and the Poles continued to press for unequivocal recognition. The two allies placed different values on the same issue; what was a sine qua non for Poland was an issue on which compromise was possible for the USSR. The central issue to the GDR, recognition by the FRG and the West generally, was one which Poland adopted as her own until such time when it proved convenient to drop it in order to gain Poland's primary objectives.

Whether or not the resolution of the German issue marks the beginning of a new type of Soviet-East European relationship, in the short run it does seem to have provided the impetus for a more aggressive foreign policy on the part of Poland. Having secured its place in Europe, Poland is able to turn her attention to broader European questions and to take initiatives on them. Within a more flexible and dynamic European situation, Jan Szczepanski has suggested, Poland could be more assertive about her national interests and assume a more active international role.[31] An analysis of several articles by Poland's leading commentators on international affairs concludes that "The new guarantee of its national existence represented by the treaty and the prospect of an emerging equilibrium in Europe are . . . perceived as a turning point which, while holding to the pivot of the Soviet alliance, provide new opportunities for an independent momentum in Polish foreign policy. 'We can pause, . . . wipe the sweat from our brows, and look around—throughout Europe—with the feelings of a man who has finished laying the foundations and can now build the house.' "[32] The treaty with the FRG has lessened Poland's debtor status in the alliance and has freed her to act more independently and aggressively. Whether or not she will do so depends as much on internal political stability and economic progress as it does on international factors. As Robert Dean wisely points out, however, Polish assertiveness "must not be seen in terms of the conventional zero-sum model with the gamut of Polish interests poised against those of the Soviet Union in an inherently antagonistic relationship, and any

*Whetten writes that "In the next decade, Moscow will have to assess and accept to a greater degree than before the individual interests and demands of its allies. Consensus will now have to be negotiated rather than imposed." Germany's Ostpolitik (New York, 1971), p. 190.

move toward the West perceived as one away from the Soviet Union or in conflict with Soviet interests. . . . It is clear that the Polish elite views the country as having genuine interests in both East and West. The challenge now is expanding the latter by creating conditions in Europe which will induce them, and which will make possible a less one-sided pursuit of Polish interests."[33] For example, "Poland's opposition to a stronger West European community is fully in keeping with the Soviet position . . . but the motivation differs somewhat. For the Soviets an integrated Western Europe complicates the exercise of political influence in that area; for Poland a closely integrated Western Europe threatens to relegate Poland to a permanent position on its periphery."[34]

To return to points made earlier, viewing the Soviet-East European relationship strictly along the cohesion-conflict dimension causes us to misperceive both the motivation and the nature of an East European country's foreign policy behavior. East European policies which are at variance with those of the USSR are not necessarily policies directed against the USSR. At the same time, it is important to bear in mind that policies which are in conformity with Soviet policy are not necessarily determined by the USSR. East European and Soviet stands may be similar and mutually supportive but they may be motivated by self-interest rather than by a desire to conform to an overall line. Poland especially has attached great importance to foreign policy questions because of her size, geographic position and especially sensivite international situation.* It is not surprising that even while remaining unquestionably loyal to the USSR and to the alliance as a whole, Poland has found it both necessary and possible to pursue her own national interest.

The treatment of the West German issue by the states in the area illustrates the possibilities of diversity without deviance in the Soviet-East European alliance. This is an issue on which the states had different perspectives arising from their historical experiences, geographical situations, economic needs, perceived national interests, and relationships to the USSR. The range and diversity of issues presented by West Germany to the East European states and the USSR are roughly summarized in Table 7.1. It is not surprising that such diversity exists; what must be noted is the ability of the various states to act upon that diversity without destroying or even threatening the alliance which binds them and without seriously antagonizing the hegemonic power of the alliance.

---

*Peter Bender points out that "In no other East European state has a member of the Politburo been at the head of the Foreign Ministry as in Poland since 1956 . . . " East Europe in Search of Security (Baltimore: Johns Hopkins University Press, 1972), p. 75.

TABLE 7.1

Policy Issues of the Federal Republic of Germany

Rumania	Yugoslavia
Principle of foreign policy autonomy; trade and economic aid	Principle of foreign policy autonomy; and trade economic aid
Hungary	**Bulgaria**
Trade; support Soviet foreign policy; improve East-West relations	Trade; support Soviet foreign policy
Czechoslovakia	**USSR**
Renounce Munich; Sudeten German expellees; trade	East-West relations; European settlement; trade; protect interests of client states
Poland	**GDR**
Oder-Neisse line; trade and aid; East-West relations; ethnic Germans	Legitimize existence, security; ideology

Source: Compiled by the authors.

DIVERSITY AND DEVIANCE IN EAST EUROPEAN FOREIGN POLICIES

Diversity in the foreign policies of the socialist states arises from several sources. Among them are conceptions of what international relations generally and international relations specifically among socialist states ought to be; the geographical position of a state; its international and domestic political situation; its economic position; the nature of its decision-making elite; the popular pressures to which it is subject; and the nature of the issues. Rumania and Yugoslavia—the latter not a member of the alliance as it is commonly conceived—are socialist states for whom autonomous foreign policy and the pursuit of national interest above all other considerations are matters of principle. This does not mean that they deliberately attempt to go against Soviet desires, but when those desires conflict with their own preferences they will opt for the latter if at all possible. Albania, on the other hand, is not a member of the alliance for well-known historical reasons, and her opposition to the USSR has become a matter of principle. The USSR's leadership of the socialist camp has been repudiated by Albania and her Chinese patrons, and the Albanians are assiduous in criticizing and dissenting from Soviet policy even where their own interests are not involved. For the other European socialist states conformity with the USSR's policies is generally desirable on two grounds. There is a genuine ideological commitment to socialist unity and there are shared socialist values. There are also practical considerations of economic alliance with—and even dependence on—the USSR and political alliance with the protective superpower.

As the German issue makes clear, different geographical positions, as well as historical memories, dictate different interests. The Oder-Neisse boundary was the most crucial issue of Polish foreign policy, whereas to the other socialist countries it became a matter of supporting the position of an ally and perhaps indirectly contributing to their own security. The historical memories of Rumanians and Hungarians regarding Germany are different from those of the Poles and Czechoslovaks. This meant not only a difference in elite attitudes and sentiments but also that the popular feelings and pressures around the issue were qualitatively different. All of the countries are interested in the role that the Federal Republic can play in efforts to improve their economies, but the importance of the FRG to this effort depends on the particular needs of the country and its dependence on foreign trade and credits.

The type of issue being dealt with is crucial in determining how much diversity there will be in the socialist camp. As a general rule it may be stated that on issues which are not perceived to be at the core of their own interests the socialist states will line up with the USSR. As a global power and the hegemonic regional power the USSR must take a stand and be actively engaged on many more issues than the other countries, and she can generally count on the support of her allies. On the Arab-Israeli conflict, for example, an issue which is farily remote from the basic interests of the East European states, they have lined up with the USSR. Rumania has not done so because of her principle of maintaining relations with all protagonists in international disputes. The Yugoslavs have been on the same side as the Soviets but only because their determination of their position has coincided, at least in outcome, with the Soviet one. The Arab-Israeli issue has been used differently for internal purposes in Poland (1968) and in Czechoslovakia (when it was made an issue by reformers in 1968 and then turned around by the regime after 1969), from the way in which it was used in Hungary and Bulgaria (where it had no domestic consequences to speak of). But the external positions taken by these states were very much the same.

There is a second class of issues, those that are of greater immediate relevance to the East Europeans but which are either remote enough or of sufficiently large dimension so that only limited initiatives can be taken, and they must defer to the Soviet lead. Relations with the United States are important to these countries because they have economic, security, and cultural consequences. But it is the Soviet-American relationship which is most important since it is not simply a question of bilateral relations but of the general state of the international system. Therefore, there is general deference to the Soviet lead in this area.

A third class of issues is typified by the one we have used here, however sketchily, for illustrative purposes. These are matters which go to the core of the national self-interest. On such matters there is the most strain toward, not necessarily independence of the USSR, but the independent formulation of the problem and of the policies designed to meet it. While the USSR may prefer multilateral approaches to such problems, which, among other things, add legitimacy to the views advocated by the USSR, on matters which are of intense concern to one or more of her allies she may have to countenance a number of bilateral processes which may not in any ultimate sense weaken the alliance and may in fact strengthen it.[35]

CONCLUSION

The existence of bilateralism, both between East and West and within the East (as, for example, relations between the GDR and Poland, a subject worthy of extended study), makes all the more necessary an attempt to study the foreign policies of the socialist states and to do so comparatively. There is probably enough autonomy in Eastern Europe to warrant the systematic study of the various countries' foreign policies, rather than noting those occasions when policies appear to deviate from the Soviet or general line. A comparative approach to foreign policy will deal with diversity not simply as deviance but will illuminate the calculus of each actor and thereby illustrate why there is diversity or conformity. It would also bring into sharper relief the detailed pieces which go into making up the larger mosaic of integration-disintegration in the area. Finally, such an approach would bring yet another aspect of Communist studies into closer touch with the discipline and might improve the generalizations and concepts developed so far by adding to the number of cases and variations that are taken into account.

The policy analysts and some area specialists have been treating the East European states as separate entitities for some time, and their work has demonstrated the correctness of such an approach. The political scientists by and large have done this only for the obviously deviant cases. If this effort were extended to all the socialist countries we would have a far more complicated—and hence, accurate—picture of the Soviet-East European alliance. Our generalizations about it and attempts to conceptualize this alliance would be more firmly grounded in reality. The integration approach to the study of Soviet-East European relations would be complemented by one which examined the individual trees in the forest and tried to ascertain why the forest assumes the general configuration that it does. The relations between the USSR and Eastern Europe promise to be ever more complex both to the policy maker as well as to the scholar. The study of these relations should proceed on several fronts at once.

NOTES

1. On the characteristics of an empire, see Ghita Ionescu, The Break-up of the Soviet Empire in Eastern Europe (London: Penguin Books, 1965) pp. 7-8.

2. Zbigniew K. Brzezinski, Alternative to Partition (New York: McGraw Hill, 1965) p. 28. See also William Zimmerman, "The Transformation of the Modern State-System: The Exhaustion of Communist Alternatives," Journal of Conflict Resolution 16, no. 2 (June 1972).

3. See, for example, Sh. P. Sanakoev, Morovaia sistema sotsializma osnovnye problemy i etapy razvitiia (Moscow: Mezhdunarodnye Otnosheniia, 1968) and Nish Jamgotch, Jr., Soviet-East European Dialogue: International Relations of a New Type? (Stanford, Calif: Hoover Institution on War, Revolution, and Peace, Stanford University, 1968).

4. William R. Kintner and Wolfgang Klaiber, Eastern Europe and European Security (New York: Dunellen, 1971), p. 207.

5. On bargaining within the Warsaw Pact, see Robin Alison Remington, The Warsaw Pact (Cambridge, Mass.: M.I.T. Press, 1971) p. 169, and Thomas W. Wolfe, "The Warsaw Pact in Evolution," in Kurt London, ed., Eastern Europe in Transition (Baltimore: Johns Hopkins Press, 1966) pp. 221 and 225.

6. R. V. Burks, "The Communist Polities of Eastern Europe," in James N. Rosenau, ed., Linkage Politics: Essays on the Convergence of National and International Systems (New York: Free Press, 1969).

7. Zvi Gitelman, The Diffusion of Political Innovation: From Eastern Europe to the Soviet Union (Beverly Hills: Saga Publications, 1972) p. 9. On consensual and cooperative relations, see Kenneth

Jowitt, "The Romanian Communist Party and the World Socialist System: a Re-definition of Unity," World Politics 23, no. 1 (October 1970).

8. Thomas W. Wolfe, Soviet Power and Europe, 1945-1970 (Baltimore: Johns Hopkins Press, 1970) p. 296. Melvin Croan remarked earlier that "it is difficult even to find a label for the present international system in the area, let alone conjecture on its future." "Moscow and Eastern Europe," Problems of Communism 15, no. 5 (September-October 1966): 63.

9. George Modelski, "Communism and the Globalization of Politics," International Studies Quarterly 12, no. 4 (December 1968): 384-85.

10. The classic study is Zbigniew K. Brzezinski, The Soviet Bloc: Unity and Conflict rev. ed. (Cambridge, Mass.: Harvard University Press, 1967). Other examples are P. Terry Hopmann, "International Conflict and Cohesion in the Communist System," International Studies Quarterly 11, no. 3 (September 1967); Cal Clark, "Foreign Trade as an Indicator of Political Integration in the Soviet Bloc," International Studies Quarterly 15, no. 3 (September 1971); Barry Hughes and Thomas Volgy, "Distance in Foreign Policy Behavior: A Comparative Study of Eastern Europe," Midwest Journal of Political Science 14, no. 3 (August 1970).

11. See, for example, William Zimmerman, "Hierarchical Regional Systems and the Politics of System Boundaries," International Organization 26, no. 1 (Winter 1972).

12. Herbert A. Dinerstein, "The Transformation of Alliance Systems," American Political Science Review 59, no. 3 (September 1965): 597.

13. Some of the better known works are Michael Kaser, COMECON: Integration Problems of the Planned Economics, 2nd ed. (London; New York: Royal Institute of International Affairs, Oxford University Press, 1967); Andrzej Korbonski, "COMECON," International Conciliation, no. 549 (September 1965); Kazimierz Grzybowski, The Socialist Commonwealth of Nations (New Haven: Yale University Press, 1964); Henry W. Schaefer, Comecon and the Politics of Integration (New York: Praeger, 1972); and Robin Remington, op. cit.

14. Charles Pentland discusses the pluralist, functionalist, neofunctionalist and federalist approaches to regional integration in his International Theory and European Integration (London: Faber, 1973).

15. A thorough survey of the literature on integration in Eastern Europe can be found in Roger Kanet, "Integration and the Study of Eastern Europe." paper for an "intensive panel" on East European Integration, International Studies Association Meeting, St. Louis, March, 1974.

16. Cal Clark, "The Study of East European Integration: Method, Madness, or Mundanity?" paper for the "intensive panel" on East European Integration, ibid., p. 15.

17. James N. Rosenau, "Comparative Foreign Policy: Fad, Fantasy, or Field?" International Studies Quarterly 12, no. 3 (September 1968): 308.

18. Barry Farrell, "Foreign Policy Formation in the Communist Countries of Eastern Europe," East European Quarterly 1, no. 1 (March 1967):39.

19. Neal Ascherson, "Poland's Place in Europe," The World Today 25, no. 12 (December 1969): 521-22.

20. For useful summaries of Polish-West German relations, see A. Ross Johnson, "A Survey of Poland's Relations with West Germany, 1956-1967," Polish Background Report 5, Radio Free Europe Research, February 26, 1968; Otto Stenzl, "Germany's Eastern Frontier," Survey no. 51 (April 1964); and Brzezinski, op. cit. A Polish overview is Marian Dobrosielski's "Poland's Contribution to the Security of Europe," Studies on International Relations no. 1 (Warsaw 1973).

21. Remington, op. cit., p. 155.

22. Philip Windsor, Germany and the Management of Detente (London: Chatto and Windus for the Institute of Strategic Studies, 1971), p. 38.

23. Karl E. Birnbaum, East and West Germany: A Modus Vivendi (Lexington, Mass.: Lexington Books, 1973) pp. 5-6.

24. For documentation, see A. Ross Johnson, "A New Phase in Polish-West German Relations," part 1, background report 13, Radio Free Europe Research, June 20, 1969.

25. A. Ross Johnson, "A New Phase in Polish-West German Relations," part 3, background report 17, Radio Free Europe Research, August 14, 1969.

26. A. Ross Johnson, "The Warsaw Pact's Campaign for 'European Security,' " RAND memorandum R-565-PR, November, 1970, p. 57.

27. Ascherson, op. cit., p. 528.

28. The text of the treaty and some of the statements supplementing it can be found in Lawrence Whetten, Relations Between the Federal Republic and the Warsaw Pact Countries (London; New York: Oxford University Press for the Royal Institute of International Affairs, 1971), pp. 227-31, and Birnbaum, op. cit., pp. 117-24. For a Polish view of the negotiations with the FRG, see R. Markiewicz, "Polska-NRF-bezpieczenstwo europejskie," Sprawy Miedzynarodowe, 1971, no. 1. For legal aspects of the treaty and a Polish interpretation, see Alfons Klafkowski, Uklad Polska-NRF z 7 Grudnia 1970 r. (Warsaw: Wydawnictwo Ministerstwa Obrony Narodowej, 1973) and an English

summary in his "The Treaty Between Poland and the German Federal Republic Concerning the Bases of Normalization of their Mutual Relations as an Element of the Recognition of the Status Quo in Europe," Studies on International Relations no. 1 (Warsaw, 1973). An article-by-article interpretation is Jerzy Sulek, "The Main Directions of the Political and Legal Interpretations of the Polish-West German Treaty of 7 December 1970," in ibid. On Polish foreign policy generally, see Eugeniusz Gajda, Polska polityka zagraniczna 1944-1971 (Warsaw: Wydawnictwo Ministerstwa Obrony Narodowej, 1972).

29. Mieczyslaw Rakowski, "How We Understand Normalization," Polityka, March 30, 1974. Translated in Radio Free Europe, Polish Press Survey no. 2445, April 16, 1974.

30. Lawrence Whetten, Germany's Ostpolitik (New York: Oxford University Press, 1971), p. 188.

31. Jan Szczepanski, "The Fate of Poland and the Polish Character," Zycie Warszawy, June 4, 1970, cited in Michael Costello, "The Poles Look at Their Country and at Themselves," Polish Background 14, Radio Free Europe Research, September 16, 1970.

32. Robert W. Dean, "Polish Foreign Policy Perspectives and European Security," Polish Background 10, Radio Free Europe Research, May 25, 1973. The quotation is from Wieslaw Gornicki, "Can the Poles Fight Themselves Free?" Zycie Warszawy, June 18-19, 1972.

33. Ibid., pp. 13-14.

34. Ibid., p. 14.

35. On the Soviet preference for multilateralism, see Richard W. Mansbach, "Bilateralism and Multilateralism in the Soviet Bloc," International Organization 24, no. 2 (Spring 1970).

CHAPTER

8

ACTUAL PROBLEMS OF POLITICAL RELATIONS BETWEEN THE USSR AND THE GDR

Peter C. Ludz

An adequate assessment of the political relationship between the USSR and the German Democratic Republic (GDR) requires a broad framework of reference. Clearly economic ties exist alongside the political bonds; in addition both must be related to the larger political structure that defines the position of these two countries within the Eastern bloc as a whole. Relevant also is the complex interrelationship which exists between foreign and domestic policy in the GDR. Here the security motive of the Socialist Unity Party (SED) leadership, the foreign policy functions of domestic policy, and the GDR's lack of legitimacy are salient factors. We suggest that an understanding of these last problems is most essential to an evaluation of the political relations between the USSR and the GDR.

THE GDR'S POLITICAL POSITION WITHIN THE EASTERN ALLIANCE

Since the conclusion (1970-1972) of treaties between the Federal Republic of Germany (FRG), on the one hand, and the USSR, Poland, and the GDR, on the other hand, East Germany's position within the Eastern alliance has begun to undergo thorough changes. This was evident at the Helsinki Conference on Security and Cooperation in Europe (CSCE) in the summer of 1973. The changes do not mean, however, that the GDR has loosened its strong ties with the USSR, the Warsaw Pact and COMECON. Rather, the GDR's relations with each of its allies have become more distinctive, and thus more complicated, in the same way as have its relations with the FRG and with other Western countries. The growing differentiation in its political situation affords the GDR both more and less room to maneuver in its foreign policy.

To analyze properly the changed international position of the GDR, it is especially necessary to examine that country's relationship with the USSR. Among the most striking consequences of the tranfer of power from Ulbricht to Honecker in 1971 is that East Germany has been modeling itself on the USSR even more closely than before. This holds both for the political and economic spheres. In contrast to Ulbricht, Honecker explicitly renounced any attempt at designing a unique model of socialism (either political or economic) for the GDR. Also, under Honecker the composition of the SED Politburo paralleled the lines of the CPSU Politburo more closely than was the case under Ulbricht. For example, after 1970, leaders of the military and the security apparatus were admitted to the CPSU Politburo as well as to the SED Politburo. In his speech to the eighth congress of the SED, in June 1971, Honecker particularly stressed the GDR-USSR relationship. Using the formula of "socialist internationalism" which had been adopted in the GDR Constitution of 1968, and clearly assigning a higher priority than theretofore to relations with the USSR, Honecker renewed the GDR's commitment to the USSR and strengthened an association which the GDR by itself will not be in a position to sever, at least for the foreseeable future. Speeches of the SED party leadership increasingly portray the USSR as the country which has attained the "greatest success" in the process of building a socialist/communist society. The strengthening of Soviet-GDR ties is further reinforced insofar as both the USSR and the GDR tend increasingly to regard the principles of "socialist internationalism" not only as fundamental guidelines for all Communist parties, but also as norms of international law.[1]

After Ulbricht's departure, Honecker shifted the GDR's priorities; the national question and the emphasis on the GDR's own national way toward socialism and communism were pushed into the background. During the 1960s Ulbricht, while bowing to Soviet wishes and interests, increasingly laid explicit stress on the GDR's own road toward socialism and even recommended the GDR, in some respects, as a model for other countries in Eastern Europe. Probably his clearest statement to this effect was given at the meeting of the Central Committee of the SED in February 1964, when he pointed out

> Our new economic system is not an invention out of the blue. It could be characterized as the concrete application of an advanced version of Leninist principles of socialist economic management to conditions in the GDR, a highly developed industrial country. We are aware of the fact that in the German

> Democratic Republic we have handled and continue to handle the transition from capitalism to socialism in accordance with our national conditions. These conditions must be distinguished from those that prevailed in the Soviet Union when it proceeded from capitalism to socialism.[2]

In contrast to Ulbricht, Honecker does not claim a special mission for the GDR, and endeavors to make East Germany's foreign policy conform more closely to the Soviet design. Horst Sindermann, chairman of the Council of Ministers and member of the SED Politbureau, made this clear in a speech delivered on the occasion of the 25th anniversary of the founding of COMECON. He emphasized that "only through their drawing together and through the strengthening of their collective forces can the (socialist) brother-countries fully develop their national sovereignty." All crucial issues of international politics are dealt with in the context of the relationship with the USSR. For example, the GDR clearly supports the Soviet policy towards the People's Republic of China (PRC), and follows the USSR in its anti-Israeli and pro-Arab positions. Furthermore, the USSR can count on the GDR's support for problems which it classifies under the heading of "peace policy," including its CSCE and MBFR strategies. The SED leadership under Honecker does not, however, appear inclined to renounce outright a national political stand. To be sure, such attitudes are expressed much less firmly than they were in the Ulbricht era. It is not longer claimed, in so many words, that the GDR should be recognized as a model for other socialist countries, in particular the USSR. On the other hand, encouragement is given to efforts to develop the GDR as a kind of model-state of the Soviet type. This may well be intended to meet the GDR's sociopolitical and ideological need to compete with the FRG in domestic affairs. Yet, on the whole, it is difficult to believe that Honecker has willingly abandoned the scope of the GDR's foreign policy to the USSR—especially at the present time when this scope is broadening.

The principles of future GDR foreign policy—while following closely the Soviet line—will need to strike a difficult balance between the twin poles of more extensive integration into the Eastern alliance and coexistence in varying forms of cooperation with the West. Aspects of the GDR's integration should be examined first. Since the 25th meeting of COMECON in July 1972, when the so-called "Complex Integration Program" was adopted, the GDR, together with the USSR, has sought to accelerate the economic growth of Eastern Europe, on the basis of both common political aims and economic interests. The USSR is regarded as the model, that is, the body politic which since 1917 has established and developed the union of "autonomous" Soviet republics as an example of interstate integration.

To what extent the Soviets themselves at present want such far-reaching integration in Eastern Europe is uncertain. Nevertheless, they can hardly disregard the various pressures toward national independence in Eastern Europe; they cannot ignore those developments which clearly demonstrate a strengthened self-confidence on the part of the Eastern and Southeastern European states, especially Rumania and Poland. Moreover, in the circumstances it seems likely that the CPSU leaders may use "integration" (in the sense of "socialist internationalism") as a watchword in order to renew unmistakably their claim to political superiority in Eastern Europe. The USSR's assertion that it is the best qualified of the East European countries to generalize experiences of socialist construction and to incorporate them into binding guidelines can be regarded as an effort to counter centrifugal tendencies in Eastern Europe. The concept of integration is also used to promote Soviet interests in the sphere of political economy. At present, the USSR is in need of financial support from East European allies to meet the high costs of its investment and development plans (for example, for developing new territory, for the exploitation of its mineral wealth, and for the construction of new industrial enterprises).

The level of East German support for Soviet policy can be gathered from some figures on the economic, technical, and scientific cooperation between the two countries. In 1972, East German exports to the USSR reached a total of 9.6 billion valuta-marks,* while imports totalled 8.0 billion valuta-marks. These figures represent about 40 percent of the total value of East German exports and 35 percent of imports.[3] Also, at present there are some 60 intergovernmental agreements that were drawn up under the auspices of the 'Joint-Governmental Commission for Economic and Scientific-Technological Cooperation' (set up in 1966).[4] Evidently, the SED leaders tend increasingly to view themselves as strong junior partners of the USSR in politial and economic matters. This junior role is accepted by the Kremlin, in the well-understood sense of the 1964 GDR-USSR Treaty.

East Germany's relations with other Eastern and Southeastern European countries closely follow the pattern of its relationship with the USSR. The GDR's particular political situation enables it better than any other East European country to subordinate its own interests to those of the USSR. While faithfully assisting the USSR to exert political control over Eastern and Southeastern Europe, the GDR is at the same time strengthening its own position with regard to the other socialist states. In this respect, the GDR's political

---

*Roughly speaking, 1 valuta-mark is equal to DM 1.

role is determined in large measure by its conspicuous failure to establish a national identity. As a Soviet watchdog, devoid of patriotic purpose, it is able to concentrate on the deviations of its socialist brethren, while evoking ideological purity and reliability on its own behalf. A second factor that conditions the GDR's relationship with the other East European states stems from the fact that—today as in the 1960s—the GDR is able to boast greater economic achievements than, for example, Czechoslovakia, Poland, or Hungary. This is accentuated by the GDR's standard of living, which has, for many years and by a large margin, been the highest in the Eastern bloc.

The tense and rather complex relations between the GDR and Eastern Europe—which, of course, vary from country to country—have come about mainly because of East German ambivalence regarding politico-economic matters. On the one hand, proposals for economic reforms launched in other states—as, for example, in Czechoslovakia in 1968, or in Hungary in 1970-71—were subjected to intensive criticism in the GDR and, occasionally, even denounced as a reversion to capitalism. On the other hand, in the GDR itself, the nationalization of private firms was not completed until the spring of 1972, when the last elements of private and seminationalized enterprises were transferred into "people's property." Moreover, the GDR constantly warns its Eastern allies of the danger of contacts with the imperialist West, especially the FRG, notwithstanding the fact that the GDR itself continues to develop its relations with the West. Thus, East Germany has increased the value of exports and imports traded with the FRG to more than 10 percent of its total foreign trade; but it has not shared the benefits of this intra-German trade with its allies.

THE SECURITY MOTIVES OF THE SED LEADERS

The political stance of the GDR, both in domestic and in foreign policy towards the USSR, cannot be fully understood without considering the basic motives of the SED politicians. These motives center on the need for security. In this repsect security does not mean simply military or strategic problems; the presence of Soviet divisions on East German soil ensures the minimum of political stability that any state needs to survive. The withdrawal or reduction of these troops in the GDR is out of the question in the foreseeable future.

The GDR's National People's Army (NVA) is quantitatively inferior to its West German counterpart, though the NVA may now be better trained and more integrated politically than it was formerly. This was acknowledged in 1967-68 when GDR troops were admitted into the Warsaw Pact's first detachment, which comprises only politically reliable units. In 1970, the GDR spent 390 marks per capita for defense purposes (these are the published figures); this represented about 5.9 percent of the GNP. West Germany spent 368 marks or 3.8 percent of the GNP in the same year.[5]

Security is not only protection against annexation by an enemy or against war. Security means much more, especially for the GDR. It means the preservation of the political and, by the same token, personal rank of the SED leaders, the maintenance of a single party's monopoly of power, the continued development of East German society along the guidelines set by the SED, and protection from ideological "deviation" and "subversion" influences from either the West or the East. The GDR, even more than the USSR (but still with the expressed consent of Moscow) vehemently attacks all ideological deviations from Soviet-style Marxist-Leninism—whether they come from the West in the form of social democracy or the East in the form of revisionism. Any political deviation is suspect. The GDR emphasizes the existence of a clear social and political demarcation line (Abgrenzung) on the West, and such concepts as democratic socialism and socially-oriented market economy. It also follows, to a certain degree and with various nuances, a policy of Abgrenzung toward certain aspects of political and intellectual life of its Eastern neighbors.

For the SED leadership the term security has maintained first and foremost a connotation of political ideology and national economy. As the second state on German soil, the military and strategic components of the GDR's security are left out of the debate, for no East German politician of standing would call them into question. It is evident that the political ideology component of the search for security is by its very nature a close combination of defensive and offensive elements. The present ideological strategy of the SED can best be described as offensive from a defensive position. The SED has been put on the defensive by the Ostpolitik of the West German government; it reacted offensively to these factors by increasing the number of agreements and intensifying joint ideological planning with its East European neighbors, and especially with the Soviets.

It is the SED leadership's need for security in this vital respect that is determining the currently growing tensions between the GDR's interests and its goals, the complicated problems of integration into the Eastern bloc, and the possibilities of cooperation or conflict with the West.

PROBLEMS OF THE GDR WITHIN COMECON

The GDR became a member of the Council for Mutual Economic Assistance (COMECON) in 1950, only one year after its foundation. The close ties that have developed within this East European economic community have become a source of problems for the GDR. In 1972, about 72 percent of the GDR's foreign trade was with COMECON members, the USSR being by far its most important trading partner. At present, however, the USSR is tending, within the framework of detente, to intensify its economic relations with the leading industrial nations of the West. The other COMECON states, for their part (the GDR is to an extent an exception), have hardly been able to escape continued Soviet pressure for COMECON integration.[6] The Soviets need the support of the Eastern bloc countries as much as ever, particularly in view of the fact that the economic and technological gap with the West is widening instead of narrowing.

COMECON membership presents the GDR with a number of specific advantages as well as difficulties. On the one hand, the much less industrialized countries of the Eastern bloc, and especially the USSR, constitute an ideal market for highly developed East German industries. At least until the first economic consequences of detente became apparent, the specialized industries of the GDR hardly had to fear serious competition within Eastern bloc markets. There was even less cause for concern after the mid-1960s, when the already extensive economic expansion in the COMECON area was succeeded by a period of intensive growth. The GDR enhanced its position by monopolizing the export of certain industrial goods, such as marine diesel engines, metallurgical equipment, dredging and road-making equipment.[7] Lastly, the GDR benefits from its chairmanship of three of the COMECON's 21 Standing Commissions: chemicals, construction, and standardization. East Germany's economic planners constantly try to exploit this advantage by presenting mainly those concepts of specialization and conditions for cooperation that are most favorable to the GDR. A good example is the planning of a uniform electronic data system for the COMECON area, which has been strongly influenced by the GDR. The GDR already has an excellent place in the field, for it possesses a relatively advanced computer industry. Similarly, it plays an essential role in the planning of container transport.

On the other hand, the GDR's firm economic integration in COMECON has not prevented the country from expanding its trade with the West. Although in 1973 foreign trade with the socialist countries was more than twice as high as with the capitalist industrial countries, the growth rates for the latter have been higher as evidenced in Table 8.1. The increase in the FRG-GDR trade is the main factor in this development.*

TABLE 8.1

GDR Foreign Trade 1960-1973
(in millions of valuta-marks)

	Imports and Exports			1973 as percent
	1960	1970	1973	of 1960
With socialist countries	13,798.8	28,340.1	36,779.8	266.5
With capitalist industrial countries	3,897.2	9,656.0	14,904.1	382.4

Source: *Statistisches Jahrbuch 1974 der Deutschen Demokratischen Republik* (East Berlin: Staatsverlag der DDR, 1974), pp. 282f.

The fact remains, however, that the GDR has had to make up for a lack of raw materials and, out of necessity, has over the years moved into the position of the second most important exporter of industrial goods in the Eastern bloc. The size of this export activity, not only strains considerably the productive capacity of the GDR, but also obliges the economy to concentrate on those industrial sectors most needed by the USSR and other Eastern bloc countries. In turn, this increases the GDR's economic dependence on the Eastern bloc markets, with the concomitant effect that the high level of exports has led to a permanent surplus of capital export goods of between 3 and 4 billion marks annually.† The GDR is also called upon increasingly to participate in bilateral efforts to open up new raw material resources and to provide capital for such undertakings.

---

*In 1973 the value of traded goods amounted to DM 5.29 billion.

†My estimate, based on data from the Deutsches Institut fuer Wirtschaftsforschung, Berlin (West), 1973.

Because of its relatively highly developed industrial base and its severe labor shortage, where possible the GDR has attempted to transform bilateral economic agreements with individual partner countries into multilateral arrangements. While Eastern bloc propaganda currently claims to have increased labor mobility and to have created multilateral industrial complexes within COMECON, the reality is in fact quite different.[8] The pronounced specialization in individual COMECON states, and the backward state of their industrial equipment compared to that of the West, necessitated seeking for new resolutions in the late 1960s. The GDR, like most other Eastern bloc countries, however, lacked the foreign currency needed to gain access to the progressive technologies of the West by way of licensing arrangements. Thus, it has been forced to resort to the alternative solution of closer scientific and technological cooperation within the Eastern bloc.

On the whole, the unwieldy structure of COMECON, based largely on bilateral instead of multilateral agreements, acts as a restraint on the GDR. The widely divergent goals and levels of development of its partner countries, as well as the principles along which the COMECON is organized, promise little prospect of effective multilateralism in the near future.

THE FOREIGN POLICY FUNCTIONS OF DOMESTIC POLICY

Although by December 1973,100 states had established diplomatic relations with the GDR, its foreign policy has remained essentially a function of domestic policy. In other words, GDR foreign policy in the first instance is not oriented toward the solution of international problems, but rather the stabilization of political control. This aspect of policy probably arises from the fact that presently the stabilization and consolidation of the GDR, to some extent, applies only in the socioeconomic, but not in the political sense. This point must be emphasized, for it has recently become fashionable in certain Western circles to regard the GDR as an industrially developed and politically consolidated modern socialist state. The GDR's exemplary performance within the Eastern bloc's socioeconomic system should not deceive anyone concerning its unsure position on the international scene and its domestic instability. For despite increased importance in COMECON and accomplishments in foreign affairs, the East German domestic situation lacks stability, even though this condition has been to a certain degree offset by foreign activities. True, this applies to other political systems as well, but rarely to really advanced industrial states.

The extraordinary attention paid in the East German media to the foreign activities of the regime underlines the special function that foreign policy fulfills in domestic affairs.

The continued instability of the GDR's political system is discernible in several areas, but most prominently in the SED's security needs. This is demonstrated by the increase in ideological schooling and political controls instituted in the autumn of 1970. In addition, the GDR's attacks on social democracy, as well as its renewed efforts in Abgrenzung, after the conclusion in 1972 of the basic treaty (_Grundlagenvertrag_) with the FRG, support this view. Despite the real increase in East-West communication, certain sectors of the GDR population have been systematically denied contact with the West, ostensibly for security reasons.

A second demonstration of the party's need for security is the reluctance on the part of the SED to permit, or facilitate, the identification of the populace with the political system. This holds true especially for the new elites and the politically active segments of the population. Even they are able to identify themselves only in part with SED socialism. The SED apparently cannot yet afford to permit more political spontaneity, participation and pluralism; in other words, to practice more political tolerance. In this sense, the SED must also maintain not only the Berlin Wall but also the fortified border with West Germany as prominent symbols. It is almost as if it feels compelled to reinforce and solidify the two.

All that has been said about East German foreign policy and its effects on domestic policy applies equally well to the GDR's policy toward German or _Deutschlandpolitik_, which in the SED's view is part of foreign policy anyhow. If Soviet influence is disregarded for a moment, the SED's policy toward Germany is essentially a consequence of domestic, or security, requirements. At the same time, the existence of a second and competing German state, and the desire of the SED leadership to cooperate with this state, at least in part, have affected the regime's situation (for example, in social policies). Such influence of foreign policy considerations on domestic affairs is, however, limited by the security needs of the party, that is, by the instability of the political system.

Thus, the GDR's domestic, German, and foreign policies are interrelated insofar as domestic policy still takes absolute precedence over foreign (including German) policy—which, in turn, can be evaluated only in terms of its function in domestic policy.

THE GDR'S LACK OF LEGITIMACY

The question of the legitimacy of a political system is by no means purely academic at a time when foreign policy is becoming increasingly dependent on, or even being supplanted by, domestic processes, in which, in any case, there is a growing interaction between foreign and domestic affairs. This is especially true in the GDR. Whatever way one formulates the problem of legitimacy, the submission of the majority of the governed to those who govern is always decisive. In this respect, the GDR still suffers from a lack of legitimacy, especially in comparison to the FRG. The political system of the FRG is based on the procedurally controlled but free participation of its citizens in an election process, as well as on the freedoms of conviction, conscience, religion, speech, opinion, and assembly. None of this applies to the GDR to the same extent. Nor has the GDR made efforts to create alternative standards of legitimacy.

The GDR's lack of legitimacy has numerous causes. The essential cause still seems to lie in the occupation by Soviet troops at the end of World War II of the part of Germany that now constitutes the GDR. The animosity of Germans towards Soviet troops, due as much to experience as to Nazi propaganda, was transferred to the German Communists, for they had allied with and were dependent upon the Soviets. Furthermore, the uncertain future of the Soviet occupation zone, mass escapes to the West, and hopes that Germany would one day be reunited (which in the years before 1961 had never been completely extinguished) helped in East European minds to counteract the efforts of GDR political leaders to have their regime legitimized by the population. Nevertheless, since 1971 when Honecker took over, the SED regime seems to have gained increased support from the population. The question of legitimacy, however, remains to be solved.

The SED leadership is fully aware of this lack of legitimacy. The fact that the grounds given by the party and state for their claim to be legitimate have changed so considerably over the years since the foundation of the GDR cannot be explained otherwise. During the 1950s the claim was based on Marxist-Leninist orthodoxy. Later, especially since 1963 and the start of the new economic system, standards of economic performance and achievement have been placed in the forefront. The GDR's preoccupation with economic performance was even incorporated in its 1968 constitution, where Article 2, paragraph 3, states "The socialist principle 'everyone according to his or her ability, everyone according to his or her performance' is applied in reality."[9] In recent years, after the 7th (1967) and 8th (1971) Party Congresses, the SED's claim led it actually to concede, and no longer only promise, the people gradual improvements in their standards of living. The USSR and other Eastern bloc states served as a basis for comparison. In fact, the GDR now enjoys a standard of living about 30 percent higher than that in those states. It should not be overlooked that efforts of the party leadership to better satisfy the material needs and desires of the population gradually act as substitutes for formal legitimacy.

In connection with these criteria of economic success and performance, the SED has since 1969, when West Germany began its *Ostpolitik*, repeatedly claimed that it alone was creating a socialist German nation. In this respect, the ideological norms and postulates of the early years have reappeared, albeit in more refined and ambitious forms. In the GDR the claim is now that the historically valuable traditions of Germany have been joined with the forces of the German working class who represent the future. The FRG, on the other hand, is described as merely another NATO State that has excluded itself from the community of the German nation by the conclusion of the Paris Treaties in 1954, by the rule of the "monopoly of the bourgeoisie," by private ownership of the means of production, and by the class struggle. For this reason there are at present two nations in Germany, the progressive socialist nation of the GDR and the regressive capitalist nation of the FRG.

In addition, the SED constantly promulgates new varieties of GDR socialism in its continually revised ideological credo. For example, at present it proclaims the "developed socialist society," even though, if compared to the USSR, it is still only beginning the road toward such a developed socialism. Within the developed socialist society, as in earlier concepts of socialism, the ideology of participation plays the main role. The motto is "plan together, work together, rule together." De facto, such first attempts toward real participation are less likely to be found in the political than in the industrial sector, where the worker has opportunities to shape aspects of his life at his work place.

A large part of the population appears hardly to have been touched by this constant change in the party's ideological claim to legitimacy. At present, observers of the GDR scene must question whether or not the problem of legitimization is not simply becoming more and more an inner-party problem, with many outside the party forced to adjust to existing circumstances, and others resigning themselves in silence to the situation. Others meanwhile have clearly contented themselves with a partial identity of interest with the political system. An explicit popular acceptance of the regime under such circumstances is as difficult to assess as is the silent development of a national identity.

In any event, the problem of the lack of legitimacy has been revitalized by the opening of the GDR, by way of the basic treaty (*Grundlagenvertrag*), to millions of visitors from the FRG. In the Abgrenzung from, and conflict with, the Federal Republic, the GDR's search for a separate identity, indeed the necessity for it to arrive at a more deeply based self-confidence, has again for many become an open question. Comparisons are again being drawn between the GDR and the FRG, and social and political aspects of the GDR are being measured against the Federal Republic, particularly with regard to the FRG's success in establishing basic human rights and legal protections. These facts, derived from numerous reports from the GDR, are a cause for concern, particularly as East Berlin's representatives are allowed to enter the international arena. In this light the GDR's entry into the United Nations in the autumn of 1973 casts a special shadow, for there are states which regard the GDR as the continuation of the Nazi Reich, and do not hesitate to say so. For example, Israel's representatives have made it clear on several occasions that they will introduce a discussion of the domestic situation in the GDR in connection with its application for UN membership. In this sense the question of the lack of legitimacy of the GDR political leadership, not only for the SED but also for the population of the GDR, may quite possibly be reopened in a more acute form in the course of obtaining international recognition.

MODERNIZATION AND THE CAPACITY OF THE SYSTEM TO ADAPT

Since the building of the Berlin Wall in the middle of 1961, the situation in the German Democratic Republic has been characterized by a basic conflict. Society has displayed considerable social and economic dynamism, and tendencies towards innovation and modernization; at the same time, there is a lack of information and communication, and a system of bureaucratic control and decision making all stemming from the effects of ideological dogma and all typical of strongly authoritarian party systems.

Today the political system of the GDR suffers from this basic conflict, which, despite the strong political dynamism of the Socialist Unity Party, was not eliminated in the early stages of social development; thus, processes of modernization of several bureaucracies, mass organizations, and numerous other institutions that were set in motion by policies of the party leadership itself, are generally checked when they are spontaneously taken up and passed on by individuals. So far, spontaneous processes of social change and individual self-expression have always been hedged in and channeled by the SED leadership, and hence modernization has been delayed. The most remarkable example in this respect is the new economic system which particularly in the years 1963 and 1964 released long-restrained vital energies in the GDR. Already in the winter of 1964, Politburo member Kurt Hager felt obliged to warn the SED of the danger of losing its political control as a result of the economic orientations set out in the new economic system. With the elimination of this in 1970, many of these energies were lost. The effects of the adaptation of the working groups in society to possibilities for job promotion, recognition of outstanding job performance, and job qualification, however, continued. As social prestige became institutionalized in connection with certain occupations, the process of job qualification was given a vigorous impetus. As a result, life in the GDR became greatly permeated by the values of work and vocation. An expression of this phenomenon is the wide acceptance among vocational and professional groups of a performance-and career-oriented society. This can also be seen in the rising generation of cadres within the SED itself. The young party cadres are today much better trained than they were five years ago, and advancement within the party is now scarcely possible without a fully qualified, continually updated and specialized knowledge.

Even when we find some limited channels of communication which show signs of a social dynamic, the inflexibility of the political and social systems remains serious. The system's lack of capacity for adaptation is shown up particularly by the fact that it does not support a variety of relatively autonomous subsystems. Hence the transmission of information as well as the production and reception of infoı mation are restricted. The stimulating effect of the partial introduction and elaboration of new techniques in planning and organization has been largely nullified as a result of a recentralization and bureaucratization of control. The capacity and the tolerance levels of the political and ideological systems thus grow only slowly—too slowly, in fact, to accommodate the processes of economic and technological modernization, lęt alone provide them with any added impulse for development.

That modernization is limited by factors inherent in the system itself can also be seen in an examination of the area of research and development. Here, since 1969, the goal has been an accelerated application of scientific knowledge in industrial production. Accordingly, research in the natural sciences has been increasingly carried out in the service of industry. The inevitable result is that basic research has declined, since the total research capacity is itself limited. The increased emphasis on direct practical application has been implemented at the expense of maintaining a broader-based research program. The economic consequences are a strong orientation toward the markets of today and neglect of the markets of the future.

Even if science and research policy introduced under Ulbricht has, since 1971 and the coming to power of Honecker, lost most of its extreme features, it is impossible to suppose that the problems inherent in the system can be quickly overcome to permit adaptation to rapidly changing economic and technological development.

CONCLUSION

During the past decade the GDR has undoubtedly developed into the most important political and economic junior partner of the USSR. In addition, since it exemplifies a state of law and order, the GDR has contributed essentially to stabilizing the Soviet influence in Eastern Europe.

On its part, the USSR has rewarded its junior partner by facilitating its worldwide diplomatic recognition. This international recognition has, however, created problems for the GDR. In its drive toward expanding trade relations with the West, the GDR must proceed very cautiously. Each initiative must take into account the interests of the other East European partners. Moreover, the GDR must assess its economic limitations realistically.

Concerning foreign policy, the GDR now as before seems to depend completely on the Soviet Union. But this pattern may soon change unless the two countries effectively coordinate their economic interests with the West. At present there are signs of a parting of ways, indicating that the GDR may in the future wish to attain a more independent position vis-a-vis the USSR in political and economic affairs.

NOTES

1. Honecker's address to the 12th plenary session of the Central Committee of the SED on July 6th, 1974.

2. Walter Ulbricht, _Zum neuen oekonomischen System der Planung und Leitung_ (East Berlin: Dietz Verlag, 1966), p. 398.

3. _Statistisches Jahrbuch 1973 der Deutschen Demokratischen Republik_ (East Berlin: Staatsverlag der DDR, 1973), pp. 286f.

4. _Neues Detschland_, May 23, 1973, p. 6.

5. _Materialien zum Bericht zur Lage der Nation 1971_, published as _Bundestags-Drucksache_ no. 6/1690, ch. 1, §15.

6. Z. M. Fallenbuchl, "Comecon Integration," _Problems of Communism_ 22, no. 2, (March-April 1973), especially p. 37.

7. Latest figures in _Statistisches Jahrbuch 1974 der Deutschen Demokratischen Republik_ (East Berlin: Staatsverlag der DDR, 1974), p. 297.

8. Heinrich Swoboda, "Produktionsverhaeltnisse und oekonomisches Grundgesetz des Socializmus im Integrationsprozess," _Einheit_ (July 1973), p. 842.

9. _Verfassung der Deutschen Demokratischen Republik_, April 6, 1968.

CHAPTER

9

DETENTE AND CZECHOSLOVAKIA

George Klein

The invasion of Czechoslovakia in August of 1968 slowed the movement toward East-West detente. Nonetheless, the Soviet occupation of Czechoslovakia did not prove an obstacle to new vistas being opened by the Nixon administration and by Willy Brandt's Ostpolitik. While the United States and the Soviet governments were moved to adopt a detente course by global considerations which spanned such transcendental issues as disarmament, increased world trade, and the shared problem of finding a reasonable modus vivendi with the People's Republic of China, (PRC), the Czechoslovak leadership was absorbed in the more mundane task of domestic crisis management. By virtue of its very location the Czechoslovak Socialist Republic is a state interested in the outcomes of the United States-Soviet negotiations and summitry. The question pertaining to the quality of the detente has been of vital interest to all European governments. The extent to which the United States and the USSR might make concessions at the expense of their bloc partners has been subject to discussion within both the North Atlantic Treaty Organization and the Warsaw Treaty Organization.[1] To what extent the USSR would be able to carry its alliance partners in its detente decisions, and what cost it would be prepared to pay have been subjects of lively controversy. What became fairly apparent through both the United States-Soviet summits, and through the treaties signed with the German Federal Republic, was a clear indication that the USSR is not willing to risk its control of the bloc for either political or economic concessions which might jeopardize its control. Leonid Brezhnev, secretary-general of the Communist Party of the USSR, apparently indicated in Prague that the USSR was interested in following a policy of disengagement in Central Europe only if this were not to threaten the power of the communist governments in Eastern Europe.[2] The 1968 Czechoslovak effort at unilateral detente could not have been reassuring to the Soviet leadership, yet, confronted by an increasingly powerful People's Republic of China across thousands of miles of open frontier and faced with the necessity of increasing its armed forces to garrison this border, the prospect of detente had its appeals to the Soviet leaders.

There was a radical variance between East and West in their reciprocal images of detente. The Soviet leadership viewed detente as a means of removing obstacles to intergovernmental contacts. It hoped that the United States would extend the most favored nations clause to its trade agreements with the USSR, and that a formula could be reached by which U.S. and Soviet armed forces could be reduced in the European arena. The Western vision of detente was more ambitious: both Brandt's Ostpolitik and detente politics in the United States hoped to initiate much broader contact between the populations and institutions of both blocs. It was hoped that both individuals and publications would be able to move more freely across boundaries. It is precisely this function of detente which the Soviet and other East European governments found the most objectionable, scoring it as an effort to interfere in their internal affairs or as a vehicle for the subversion of their political systems by ideological means.* Apart from detente, the primary objective of Soviet foreign policy was to persuade the United States to withdraw a portion of its troops from Europe. This policy was expressed through a wide variety of initiatives launched both by the Soviet and East European governments. In October of 1957 the foregin minister of Poland, Adam Rapacki, proposed a plan which envisioned the creation of an "atom-free" zone in Central Europe.[3] The Rapacki Plan died because it was unacceptable to the NATO alliance, and to the United States in particular. The specific issues of the proposal have undergone many evolutions since that time. The most recent of these has been the Soviet proposal for a Conference on Security and Cooperation in Europe (CSCE), which was launched in Helsinki in November of 1973, and the talks on the Mutual and Balanced Force Reductions (MBFR) in Vienna in October of 1973. While the conferences have led to nothing but deadlock, there is little question that the issues raised will continue to be discussed.

---

*Brezhnev, in a speech delivered in Sofia, Bulgaria, warned the West not to try to barter for concessions pertaining to the internal problems of the USSR, New York Times, September 20, 1973, p. 1.

BASES OF CZECHOSLOVAK FOREIGN POLICY

Czechoslovak foreign policy since World War II has been inextricably linked with Soviet foreign policy. Czechoslovakia's role as the most loyal foreign policy partner of the USSR predated the communist ascent to power in February of 1948. Any opposition to the Soviet foreign policy line was underground, and never surfaced as it did on occasion within Poland, the German Democratic Republic or Rumania. It was not even manifest during the Prague Spring of 1968, when the April Action Program of the Communist Party of Czechoslovakia proposed increased trade and contact with the West and greater East European input into the deliberations of the Warsaw Treaty Organization. Even Alexander Dubcek, first secretary of the Communist Party of Czechoslovakia during the Prague Spring, did not swerve far from the Soviet foreign policy line. The theory was that by close adherence to Soviet foreign policy, the Dubcek leadership would gain room to maneuver for domestic reforms. The presupposition was a miscalculation, as the Soviet "entry" (the favored term in Czechoslovakia) and Rumanian independence in the conduct of foreign policy have demonstrated.

This unswerving loyalty which Czechoslovakia manifested toward the Soviet policy line is explicable only on the basis of its domestic situation and historical experience. President Edvard Benes initiated the present course in wartime London even before his government returned from exile. This constant of Czechoslovak foreign policy was borne out dramatically in 1947 when, under Soviet pressure, Czechoslovakia refused to participate in the Marshall Plan even before a communist government had gained power. The attitudes of Benes and Jan Masaryk, the foreign minister, were shaped by the Munich experience. The USSR had been excluded from the Munich negotiations and therefore the Soviets could claim, with some justice, that like the Czechs and Slovaks, they were the victims of the great power machines of the Western states. The Soviets maintained that the abandonment of the French commitment to Czechoslovakia in effect constituted an effort to shift Hitler's expansionist drive from West to East. Notwithstanding the claim of many historians that the USSR was in reality no more willing to honor its treaty obligations to Czechoslovakia than were the French and British, the impression was gained in Czechoslovakia that the Munich Agreement constituted a new alignment in Europe which the USSR was not bound to observe, having been excluded from all negotiations. Thus, the Czechoslovaks felt that the Soviets were, at the least, justifiably entitled to ensure their own security as much as possible. The Stalin-Ribbentrop Pact certainly did not evoke the shock and hostility in Czechoslovakia that it did elsewhere in the West. The Czechoslovak elites, by now profoundly cynical, viewed it merely as the logical consequence of the Western repudiation of the security system it had built in Central and Eastern Europe. It has been frequently maintained that the British and French were buying time at Munich in order to achieve a better state of military preparedness; if that were the case, then the USSR was equally entitled to buy time for itself.

Czechoslovak foreign policy was supported by the postwar internal evolution of the state as well. In 1946 the Czechoslovak Communist Party polled 38 percent of the votes in the last free elections. Even more important was the communist control over key segments of society and government. Benes had actually bartered away the few remaining elements of strength which would have militated toward the creation of a democracy. The Kosice Program of 1945 settled such issues as the nationalization of major industries in Czechoslovakia and the number of permissible parties even before the electorate could be consulted. The policy of nationalization, carried out with the approval of the preponderant majority of the population, so demoralized the remaining bourgeois forces within the state that they were incapable of rendering effective opposition to the tightening communist control. The February 1948 coup merely put the Communist Party into power officially. The Czechoslovak Communist Party did not have to contend with any important oppositional forces within the Czechoslovak society, for the church was not a potent force as in Poland, nor did the nationality problem circumscribe the centralizing power of the party as it did in Yugoslavia. Communist Party membership in Czechoslovakia was always large, and the party could follow its chosen path with little regard for dissenting minorities.[4] Opposition was scattered and ineffective.

Czechoslovak dependence on Soviet foreign policy makers was reinforced by the decision to expel the three million Sudeten Germans who historically had inhabited the territory of Czechoslovakia. While the Western allies did not actively encourage the Czechoslovak removal of the Germans, they did not oppose it. The most avid supporter of German expulsion was the Soviet leadership, well aware that the Czechoslovak action would result in a dependence on the USSR for the maintenance and preservation of the territorial integrity of the reconstituted Czechoslovak state. The Czechoslovak relationship with Germany is thus the keystone of Czechoslovak foreign policy.

German-speaking peoples surround the Czech lands, and the removal of the German population added a special dimension of tension to a long history of antagonism. Moreover, the German Federal Republic (GFR) was unwilling to denounce the Munich Treaty or accept the expulsion as permanent until Willy Brandt initiated the Ostpolitik. Until August of 1968, the German Democratic Republic (GDR) seemed a tame partner within the context of the Soviet bloc and therefore posed no threat from the point of view of the Czechoslovak government. On the other hand, the German Federal Republic, due to its location, size, population, and integration into the North Atlantic Treaty Organization (NATO) seemed a plausible threat to the status of Czechoslovakia, not only from the perspective of the leadership, but also in the eys of a substantial portion of the populace. Moreover, Ostpolitik was not greeted with enthusiasm by all Germans, as indicated by the Bundesrat's failure to ratify the treaty signed by Czechoslovakia and the German Federal Republic in 1973, which normalized relations between the two states.[5] This confirmed the fear of many Czechs and Slovaks that there are forces in the German Federal Republic which do not regard the boundary settlements arising from the World War II as final. In the minds of many Czechs and Slovaks there is the suspicion that, in the event of an armed confrontation between the Warsaw Treaty nations and the NATO nations, the Western allies would not be able to restrain their German alliance partners from taking advantage of an opportunity to revise the status of East Central Europe at the expense of the Czechoslovak state. While Czechs, Slovaks, and Poles may chafe within the Soviet bloc, the policy makers in both countries cannot envision any alternative to the USSR as the guarantor of their respective territorial status. Communists and non-Communists alike recognize this fact, which has produced a consistent policy line, transcending mere political rhetoric; even the most avid anti-Communists cannot advance an alternative solution for this complex problem. This is the major reason why the Polish and Czechoslovak governments have consistently dramatized the German threat and pointed to the threat of ever-present German revanchism as the basis of their foreign policy. There is an additional advantage in that it has been a foreign policy around which a measure of national consensus could be built. The participation of the German Democratic Republic in the invasion of Czechoslovakia in August of 1968 has had a disorienting effect on the question of which Germany represented the real threat. According to Peter Bender,

> The participation of the Volksarmee in the invasion of 21 August pushed hostility to the GDR to its peak. I will never forgive the Russians for having the Germans march in with them, were the words of one Communist. . . . The 'good' Germans had turned out by no means so good, and the 'bad' no longer seemed so bad. On the contrary, they most showed genuine sympathy for the fate of Czechoslovakia. Of course this development must not be allowed to conceal the fact that the Federal Republic will

> continue to be a source of anxiety in Prague, for both the present and future regimes.[6]

Nevertheless, the fear of Germany is still alive, and despite detente policies the German question remains very much at the center of all Czechoslovak considerations. It is still used by the leadership as a means of building consensus.

THE DIMENSIONS OF INTERNAL POLITICS

In the post-"entry" period the present Czechoslovak Communist Party leadership, presided over by Dr. Gustav Husak, has found itself in the position of carrying out the foreign policies of Dubcek's reform movement internationally while practicing prereform conservatism domestically. It has been stated that de Gaulle, by giving independence to Algeria, carried out a policy of the left through an essentially conservative regime. The same hyperbole could be applied to the current situation in Czechoslovakia. Many of the present leaders are survivors of the reform movement, including Prime Minister Lubomir Strougal and Husak; they are the leaders who demonstrated the greatest adaptability to the "new realities" dictated by the Soviet "entry". They mercilessly purged those who were not quite as flexible, trimming the Czechoslovak Communist Party membership rolls by close to 500,000.[7] The individuals who were expelled or crossed off the party rolls included some of the principal intellectuals, and in general, the best trained element within the Communist Party. These individuals constituted the most viable public opinion leadership within the country. By and large those who have remained in the Party do not possess the charisma or the intellectual stature of those excluded. The purge was undertaken at Soviet prodding, and the leadership is faced with the difficult task of "normalizing" the political situation with a party membership which is less capable of popularizing the present policies than those it has expelled from its ranks. Moreover, the underground influence of the personalities of 1968 is still strong, although they remain in internal exile. This gives the present leadership a sense of insecurity. Any internal liberalization might bring this vocal element back into office and lead to a repetition of the events of 1968. These are the reasons why the Czechoslovak leadership views detente politics as an internal threat. It involves the present leaders in the contradiction of presiding over the liberalization of Czechoslovak relationships with the German Federal Republic, the United States and other NATO members while following a restrictive course at home.

These are also the reasons why the responses to increased exchange between individuals and nongovernmental organizations of Czechoslovakia with their Western counterparts are greeted with such expressions of overt hostility. The signing of the treaty with West Germany was immediately followed by disclaimers from the Czechoslovak leadership that economic cooperation with the capitalist countries would not be pursued at the cost of "ideological erosion." Leaders such as Strougal warned against cultural exchange as an "instrument of alien penetration" and charged that this was precisely what the "right-wingers of 1968" sought at the expense of eroding the alliance with the socialist countries.[8]

The present Czechoslovak leadership obviously feels that it must preside over a state which is a reliable and trusted partner to the USSR and the Warsaw Treaty Organization before it can regain any room for maneuver both domestically and in the international arena. Any regime which removes "undesirable" publications from all public libraries can not logically support the free flow of mass media materials between East and West. This was one of the principal reasons for the deadlock of the CSCE conference.[9] In any case, the limits of the permissible in Czechoslovak foreign policy are set by the USSR, and if anything, the Czechoslovak government is more conservative in its position than the USSR.

ECONOMIC FACTORS

Many of the political crises which Czechoslovakia faced during the last decade were generated by an economy which did not satisfy the aspirations of much of the population. The autarkism practiced throughout the COMECON bloc did not seriously hamper the development of those states which were in the early stages of industrialization. The Czechoslovak economy, however, differed sharply from the other Eastern European states; for the Czechoslovak Communists inherited a mature industrial society, to which the universally applied lessons of Stalinist development were not particularly applicable. There is substantial agreement among Czechoslovak economists that the uncritical implementation of the Soviet model caused the negative growth rates of 1961-62. These in turn caused the Novotny leadership to turn to the intellectuals and academic economists for solutions. It was this alliance of intellectuals and innovative party functionaries which ultimately brought about the Prague Spring.

The projected economic policies of the Prague Spring essentially relied on the lessons which could be gleaned from Yugoslav experience. These were the establishment of market socialism, the abrogation of a detailed economic plan, and above all, a significant boost in per capita productivity. Czechoslovakia suffered from a chronic labor shortage, but because it was already industrialized it could not effect massive labor transfers from the agricultural to the industrial sector. This left a dramatic increase in individual productivity as the key to the satisfaction of pent-up consumer demands. It was clear to the reforming economists that much of the technology and processes which were necessary to achieve this result had to be obtained in the West. Yet, Czechoslovakia was bound by its own integration into the COMECON bloc, which had faced the Common Market with a measure of hostility on ideological and political grounds.[10] Much of Czechoslovakia's industrial capacity was tied to fulfilling long-term contracts with its bloc partners. Moreover, Czechoslovakia's trade dependence was remarkably low for a state which was more comparable to those of Western Europe than to the USSR in its internal economic structure. Czechoslovak trade dependence represented only 11.7 percent of Gross National Product (GNP) which is substantially lower than the share of imports in the advanced industrial states of Western Europe.[11] The Czechoslovak crisis of 1968 brought the Soviet leadership to the conclusion that Czechoslovak economic performance would have to be substantially improved if the present holders of power were to enjoy a measure of legitimacy and stability. The Soviets were obviously willing to encourage those exchanges with the West which would stimulate economic progress without undermining the ideological position of the present leadership. This policy was also very much in line with the overall political goals of detente. In this regard, the economics of Husak were remarkably similar to those proposed by the reformers, despite his disclaimers.

Czechoslovakia of course could not move in this direction beyond the boundaries dictated by COMECON policies or those acceptable to the Common Market. In order to facilitate increased trade, the Soviet leadership had to depart from the policy of attacking the European Economic Community as a foil for U.S. monopoly capitalism, and had to assume a posture of detente toward the EEC as a legitimate and autonomous agent. This was mandated by the very success of the EEC in stimulating West European cooperation, which went beyond what had been achieved within the framework of COMECON where the small nations rebelled with some frequency against the roles assigned to them in the socialist division of labor.[12] In January of 1973 the European Commission adopted a united commercial policy toward the COMECON bloc. Their communique stated,

> In order to promote detente in Europe, the Conference reaffirmed its determination to follow a common commercial policy towards the countries of Eastern Europe

> beginning January 1 of 1973; the member states declared their determination to promote a policy of cooperation founded on reciprocity. This policy is, at present, closely linked to the preparation and progress of the Conference on Security and Cooperation in Europe, to which the enlarged Community and its member states are called upon to make concerted and constructive contribution.[13]

It is obviously intended that the Conference on Cooperation and Security in Europe should establish institutionalized machinery for the facilitation of commerce between the two blocs. This in effect carries with it the implication that both sides recognize the legitimacy of the two dominant European organizations. What scope the individual East European states such as Czechoslovakia will have in such a framework remains unclarified.

The Husak leadership has maintained a measure of economic flexibility along with a political hard line in domestic affairs. Spurred by substantial Soviet credits and by a dramatic increase in international trade, both East and West, Czechoslovak economic performance has improved consistently over the past few years. The total share of Western trade in the Czechoslovak market has risen in the last few years. Trade with non-Communist countries rose by 26 percent in 1973, accounting for 32 percent of the total trade.[14] West Germany is now Czechoslovakia's fourth largest trade partner. Trade with the United States rose by 69 percent in 1973. These increases were achieved after some initial deterioration of trade with the West in the immediate aftermath of the 1968 Soviet invasion, during the years 1969-72.[15]

Czechoslovak per capita income increased dramatically within the last four years, even though Czechoslovakia slipped from its leading position to second place in the bloc in terms of per capita income. The regime has succeeded in providing the country with a fairly substantial growth in standard of living coupled with a far-reaching expansion in international trade, which makes Czechoslovakia more dependent on the prosperity of Western markets. This policy must be viewed as part of a deliberate effort by both the Soviet and Czechoslovak leaderships to maximize the gains which can be obtained from economic detente.

The problem for the Czechoslovak leadership will be to insulate the country from the inflationary trends of the West. The increasing Czechoslovak dependence on imported Middle East oil may have a destabilizing influence on the otherwise carefully maintained noninflationary price structure of the economy.* The Czechoslovak leadership may not be able to maintain the domestic hard line in the face of growing prosperity which will demand a rational use of human talents within the society. At present, the leadership has leaned toward exclusion of those who represent even a potential threat of the revival of the policies of 1968. The possible solutions to these problems depend more on the noneconomic content of detente policies.

DETENTE AND THE FEDERAL REPUBLIC OF GERMANY

Brandt's Ostpolitik was the forerunner of detente politics on a global scale as practiced by the Nixon administration. The Ostpolitik signaled that Germany had cast off from the moorings of American foreign policy. The moves toward a rapproachement with Eastern Europe reestablished Germany as a power capable of major initiatives in the international arena. This shift in policy was reinforced by a corresponding change in German public opinion which no longer viewed the USSR as West Germany's greatest enemy or the United States as its sole protector and friend.[16] These shifts, heralded by American detente moves in the field of disarmament, created a new atmosphere in which Germany, under Brandt's prodding, sought national solutions to the international tangle which bound her people and leadership to an unsatisfactory status quo. The question which animated German public opinion was reunification, or at least reaching a satisfactory modus vivendi with the German Democratic Republic. The Berlin question commanded immediate attention because of West Berlin's isolated situation. These major issues could find peaceful solutions only through an overall settlement with the USSR and the GDR. The relationship of Czechoslovakia's detente with the German Federal Republic has to be viewed through this particular prism.

The policy makers of both the German Federal Republic and Czechoslovakia had to bear in mind the larger picture. Czechoslovakia

---

*The Adria pipeline from the Adriatic port of Sisak will, when completed in 1977, supply Czechoslovakia with five million barrels of Mideast oil. [Quarterly Economic Review: Czechoslovakia and Hungary no. 1 (1974): 6].

obviously could not transcend the limits placed on detente by the USSR, which drew the line at any danger of ideological penetration. At the same time, the Czechoslovak agreements with the West Germans could not transcend the limitations of the priority which the Czechoslovak leadership had to place on its relationship with the GDR. Thus, Czechoslovakia obviously would have been loath to grant concessions on the special status of Berlin to the GFR, which went beyond what the GDR was willing to concede. The question of the right of West German representation regarding West Berlin interests constituted one of the real snags in the negotiations of a settlement with the GFR. This relationship was at least as close to the concerns of SPD policy makers as was the question of relations with Czechoslovakia. The price paid by West Germany for the normalization of relations was not as great as the CDU-CSU coalition (which enjoyed a majority in the Bundesrat) implied. At the root of the issue was the simple recognition of the changes that World War II had wrought in the heart of Central Europe. The expulsion of the Germans from the Sudetenland was an accomplished fact. The repudiation of the Munich agreements stirred some emotion in West Germany but did not require the GFR to make any substantive concessions. Once a West German leadership abandoned its aspirations for a German state restored to its prewar territorial boundaries, detente with Czechoslovakia and Eastern Europe could proceed. The immediate consequence was the reorientation of a measure of Czechoslovak foreign trade to West Germany. The present Czechoslovak leaders claimed that they followed a policy opposite to that of the Dubcek reformers. They charged that the Dubcek leadership placed its primary emphasis on the accelerating economic relationship with the West. While the present leadership places its primary interest on a health relationship with the East, Strougal has stated that only from such a platform will Czechoslovakia be able to expand its trade with the West.[17] The difference seems academic because the preponderant trade activity in Czechoslovakia was and is with the COMECON states. Despite this, the present government has dramatically increased its trade with the West in general, and with the GFR in particular. This policy was initiated by Dubcek and has been continued under Husak's direction. The post-1968 economists obviously agree with the prereform economists that the desire for increased Czechoslovak productivity requires closer ties with the West.

It is fairly apparent that the USSR is less willing to assume economic support in instances where Western trade proves more economical. It is generally acknowledged that the USSR has counseled moderation to Communists in their Western economic relations, from Cuba to Portugal and Italy. The USSR does not wish these leaderships to undergo any breaches with the West which would add to the burdens of the Soviet economy. These lessons are being finally applied to Eastern Europe, where the USSR now actively encourages expanded economic relations with the West, thereby increasing consumer satisfaction within the East European states as well as the need for trade with adequate economic rewards within the bloc. The Czechoslovak leaders capitalized on these Soviet trends to the fullest extent by taking advantage of the breathing space granted them by the Soviets.

On February 24, 1973, Brezhnev visited Czechoslovakia and declared that the country had returned to normalcy and the leading role of the Czechoslovak Communist Party had been consolidated.[18] He then urged the leadership to resume its diplomatic negotiations with the German Federal Republic. With this encouragement, the Czechoslovak foreign minister, Bohuslav Chnoupek, and Walter Scheel, foreign minister of the German Federal Republic, initialed a treaty on the resumption of diplomatic relations between the German Federal Republic and Czechoslovakia on June 21, 1973. The treaty was finally signed by Chancellor Willy Brandt and Prime Minister Lubomir Strougal on December 11, 1973, after two previous attempts had failed.[19] In the instrument both states declared that the Munich Agreement of 1938 was null and void with regard to their mutual relations. The Czechoslovak government initially demanded that the Munich Agreement be declared invalid retroactively and abandoned its insistence that the Munich Agreement be declared invalid from its inception only under Soviet pressure. The Soviet leaders felt that Czechoslovak insistence might weaken the Brandt government's position and place an obstacle in the path of the larger issues of detente, which the USSR was pursuing actively. Another stumbling block in the negotiations was the issue of Berlin. The Czechoslovak government wished to restrict German consular representation to the citizens of the German Federal Republic, excluding the business organizations and citizens resident in West Berlin. The issue was settled by a Soviet-sponsored compromise in which Czechoslovakia and West Germany agreed that West Berlin representation would be negotiated case by case.

On March 8, 1974, the Bundesrat, which is dominated by the CDU-CSU coalition, refused to ratify the treaty, in effect negating Brandt's efforts at compromise. The reasons for the rejection were precisely those which Czechoslovak propaganda had used so effectively in its effort to depict the German Federal Republic as a power which did not wish to repudiate the Munich Agreement because it still entertained designs for the revision of the realities created by World War II. The stated reasons were that the treaty did not clarify whether the Munich Agreement was null and void from the inception or only henceforth.[20] The Bundesrat also rejected the preamble, which stated that the Munich Agreement was forced on Czechoslovakia, without dealing with the question of German self-determination. The Bundesrat did not wish to legitimize the postwar expulsion of the Germans or the confiscation of their property. Its members further objected that there were no humanitarian provisions guaranteeing the exit of Germans still resident in Czechoslovakia. They objected strenuously to the lack of any guarantee that Czechoslovakia would accept the German Federal Republic's consular representation for West Berlin. The treaty was ratified by the Bundestage on June 20, 1974, overriding the Bundesrat, 232-190. This represented a victory for the SPD policy, but the CDU-CSU coalition which had effectively blocked it in the Bundesrat had made the point that there exists a large segment of responsible opinion in the German Federal Republic which is not willing to resign itself to the settlements arising from World War II. This plays directly into the hands of the Czechoslovak leadership by demonstrating their often repeated charge that there were still revanchism elements within Germany which were opposed to recognizing the German losses as final. Nevertheless, the treaty provides the backdrop for a new start in a relationship which is important for the future of Europe. It should be considered an important achievement, perhaps the most important achievement, for detente politics regarding Czechoslovakia.

THE UNITED STATES AND CZECHOSLOVAKIA

The United States effort to seek bilateral solutions to world problems with the USSR provided a rationale for Willy Brandt's Ostpolitik. The U.S.-Soviet SALT agreements had their primary impact on Europe in that they were based on an assumption of continuing stability in that area.

Willy Brandt's Ostpolitik released the United States from the rigid obligations inherited from the Adenauer-Dulles cold-war era. By the pursuit of bilateral solutions with the USSR both the United States and the German Federal Republic freed their respective foreign policy makers to seek new solutions. Issues which formerly had been nonnegotiable, such as the status of West Berlin, the recognition of the German Democratic Republic, or the Oder-Neisse line, were now open to direct negotiation between the two German states. This had the further effect of freeing the United States to seek solutions in Eastern Europe. The U.S. policy of accepting the present European division was highlighted by the acceptance of the Soviet invasion of Czechoslovakia in 1968. The token reaction of the United States tacitly acknowledged that Czechoslovakia was in the Soviet sphere of influence, in which the U.S. policy makers had no intention of interfering. It was understood at the time that the 1968 invasion would temporarily slow the process of detente, but would not halt it. Subsequent events have

have confirmed this. Neither the German Federal Republic nor the United States were willing to let this local issue becloud their long-range objectives, a part of which was the desire to insulate the European area from non-European conflicts in the Middle East and Southeast Asia. The net effect was to free the Soviet leaders for bolder actions requiring the use of force to maintain the integrity of the Warsaw Treaty Organization bloc. Insofar as the United States protest against the bloc invasion of Czechoslovakia was only token, the United States was in a good position to resume talks for the settlement of the outstanding issues between the two states.

The issues which posed problems for the U.S.-Czechoslovak relations can be categorized into three areas: the extension of diplomatic contacts, the negotiations of agreements which would promote increased trade, and programs accelerating cultural and scientific exchanges and people-to-people contact. The first issue was settled by the July 1973 consular convention establishing a United States Consulate in the Slovak capital of Bratislava and a Czechoslovak Consulate in Chicago. On both sides the normalization of economic relations was based on the desire to settle the economic issues arising from the presence of Czechoslovak assets in the U.S. banks and the Czechoslovak desire to repatriate them. On the other hand, the United States demanded settlement for the losses sustained by U.S. citizens from the nationalization of foreign properties in Czechoslovakia. Talks for the settlement of these issues were initiated in July of 1973 when U.S. Secretary of State William P. Rogers visited Czechoslovakia to sign the consular convention. After 25 delegation meetings of the two respective countries and numerous consultations of experts, a settlement agreement was signed on July 5, 1974. Rude Pravo of July 6 declared, "We have succeeded in overcoming the remainders of World War II and thus we have established the preconditions . . . the normalizations of mutual relations. . . .[21] The successful conclusion of these negotiations established the possibility for the extension of contacts covered under the third point, but this area is the least acceptable to the Czechoslovak government, because it carries with it the threat of ideological penetration, denounced by official spokesmen of the Warsaw Treaty Organization.[22] The initiation of programs which would lead to greater people-to-people contacts must await the outcome of the Conference on Security and Cooperation in Europe.

DETENTE AND THE VATICAN

Detente politics has also brought about the renewal of a dialogue with the Vatican. The Roman Catholic Church has been conducting its own version of detente politics in Eastern Europe since the 1960s. The Vatican has achieved a measure of normalization of relations with Poland and Hungary; in both of these societies the Church represents a powerful political force which has on occasion acted as an effective veto group. This is particularly true in Poland. The Church did not occupy a similar position in Czechoslovakia. The Czechoslovak Communist Party enjoyed such strength that it did not have to accomodate any competing bodies, including the Church. The Church's principal bases of support lay in the rural agricultural areas, which encompass only a minor proportion of the total population of Czech lands. In Slovakia the Church wielded much greater power and influence because of the lesser degree of industrialization in that part of the country, and also because Slovak Catholicism resembles the Polish mode. Since religious activity was one of the few tolerated means of registering protest, open manifestations of belief became tokens of resistance. The reform movement promoted policies which would have granted freedom of conscience to all segments of the population, and the Church would have been one of the principal beneficiaries. Thus, the suppression of the reform movement also affected the prospects of the Church in Czech lands.

Within the general framework of bloc detente politics, the successors to the reform movement also engaged in negotiations with the Vatican because many of the clerical posts in Czechoslovakia remained unfilled, due to the conflict between the Vatican and the state over the right to appoint.[23] By improving relations with the Vatican the present regime could come to domestic accommodation with a significant portion of the population without running any of the major political risks implied by the rehabilitation of the reformers who had a much broader national consensus behind them. Even this low-risk option faces difficulties due to the generally restrictive policies followed domestically. The state has consistently attempted to depoliticize the Church and has made efforts to restrict the Church's access to the socialization processes which are essential to its perpetuation. While secret negotiations were in progress with the Vatican, incidents tended to mar the delicate relationship. In 1973 secret negotiations with the Vatican led to the appointment of four new bishops, which still left several unfilled bishoprics in Czechoslovakia. Relations with the Vatican cooled the following year, when on April 7 Stefan Cardinal Trochta, Archbishop of Litomerice, died of a heart attack after a lengthy discussion with a state official. Western Catholic publications claimed that Trochta was so traumatized by the interview that it brought about the fatal attack. Czechoslovak authorities deny this. It was nevertheless symptomatic of the relationship that such an accusation could be made. In September of 1974, according to a Prague radio report, talks were resumed between Vatican negotiators and the Czechoslovak government.[24] It was hoped that these talks would lead to the appointment of more bishops as well as the safeguarding of seminaries and religious orders.

CONCLUSIONS

The effects of detente politics are eagerly awaited in Czechoslovakia by the populace and the government. There is a general realization that the prevailing political climate in the country will not be determined by its leadership, but rather in Moscow and by the international situation. The liberalizing forces hope that a change in the international climate will cause the leaders in Moscow to liberalize internally and that an internal liberalization in the USSR will be felt throughout the Soviet bloc. This represents one of the sources of hope for those who have been banished, at least temporarily, from Czechoslovak public life.

The source of hope for the liberals becomes the source of anxiety for the present wielders of power. Many of them contributed to the downfall of Novotny when he lost the support of the Soviet leadership. They cannot help but wonder about their fate should they become the source of embarrassment to the Soviet leadership's quest for detente and for a better relationship with the West European Communist Parties, which have not forgotten the final outcome of the Prague Spring. These leaders know that they do not enjoy the support of large segments of the Czechoslovak population, and that they face opposition within the party itself. They therefore depend on the Soviet continuance of a stiff line both in international and domestic matters for their legitimacy at home.

Czechoslovakia is a state which is vulnerable to any destabilization of the central European area and is governed by a domestic regime which rests on a brittle foundation. The initial Bundesrat rejection of the treaty normalizing relations between the German Federal Republic and Czechoslovakia demonstrated that the status of the Sudetenland and the Munich agreements still can become a live issue in German politics. Even the eventual ratification of the treaty will not alleviate Czechoslovak fears. The security of the Czechoslovak government will depend on the continuing stability of Europe and the support which the USSR will be prepared to render to this regime, both domestically and in its foreign policies. Only as its security increases will it be able to extend the fruits of detente to domestic and international policies, such as increasing contact with the West and providing a measure of liberalization at home. The normalization of relations with the United States and increased trade are low-risk policies for the present Czechoslovak leaders. Their effect is to stabilize the regime domestically and internationally.

True detente, as viewed from a Western perspective, does not depend solely on the volume of trade or intergovernmental contacts, but on the very quality of the domestic situation within the Soviet bloc. At present, a general tightening has affected Czechoslovakia, Hungary, and Rumania, and is placing increasing pressure on Yugoslavia. Under the circumstances detente can influence foreign policy at best; there is little evidence that the Soviet leadership is desirous of more. Obviously the Czechoslovak leadership will not be able to transcend the Soviet definitions of detente.

NOTES

1. For a discussion of the debate within the Warsaw Treaty Organization see Mojmir Povolny "The Soviet Union and the European Security Conference," Orbis 18, no. 1 (Spring 1974); and Charles Ransom, The European Community and Eastern Europe (Totowa, N.J.: Rowman & Littlefield, 1973), pp. 88-100.

2. Richard Davy, "The ESC and the Politics of Eastern Europe," The World Today (July 1972).

3. "Summary of the Debate, U.N. General Assembly," United Nations Review 4 (November 1957): 84-85.

4. Jaroslav Krejci, Social Change and Stratification in Postwar Czechoslovakia (New York: Columbia University Press, 1972), p. 145.

5. New York Times, part 4, March 10, 1974, p. 16.

6. Peter Bender, East Europe in Search of Security (London: Chatto and Windus, 1972), p. 87.

7. While no comprehensive membership statistics have been published in the aftermath of the expulsions, Rude Pravo stated that overall membership had declined by 473,731 (December 15, 1969). The estimates are that overall Party membership declined by 27.8 percent. Richard F. Staar, ed., Yearbook on International Communist Affairs, 1971 (Stanford, Calif.: Hoover Institution Press, 1971), p. 27.

8. Rude Pravo, December 14, 1973, pp. 1, 3-4.

9. For further discussion, see Radoslav Selucky, Czechoslovakia: The Plan That Failed (London: Thomas Nelson & Sons Ltd., 1970), pp. 27-47.

10. Gerhard Mally, "Regionalism in Western and Eastern Europe," World Affairs 137, no. 2, (Summer 1974): 48.

11. Michael Kaser, "Comecon's Commerce," Problems of Communism 22, no. 4 (July-August 1973): 3.

12. Mally, op. cit., p. 50.

13. Ibid., p. 48.

14. Quarterly Economic Review: Czechoslovakia and Hungary no. 2 (1974), p. 5.

15. Charles Gati, "East Central Europe: Touchstone for Detente," Journal of International Affairs 28, no. 2 (1974): 164.

16. Werner Kaltefleiter, "Europe and the Nixon Doctrine: A German Point of View," Orbis 17, no. 1, (1974): 92.

17. Rude Pravo, December 14, 1973, pp. 1, 3-4.

18. New York Times, October 27, 1974, p. 17.

19. New York Times, December 12, 1973, p. 1.

20. Kiessings Contemporary Archives (London: Kiessings, Longmand Group, Ltd., April 22, 1974), p. 2682.

21. Rude Pravo, July 6, 1974.

22. See Husak's interview for Reuter, Rude Pravo, December 12, 1973, pp. 1-2.

23. Quarterly Economic Review: Czechoslovakia and Hungary no. 4 (1974), p. 2.

24. Ibid.

CHAPTER

10

HUNGARY'S ROLE IN DETENTE

Richard C. Gripp

To determine what Hungary's role might be in the East-West detente, we must first ascertain just what functions the USSR has assigned Hungary to carry out with respect to detente and, secondly, we should try to determine what benefits and what risks might result from Hungary's participation. A number of questions can be posed. Is detente truly important to Hungary? Was Hungary ready for detente by the 1970s, or did the policy unfold before she could allow a more satisfactory relationship with the USSR to evolve? Will detente measurably affect either Hungary's internal or foreign policies? What will be the results of detente on the personal political fortune of Janos Kadar? How will detente affect Hungarian relations with the USSR, the Soviet bloc, the Federal Republic of Germany, other nations in Western Europe, the United States? Could there be detente for Hungary if the USSR were not involved? These questions appear appropriate to any treatment of the problems and prospects which detente may present for Hungary. To set the scene, however, the current Hungarian-Soviet relationship, which has been in effect for some time, should be stated briefly.

Internally, Soviet advisors continue to operate within Hungarian party, government, and economic institutions, and the ongoing policy consultations which are held between Hungarian and Soviet leaders reflect just a few of the various Soviet inputs into Hungarian national

---

The research assistance of Dr. Andrew Szabo is gratefully acknowledged.

life. With respect to foreign policy, Kadar noted succinctly in early 1974 that "we have always openly sided with the Soviet Union even in the most difficult times."[1] In September, 1974 a Hungarian delegation headed by Kadar, Premier Fock, Politburo members Nemet and Benke, and Foreign Minister Puga visited Moscow and Leningrad in a much publicized official six-day visit which ended with a joint communique of the two governments reaffirming peaceful coexistence, as expressed in the improved European situation, the significant normalization of Soviet-American relations, and the "developing constructive dialogue between socialist and capitalist countries. . . ."[2] During these meetings Kadar noted that on all basic questions of international life "we hold positions and views that are totally identical with those of our Soviet friends; therefore we act in the same way. . . . We take precisely the same attitude toward the European Conference on Questions of Security and Cooperation."[3] Finally, Hungarian Foreign Minister Frigyes Puja observed that because the foreign policy of the USSR "acts as a compass that guides us, efforts will therefore continue to be made to coordinate foreign policy activity with that of the Soviet Union."[4] The picture which emerges, then, is that of two nations, Hungary and the USSR, whose foreign policies, in all significant aspects, are closely aligned in a tandem relationship, supposedly for their mutual benefit. The picture also reveals that the USSR clearly is the dominant partner and that Hungarian officials fully accept Soviet leadership in all important areas of Hungarian foreign policy.

Hungarian desires for more independence from Soviet and Bloc alliances, despite official disclaimers to the contrary, first surfaced during the 1956 revolution. There were at the time aspirations for a third road between communism and capitalism, a road which would embrace political pluralism (including constitutional government) as well as neutralism in international affairs.[5] These desires may well remain today. In a 1974 statement, for example, which referred to European security in general, the Hungarian foreign minister seemed to dwell uncommonly long on one theme. He argued that the socialist countries want to respect the inviolability of frontiers, the sovereignty of countries, renunciation of the use of force, and noninterference with the internal affairs of others "in a clear and unambiguous wording."[6] One might suspect that Puja was registering an unofficial protest to the Brezhnev doctrine which rationalized the 1968 invasion of Czechoslovakia by fellow socialist nations, done in order to preserve socialism. Any possible increase in Hungarian independence from Soviet controls, however, might depend in part on some of the internal political and economic reforms that have been introduced recently within Hungary.

INTERNAL REFORMS

It took some time after the 1956 revolution, which was quashed by the Soviet Army, before Hungarian leadership felt confident enough to initiate internal reforms within political and economic spheres. Several of these reforms deserve examination.

In the latter half of the 1960s, a number of modifications geared toward liberalization of Hungarian legal and political practices were attempted. Censorship in the film industry and of literature generally was ended during this period, and limited private publishing of books was authorized in 1962. Restrictions on citizens' gifts into and out of Hungary and the carrying of currencies abroad were eased.[7] Just what does and what does not constitute a crime was reexamined, and punishment for certain crimes (such as attempted escape across the border) was lightened, and the use of torture to extract confessions was itself made a crime.[8]

The duties of Parliament were increased in 1966 and 1967 and its responsibilities were enhanced by authorizing more parliamentary controls over the executive budget, as well as in the area of general legislation. Permission was granted to provide for multiple candidates in some districts for elections to the National Assembly.[9] Other efforts supported by the nation's leaders since 1966 to provide for a more open society, politically, have included the easing up on party controls over governmental and societal organizations, the opening up of governmental and industrial institutions to more inquiries from citizens, and the granting of freer expression of public opinion on various aspects of national life, including the Communist Party.

Economic reforms were launched throughout Eastern Europe in the 1950s and they continued into the 1960s. One of the most heralded of these was Hungary's New Economic Mechanism (NEM), which took effect at the beginning of 1968. Even prior to this date, however, Hungarian leaders had resisted those coordinated planning efforts of the Council for Mutual Economic Assistance (CMEA) which they believed to be economically detrimental to their nation, while simultaneously calling for improvements in the overall CMEA system, chiefly those which would accommodate decentralized intraenterprise contacts between member nations. Among Hungarian criticisms of CMEA were: the retention of fixed long-term prices which frequently were unrealistic when compared with world market prices; restrictions on the smooth flow of goods which would result if greater emphasis were placed on the concept of supply and demand; and the lack of adequate national incentives for product specialization which was being called for in the Bloc-wide division of labor among CMEA members.[10]

NEM was designed, in part, to stimulate output by grafting on to the command economy some of the attributes (and hopefully thereby some of the advantages) of a Western-type market economy, such as the institution of free prices. Specifically, management and planning details were to be decentralized to the production enterprises, rationing was to be abolished, profits were to be maximized, and the market was to replace administrators in the determination of prices.[11] Of course, for the Hungarian leadership the justification for planning continues, since without government planning no purposeful development can be achieved. But without market relations, national allocation cannot be realized efficiently. The objective, then, is a "controlled market economy."[12] What was anticipated by the party leadership was that an improvement in the nation's foreign trade would be one of the early results of the NEM.

The desired results of these reforms, both political and economic, are questionable in part because of the long institutionalization of communist ideology which, while giving voice to what are perhaps genuine desires for some reform, inevitably confines many of the proposals to simple form rather than deep substance. To this can be added the natural conservatism of entrenched bureaucrats and leaders. Consequently, the political reforms that have taken place have been modest ones, in the main involving a strengthened position enjoyed by labor leaders, more power for local governmental councils, a slight increase in the responsibilities of the National Assembly, and some legal advances. All of these reforms, incidentally, have in some measure their Soviet counterparts, so that prior Soviet approval for the Hungarian versions might have been fairly easy to gain. Moreover, with respect to the USSR, Hungarian leaders have been quite careful to reassure everyone that the reforms do not signal any break with the past, nor disagreement with Soviet insistence on a communist party-dominated political system.

After three years of the NEM, Granick concluded in 1971 that, at best, it had had little of either a positive or negative demonstrable effect on the economy.[13] The dilemma of real versus ersatz reform may come down to the question, as Gati phrases it, of whether to shelve the NEM entirely or merely to slow its momentum. Criticism of the NEM within Hungary focused on its resultant inequality in wages, specifically the lower wages for workers in proportion to higher wages for some other occupations. Accordingly, the NEM did not promote proleterian equality and it therefore contributed to a rise in the strength of workers' opposition. One analyst argues that the central fact of the NEM is that it produced a redistribution of income away from factory workers in favor of the small peasantry and of workers in small-scale cooperatives.[14] At a March 1974 plenum of the Party's Central Committee, two Politburo members (who had been economic reformers) were removed from their positions as Central Committee Secretaries.[15] Interestingly, political pressure from workers seems to have forced their removal (somewhat reminiscent of Polish leader Gomulka's fall from power following the riots of Polish shipyard workers in December, 1970).

The progress of economic and political reforms, or the lack thereof, relates to detente in an indirect, but nevertheless positive way. While one supports the other, the absence (or even weakening) of one would not necessarily cancel out the other. Thus, without internal economic and political reforms, detente probably would be limited to shaping only a few features of foreign trade and of foreign policy for Hungary. Without detente, internal Hungarian reforms might well suffer from considerably more resistance both from conservatives within the Hungarian ruling elite as well as from Soviet advisors to that nation.

FOREIGN TRADE AND FOREIGN POLICY

Apart from obvious Soviet domination over major Hungarian foreign and domestic policies, what correlations might there be between current foreign policies of the USSR and the long-range interests of Hungary? In addition to mollifying Soviet leaders because of Hungary's subordinate position, are there not, on the other hand, certain common organizational issues and geographical areas with which Hungary could be expected to retain as much of an innate, even narrow interest, as does the USSR itself? In attempting to answer the question we might give the important international organizations and geographical areas which concern Soviet policy makers and then try to determine which of these are of considerable importance in and of themselves to Hungary as well.

International organizations of common Soviet and Hungarian interests are the CMEA, the Common Market, NATO, European Security (including the Mutual and Balanced Force Reduction Talks—MBFR). and the United Nations.

Geographical areas of common interests are Eastern Europe, Western Europe, and the United States.

An international organization of Soviet concern, but of only slight Hungarian interest is the Warsaw Pact.

Geographical areas which are of Soviet concern, but are of only slight Hungarian interest are Asia, Africa, the Middle East, and Latin America. (Hungarian interest in Middle Eastern oil has increased dramatically within the past year.)

If the foregoing organizations and areas at all accurately represent significant versus moderate concerns of Hungarian foreign policy, then her identification with a number of Soviet policies might well be interpreted as being in the interests of Hungary at least as much as being merely supportive of the USSR. Accordingly, vigorous and enthusiastic pursuit by Hungary of certain common Soviet-Hungarian policies (for example, aid for North Vietnam, or criticism of Mao's leadership of China) are simply to support Soviet policies. In these cases, presumably, Hungarians are not greatly concerned with the particular issues; their relative indifference means that Hungarian support is provided at little if any political cost to Hungary. In one other very limited area we might conclude that Hungary's backing of Soviet international actions is detrimental to Hungarian national interests both in the short and the long run. This is best seen in the case of the invasion of Czechoslovakia in 1968. This Hungarian endorsement of and complicity with Soviet actions must have involved considerable political cost to the Hungarian leaders' images domestically.

One might conclude, consequently, that there are some Hungarian foreign policies which fall within the sphere of Hungarian national interest even though these policies are similar if not identical to counterpart Soviet policies. A number of these policies focus on detente. Thus, the first two questions raised at the beginning of our discussion can be answered affirmatively, that is, that detente is important for Hungary and that she probably was more than ready for such a development in the 1970s.

On positve effect of the NEM anticipated by Hungarian leaders was a measurable improvement in the foreign trade balance as well as in its commodity assortment, including especially an increase in trade with Western nations. In a statement reminiscent of the long-range goals of CMEA, the father of the NEM, Rezso Nyers, noted that progress was being made toward a future "when the socialist and the capitalist world market will not only be in closer contact, but developing market relations will create a kind of division of labour as well."[16] There are some anticipated internal changes regarding CMEA also, in that competition among the member nations will increase. Demands of CMEA members for raw materials cannot be satisfied by the USSR alone, so that the members must look to new sources among the capitalist nations in the future. Thus, in the realm of cooperation among socialist nations, the demands of the market should assume more importance.[17] In one respect the CMEA might assist its members in attaining a more advantageous position in the world market. It can be argued that the combined economic and political strength of the socialist community makes it possible for a small nation such as Hungary to enjoy more of an equal trading status with nations in the capitalist world.[18]

It is expected that Hungarian industry can modernize by acquiring scientific and technological knowledge in both new products and managerial techniques from Western nations. However, the achievement of this particular goal requires Hungary to export commodities which will be more competitive in the West than they were previously, and that will mean the export of greater amounts of finished industrial goods as compared with raw materials and agricultural products. New sources of outside investment capital are needed and Hungarian exports to noncommunist nations must not suffer from trade restrictions imposed by those nations.[19] Other efforts that Hungary has expended toward reaching her foreign trade goals have included joining the Council of the General Agreement on Trade and Tariffs (GATT), agreeing to place trade on a convertible basis with Austria and Yugoslavia, opening a bank in Vienna, entering the Eurodollar market, forming partnerships with foreign firms to produce commodities in Hungary, such as the one with the American Tyler Corporation to produce refrigerators, entering into deals with the EEC in 1971 and 1972 for the sale of pork, wine, and dairy products, and arranging with 25 Western banks, mostly American, for a loan of $100 million.[20] During the four-year period from January 1964, to January 1968 (the start of the NEM), Hungary signed 27 cooperative agreements in industry and agriculture with Western nations. In the two and one-half year period from January 1968 to July 1970, there were 89 such agreements signed with Western nations, including some 150 economic agreements on cooperation between Hungary and the Federal Republic of Germany.[21] A new 10-year agreement for economic, industrial, and technical cooperation between Hungary and the Benelux countries was concluded early in 1975. Under the agreement the two sides will give most favored treatment to each other in the appropriate fields of cooperation, especially with respect to engineering, metallurgy, the chemical industry, pharmaceuticals, agriculture, agricultural machinery, and in the service industries.[22] By the 1970s, then, even prior to the launching of detente, Hungary had initiated a broad increase in contacts on a number of fronts with nations which were in a position to help her achieve some of her economic goals. But will this flurry of activity result in measurable improvements for Hungary?

The importance of foreign trade for Hungary's economy (40 percent of her national income) cannot be overestimated. Among the communist nations, Hungary ranks third in the per capita volume of foreign trade.[23] The majority of her foreign trade is with other communist nations; 70 percent of the total is with CMEA members. Her desire to increase trade with the West, in particular to export more finished industrial goods to these nations, has not yet been realized. As shown in Table 10.1, Hungarian imports and exports with both communist and noncommunist nations in 1972 compared with 1960, as percentages of total foreign trade, have not changed dramatically.[24]

TABLE 10.1

Hungarian Foreign Trade in 1960 and 1972
(in percentage)

	Communist States	Noncommunist States
Imports from		
1960	70.4	29.6
1972	65.8	34.2
Exports to		
1960	71.3	28.7
1972	69.8	30.2

Source: Statistical Pocketbook of Hungary, 1973.

Moreover, despite the offical desire to increase the export of finished industrial goods, this goal has not been achieved in Hungary's trade, even though she continues to be the Soviet Bloc's most trade-dependent member. The export of machinery, transportation equipment, and other capital goods to fellow communist states declined in the 1960-1972 period by almost 9 percent, and it also was unchanged with respect to the noncommunist states. There was, to be sure, a slight increase in this same period of exports to communist states in consumer goods of a little more than 6 percent. In addition, for the planned exports to the People's Republic of China during 1973, machine tools, trucks and vehicle components, medical equipment, and aluminum cables were to be included. In return, Hungary was to have imported from China nonferrous metals, chemicals, agricultural products, and certain consumer goods.[25]

Hungarian exports to the USSR emphasize finished industrial goods (68 percent of the total), while 66 percent of Hungarian imports from the USSR constitute raw materials and semi-finished goods.[26] Ninety percent of Hungarian iron ore is imported from the USSR, while some other imports from that nation, such as oil and natural gas, lumber, potassium fertilizer, sulphuric acid, and heavy-duty tractors are purchsed by Hungary at less than the world market price.[27] Consequently, the USSR has tied parts of the Hungarian economy to the bloc as a whole and to the USSR specifically. This is particularly the case in energy sources, illustrated by the construction of an ethylene pipeline which joints the Tisza Combine in Hungary with the Kalnish Chemical and Metallurgical Combine in the Ukraine.[28] In 1974

Hungary planned to import from the USSR 4.2 billion kilowatt hours of electricity and 5.7 million tons of crude oil.[29]

In 1974, Hungary's foreign trade balance deteriorated because her imports from the communist nations increased by 20 percent over 1973, but her exports to these nations for the same period increased only six or seven percent. Her trade with the capitalist nations in 1974 also saw imports increased 21 percent, but exports rose only 6 percent.[30] As of the present, Hungarian foreign trade has not at all matched her stated policy goal of marked increased with the West.

As might be expected, Hungarian officials enunciate the now-traditional anticapitalist and antiimperialist caveats, and they swear fealty to the main pillars of Soviet policy. Following these customary preliminaries, the spokesmen then proceed to set forth their own objectives. In a 1972 statement, the foreign minister announced the goal of increasing Hungarian ties with Western Europe, especially with the Federal republic of Germany, as well as with the American continent. In 1974, reference was made to the European communist movement remaining loyal to the principles of internationalism, but it was noted that the movement was truly European in spirit.[31] Politburo member Kallai pointed to the many diverse forces within European society (he enumerated workers, peasants, intellectuals, communists, socialists, Social and Christian Democrats, members of secular and ecclesiastical organizations), all working to create a Europe where security and cooperation are the rule.[32] In the Helsinki Conference on Security and Cooperation in Europe, then Foreign Minister Peter noted that Hungary had established fruitful relations with Austria, France, Italy, Canada,and the United States as well as extensive cultural and economic relations with the German Federal Republic. What Hungary wants, he continued, is European cooperation for protection of the environment, a widening division of labor under the CMEA while sumultaneously increasing cooperation with other nations, expansion of European cultural relations, and the establishment of a permanent body for the protection of European security.[33] The current foreign minister has added that the main objective of Hungarian foreign policy is to ensure favorable international conditions necessary for the protection of socialist achievements and the building of a socialist society.[34] Regarding the German Federal Republic, again, a Central Committee Secretary, the late Zoltan Komocsin, stated that while friendly relations between the Hungarian Socialist Workers Party and the German Communist Party would continue, in the future it would be necessary for the Hungarian Party to carry on a dialogue on common problems with the German Social Democratic Party as well.[35] Finally, we might note a recent reference to three main pillars of Hungarian foreign policy vis-a-vis the other communist nations which included 1) proletarian internationalism, 2) socialist internationalism, and 3) peaceful cooperation between nations of different socialist systems. Significantly, none of the three, according to the source of the reference, can be allowed to outweigh any of the others.[36]

HUNGARY AND DETENTE

Just prior to the inauguration of detente a deputy minister of foreign affairs argued that the greatest obstacle to improving the situation in Europe continued to be American strategy, which was based on force.[37] This Soviet-inspired line of criticism was dropped soon thereafter, however, as Hungarian leaders moved toward full acceptance of the idea of detente. By mid-1972 Hungarian and American officials (including the United States' secretary of state) exchanged visits which later were followed by new American-Hungarian agreements (for example, contracts for hotel and soft drink franchises in Hungary). In a 1974 statement, detente was portrayed as becoming the main characteristic feature of our time, although occasional lapses in its progress were to be anticipated. Once achieved, the new era of cooperation could be expected to embody much greater investments for mankind than simply that of armaments.[38]

There are, consequently, substantial reasons for active and enthusiastic Hungarian support for both the spirit and the objectives of detente, reasons which focus on both short- and long-range goals on the part of that nation's political leadership. Detente should make it easier for Hungary to carry out certain internal political and economic reforms without greatly risking a Czechoslovak-like Soviet reaction. These reforms would seem to be called for if the nation's leaders realistically expect further modernization of the economy. The idea of detente can contribute persuasive arguments to support the position that Hungarian national reforms are complementary parts which fit in with the broader, overall and more inclusive objectives of international cooperation. That the internal economic reforms have been so slow to unfold should further allay Soviet apprehensions of drastic changes occurring in Hungary.

Successful detente negotiations which include Hungary might then permit her to deal with other East European communist nations from a position of greater stability and hence more independence. Here Hungary might well differ from some of the other nations. Some East European leaders are opposed to detente, fearing a loss to their current political power if the general climate of East-West relations were to measurably improve and hence undergo a dramatic change; the Czechoslovak leaders seem to typify this attitude. Husak apparently sees detente as threatening him personally.[39] On the other hand, Kadar has established a close working relationship with Brezhnev, so much so that Kadar probably has no personal fear of detente, so long as that process is still favored by the Soviet leaders and so long as the process makes sense for Hungary's economy.

In supporting detente, Hungary obviously is giving support to current Soviet foreign policy. This is justification enough in the view of the Hungarian leaders, of course. In addition to affirming the Soviet position in international affairs, however, national security for Hungary also emerges as a logical reason to support detente. This will particularly be so if Hungary and other East European nations are able to work out a satisfactory accommodation with the Federal Republic of Germany. In the long run such an achievement should result in two definite benefits for Hungary.

First, Hungarian leaders no longer need fear the possibility of a rearmed and neofascist Germany. This remnant fear of the cold war appears to be subsiding throughout Europe. One of the fortunate results of unfortunate international difficulties, such as the recent oil embargos, rising inflation, and general economic recession in many nations, is a growing belief that some minimal economic and even political international cooperation is necessary. Consequently, West Germans should be as interested in pursuing detente Eastward as the Hungarians have been in pursuing it Westward. Second, the mutual economic advantages to the two countries in improved interstate relations should contribute to a lessening of fears in Eastern Europe regarding a belligerent Germany, an aggressive North Atlantic Treaty Organization, a resumption of the cold war and a possible military attack from Western nations.

Another favorable consequence of improved cooperation with Western nations, particularly if this is accompanied by the expected technological and trade agreements, might be found in the further modification of the CMEA alliance. If the restrictive features of the CMEA can be eased, Hungary may well be able to negotiate a considerably broader network of Western contacts. To date, these restrictions include the requirement that Hungary sell some exportable materials to other CMEA members, and particularly to the USSR, at less than the world market price for these commodities; Hungary's failure to receive CMEA and Soviet endorsement in planning, financing, and developing some portions of the industrial sector; and the tying of the Hungarian economy too closely to that of the USSR. But even if these difficulties can be overcome or mitigated, the resultant situation may not be greatly improved.

Hungary's current rate of inflation reflects both her dependence upon imports of fuel resources as well as the fact that communist states are by no means immune from world market developments.[40]

Worldwide inflation hits hard because of Hungary's need to import most of her raw materials and energy resources, which are rising rapidly in cost, while her exportable finished commodities have not enjoyed a concomitantly rapid rise in price. The dilemma of long-run versus short-run gains now presents itself. As Hungary seeks additional Western markets for her finished industrial goods, she is thereby required to improve their quality in order to make them more competitive with higher quality Western goods. But, what of her present convenient arrangement of selling industrial goods of lower quality to the USSR and to other CMEA partners? While expanded trade with the West remains a desirable goal, Hungary may be forced to relinquish a short-run comparative advantage. In any event, a profile of Hungary's international posture for at least the latter 1970s, in light of the foregoing analysis, might now be suggested.

In the first place, the profile should reveal a nation still firmly within the Soviet-dominated East European Bloc of communist states. As such, Hungary can be expected to continue supporting the main features of Soviet foreign policy, for example, opposition to NATO and to Israel. The profile also suggests that the Hungarian economy will become measurably strengthened following the present as well as the anticipated general economic and trade agreements with developed capitalist nations. Although fervent Marxists may see in Western economic recessions the fulfillment of Marxian predictions of the decay and eventual collapse of capitalism, Hungarian Marxists probably cannot rejoice over the possibility of endangered trade agreements and technical assistance which they have long sought and now finally anticipate receiving from Western nations. Hungary should, in the next half-decade achieve somewhat greater independence from Soviet controls, although such independence can be expected to be only slight at first and only piecemeal thereafter. Here again, detente might provide the more relaxed international atmosphere, particularly with respect to the USSR, which might enable the latter to conclude that a relaxation of tight controls over Hungary is in order. Accompanying this development, if it does occur, should be greater Hungarian demands for increased independence from the CMEA restrictions so that easier trading with the West can result.

The foregoing assumptions concerning Hungary's international position for the late 1970s appear to rest, however, on at least two underlying assumptions. The first is that detente, despite some possible temporary setbacks, will continue to expand and become more widely and permanently accepted, especially on the part of its two main actors, the United States and the USSR. Secondly, the USSR will discover enough of value in detente to compensate for a Hungary less subject to Soviet controls. Thus, the positive material benefits of detente for the Russians might equal or surpass the uncomfortable psychological adjustment necessary in accepting the fact of a more autonomous Hungary. And yet, all or even most of these developments are not predestined.

With all of the talk of detente from both the American and Soviet sides, Soviet leaders retain a deep distrust of Western nations. Conceivably, the mentality of Soviet leaders might not permit them to think seriously along such lines of political reforms, greater independence for and eased controls over the East European nations as well as a more freely operating give-and-take in foreign policy vis-a-vis the West. If that is the case, then Hungarian achievements will be indeed minimal, chiefly because the Soviet leaders may be incapable of viewing detente in the way that the leaders of Western nations optimistically have viewed it.

NOTES

1. Quoted in Charles Gati, "The Kadar Mystique," *Problems of Communism* 33 (May-June 1974): 15.

2. *Pravda*, October 1, 1974, p. 2.

3. Ibid., September 26, 1974, p. 2.

4. Frigyes Puja, "Foreign Policy at a Time of International Detente," *The New Hungarian Quarterly* 15, no. 55 (1974): 32.

5. See Bennett Kovrig, "Decompression in Hungary—Phase Two," in Peter A. Toma, ed., *The Changing Face of Communism in Eastern Europe* (Tucson: University of Arizona Press, 1970), p. 195.

6. Puja, op. cit., p. 24.

7. See the discussion in William F. Robinson, *The Pattern of Reform in Hungary, a Political, Economic and Cultural Analysis* (New York: Praeger, 1973), pp. 93, 291-303.

8. *The New Hungarian Quarterly* 13, no. 48 (1972): 19-21. See also William Shawcross, *Crime and Compromise, Janos Kadar and the Politics of Hungary Since Revolution* (New York: E. P. Dutton, 1974), p. 118.

9. *The New Hungarian Quarterly* 13, no. 48 (1972): 18; Robinson, op. cit., p. 216.

10. See Istvan Friss, *Reform of the Economic Mechanism in Hungary* (Budapest: Akademiai Kiado, 1971), pp. 227ff.

11. See, for example, Bela Csikos-Nagy, *Pricing in Hungary* (London: Institute of Economic Affairs, Occasional Papers, 1968), p. 12.

12. Ibid., p. 7.

13. David Granick, The Hungarian Economic Reform (Bloomington: International Development Research Center, Indiana University, Working Paper No. 11, February 1972), p. 18.

14. The Guardian, June 1, 1974.

15. Gati, op. cit., pp. 33-34.

16. Rezso Nyers, "The Hungarian Economy in the Seventies," The New Hungarian Quarterly 15, no. 53 (1974): 12. Forty percent of Hungarian national income results from foreign trade. See Budapest, in English, in Foreign Broadcast Information Service, March 9, 1973, p. f2. Kaser states that 1971 trade may have been as high as 20 percent of the Hungarian GNP (4.7 percent of this reflecting trade with the West). Michael Kaser, "Comecon's Commerce," Problems of Communism 22 (July-August 1973): 4. Nyers was removed from the Politburo in March, 1974.

17. Janos Mandel Miklos-Muller, "Az exportorientalt gazdasagpolitika celjai," Kulgazdasag (June 1974): 417.

18. Nepszabadsag, February 18, 1975, p. 3, in Foreign Broadcast Information Service, February 21, 1975, p. f3.

19. Robinson, op. cit., p. 130.

20. Christian Science Monitor January 11, 1973; and Michael Kaser, "The EEC and Eastern Europe: Prospects for Trade and Finance," International Affairs 50 no. 3 (1974): 406. Nepszabadsag, June 29, 1974, p. 8, in ABSEES 5, no. 4 (1974): 200.

21. Robinson, op. cit., p. 130. Nepszabadsag, March 16,1975, p. 5, in ABSEES 5, no. 3 (1974): 195.

22. Budapest, Domestic Service in Hungarian, Foreign Broadcast Information Service, February 21, 1975, p. f9.

23. Mezhdunarodnaya Zhizn', no. 4, 1972, p. 151.

24. Statistical Pocketbook of Hungary, 1973 (Budapest: Statistical Publishing House, 1973), p. 202.

25. Budapest, Domestic Service in Hungarian, March 7, 1973, Foreign Broadcast Information Service, March 8, 1973, p. f4. Trade with China rose sharply in 1971.

26. Statistical Pocketbook of Hungary, 1973, op. cit., pp. 203-07; Tarsadalmi Szemle, May 1973, in ABSEES 4, no. 2 (1973): 194.

27. Nepszabadsag, February 23, 1975, p. 10, in Foreign Broadcast Information Service, February 26, 1975, p. f4.

28. Pravda, October 27, 1974, p. 3.

29. Budapest, Domestic Service in Hungarian, December 18, 1973, Foreign Broadcast Information Service, December 21, 1973, p. f1.

30. Nepszabadsag, February 8, 1974, in ABSEES 5, no. 3 (1974): 194; Budapest, Domestic Service in Hungarian, February 21, 1975.

31. Janos Berecz, "European Security and the Role of Public Opinion," The New Hungarian Quarterly 15, no. 53 (1974): 17. In 1971 the Prime Minister noted that the situation appeared to be ripe for a discussion on the main problems of European-wide economic cooperation with the participation of all European countries. The New Hungarian Quarterly 12 no. 43 (1971): 20-21.

32. Gyula Kallai, "The Responsibility of Europe," ibid. 13, no. 46 (1972): 6.

33. "Towards the Consolidation of Detente," ibid. 14, no. 52 (1973): 8-10. Particularly cordial relations are maintained by Hungary with two advanced capitalist nations—Austria and Finland. Ibid., 15, no. 54 (1974): 19.

34. Frigyes Puja, "Foreign Policy at a Time of International Detente," ibid. 15, no. 55 (1974): 30.

35. Zoltan Komocsin, "European Security and World Peace," ibid. 15, no. 54 (1974): 6. Diplomatic relations between Hungary and the Federal Republic of Germany were established in December, 1973.

36. Tamas Palos, "A diplomacia es az ideoloqiai harc," Kul-politika, February 1974, p. 17.

37. Frigyes Puja, "The Political Situation in Europe Today," The New Hungarian Quarterly 12, no. 42 (1971): 35.

38. Ibid. 15, no. 53 (1974), 3: and 15, no. 54 (1974): 3.

39. New York Times, October 1, 1974.

40. This dependency is reflected in domestic price increases for energy resources which went into effect in Hungary on September 1, 1974. These increases, however, reflect only part of the increase in cost to be borne by the government. See Magyar Nemzet, July 14, 1974.

NAME INDEX

Acheson, Dean, 8
Adenauer, Konrad, 193; government, 152
Alperovitz, Gar, 27-33, 35-42, 43-45, 49-50
Amalrik, Andrei, 110
Ambrose, Stephen, 47
Arbatov, Georgy, 106-08, 113, 116
Ascherson, Neil, 154
Aspaturian, Vernon, 109
Atkinson, Brooks, 8

Barnes, Maynard B., 39, 40, 41
Benes, Edvard, 183, 184
Beria, Lavrentii, 63, 67
Bevin, Ernest, 10, 17, 19
Bidault, Georges, 10, 14, 19
Black, Cyril E., 41
Brandt, Willy, 154, 155, 181, 182, 184, 190, 192, 193
Brezhnev, Leonid, 105, 115, 117, 118, 129, 181, 192, 200, 209
Bulganin, Nikolai, 68, 85, 89
Byrnes, James F., Secretary of State, 5, 6, 8, 9, 10, 11, 12, 14, 15, 16, 19, 22, 29, 30, 35, 37, 39-40, 41, 42, 43, 44, 45, 46, 47-48, 50

Callender, Harold, 10
Chnoupek, Bohuslav, 192
Chou En-lai, 109
Churchill, Sir Winston, 4, 30, 32, 34, 35; Iron Curtain address, 7, 8-9
Clark, Cal, 148
Clausewitz, Karl von, 107
Clay, Gen. Lucius, 12, 13, 14, 15, 22
Connally, Tom, 9
Crane, Gen. John A., 39, 40, 41

Davies, Joseph E., 30, 32, 46, 63
Dean, Robert, 157
de Gaulle, Charles, 186
De Lattre de Tassigny, 12
Deutscher, Isaac, 71
Dillon, C. Douglas, 90
Djilas, Milovan, 73-74
Douglas, Justice William, 7
Dubcek, Alexander, 183, 186, 191
Dulles, John F., 89, 193

Eden, Sir Anthony, 83-84
Ehrenburg, Il'ia, 59
Eisenhower, Dwight E., 12, 84, 87, 88, 90, 92, 94

Fleming, D. F., 16, 23
Fock, Janos, 200
Fulbright, J. William, 116

Gomulka, Wladyslaw, 153, 154, 203
Gosnjak, Ivan, 90
Granick, David, 202
Gromyko, Andrei, 112
Groves, Gen. Leslie R., 32
Groza, Petru, 42, 43-44

Hager, Kurt, 179
Halle, Louis J., 47
Hitler, Adolf, 8, 183
Ho Chi Minh, 79-80, 93
Honecker, Erich, 167, 168, 176, 179

Hopkins, Harry, 30, 32
Husak, Gustav, 186, 188, 189, 191, 208-09

Jackson, Senator Henry, 106, 114
Johnson, Ross, 153-54

Kadar, Janos, 200, 209
Kardelj, Edvard, 82, 88
Kennan, George, 44, 63
Khrushchev, Nikita S., 65, 67, 68, 70, 85-86, 91, 93-94, 105, 110, 117, 129, 146, 153
Kissinger, Henry, 116
Komocsin, Zoltan, 207
Kosygin, Aleksei I., 109

Labedz, Leopold, 104
Laqueur, Walter, 100
Legvold, Robert, 111
Leonhard, Wolfgang, 103, 104

Maddox, Robert James, 28
Malenkov, Georgii M., 60-61, 63, 67
Mao Tse-tung, 26, 109, 117, 204
Marshall, George C., 15-16, 17, 18, 19, 20, 37, 45
Masaryk, Jan, 183
Mates, Leo, 81, 90
Michael, King of Rumania, 42, 43
Mikoyan, Anastas I., 68
Modelski, George, 146
Molotov, Vyacheslav M., 4, 5, 8, 9, 10, 11, 12, 14, 15, 16, 17, 18, 19, 20, 22, 29, 45, 47-48, 68
Montgomery, 12
Moore, Jr., Barrington, 15
Murphy, Robert, 83-84

Nixon, Richard M., 101, 114, 118; presidential administration, 110, 113, 115, 181, 190
Novotny, Antonin, 187, 196

Pasternak, Boris, 59
Popovic, Koca, 90
Puja, Frigyes, 200

Rakowski, Mieczyslaw, 155-56
Rapacki, Adam, 182
Reston, James, 16
Riddleberger (U.S. Ambassador), 91
Roberts, Henry L., 42
Rogers, William P., 194
Roosevelt, Franklin D., 28-29, 33

Shcherbakov, Aleksandr, 61, 63, 64, 65, 66
Scheel, Walter, 192
Shulman, Marshall, 100, 104, 105, 111
Sinderman, Horst, 168
Smith, Bedell, 18, 84
Solzhenitsyn, Aleksandr I., 59
Stalin, Iosif V., 4, 5, 7, 8, 11, 17, 18-19, 20, 26, 29, 30, 32, 33, 34, 35, 36, 37, 39, 40-41, 42, 44, 45, 46, 49, 57-60, 61-63, 67-74, 117, 145
Stassen, Harold E., 84-85
Stettinius, Edward R., 45-46
Stimson, Henry, 30, 31, 32, 33-34, 36, 37, 49-50
Strougal, Lubomir, 186, 191, 192
Sulzberger, Cyrus L., 9
Szczepanski, Jan, 157
Szilard, Leo, 30, 47

Tito, Josef B., 73-74, 79-80, 81-84, 86-87, 89, 90-91, 93-94
Trochta, Stefan Cardinal, 195
Truman, Harry S., 6, 15, 16, 19 27, 28-30, 31, 32, 33, 34-35, 36, 37, 38, 39, 40, 42, 43-44, 47-48, 50, 80

Ulam, Adam, 111
Ulbricht, Walter, 167, 168, 179

Vandenberg, Arthur H., 3-5, 9
Voznesensky, Nikolai A., 68
Vukmanovic-Tempo, Svetozar, 84-91

Wolfe, Thomas, 112, 146

Zhdanov, Andrei A., 64, 65, 67, 68, 71
Zhukov, Georgii K., 12, 65

SUBJECT INDEX

Africa, 203
aggression, 4, 5, 7
aid, 20; U.S. to Greece, 16; to Turkey, 16; to Yugoslavia, 77-96
Albania, 85, 144, 159-60
Algeria, 186
alliances, 3, 4, 38, 81-82, 111, 144-45, 146, 147, 148, 149, 150, 151-52, 156, 157, 158-60, 162, 166, 168, 181, 187, 200 (see also, military assistance, trade, treaties)
Allied Control Council/Commission, 10, 11, 12, 14, 17, 19, 40
allied governments/powers, 12, 42, 43, 155
allies, 4, 5, 15, 156, 169, 170, 184, 185
All-Union CP (see, Communist Party)
American (see, United States)
American-Soviet relations (see, Soviet-American relations)
Anglo-American, 34, 38, 39, 43 (see also, United States and Great Britain)
Arab-Israeli issue, 151, 160, 168
arms/armaments, 6, 12, 208; control, 20, 107, 112; negotiations, 112; race, 107, 117
Asia, 203
atomic: bomb, 8, 26, 28-30, 32, 34, 40, 41, 42, 44, 45, 49; control, 49; diplomacy, 26-56, 28-29, 35-36; monopoly possession, 26, 50; stockpile, 47; testing, 28, 32, 34; use, 26, 33, 35
Austria, 19, 20, 82, 205, 207; State Treaty, 19

Balkans, 35, 38, 39, 42, 82-83, 93
Belgium, 22
Benelux, 205
Berlin, 155, 175, 178, 190, 191, 192, 193; blockade, 19; Conference, 39; Declaration, 38
Bolsheviks, 57, 66, 70
boundaries, 157, 182, 185, 191, 200; Oder-Neisse line, 152, 153, 155, 160, 193
buffer states, 4
Bulgaria, 35, 38, 39, 40, 41, 42, 44, 46, 136, 150, 151

Canada, 8, 109, 207
Central Committee (see, Communist Party)
Central Europe, 3-25, 21, 29, 32, 34, 48, 184, 185, 191, 196
China, 6, 16, 108, 109, 110, 113, 114, 115, 117, 154, 160, 168, 181, 182, 204, 206
CMEA (Council for Mutual Economic Assistance), 201, 203, 204, 209-10
cold war, 3-25, 26, 28-29, 38, 56-77, 67, 74, 78, 100, 104, 118, 193, 209
collective security, 4, 82
COMECON (Council for Mutual Economic Assistance), 122-23, 124, 128-29, 136-39, 141, 145, 148, 150, 166, 168, 172-73, 174, 188, 191

Cominform, 78, 79, 93
Common Market, 188
communism, 16, 37, 47, 58, 63, 74, 109, 149, 161, 167, 200, 208
Communist Party (CPSU), 56-77, 91, 105, 181; Central Committee, 64, 72-73; Orgburo, 72; Party congresses, 73; Politburo, 60, 63, 64, 72, 103; Secretariat, 60, 66, 72
Communists, 7-8, 41, 70, 73, 85-86, 88-89, 93, 145, 183, 185, 191, 206-07; Czech, 183, 184, 186, 187, 192, 195; German, 12, 20-21, 176, 207; Greek, 79, 93; Hungarian, 201-02, 205, 207-08; Polish, 32; Rumanian, 42, 44; Ukrainian, 68; Yugoslav, 80
CSCE (Conference on Security and Cooperation in Europe), 166, 182, 187, 189, 194, 207
Cyprus, 101
Czechoslovakia, 22, 88, 89, 110, 115, 136, 137, 149, 150, 151, 152, 156, 160, 170, 181-98, 204, 208; foreign policy, 183-86, 187

demilitarization/disarmament, 181; of Germany, 5, 6, 10, 11, 12, 16, 17, 19, 20, 21
detente, 98-121, 122, 154, 172, 181-98, 199-213

Eastern Europe, 3, 5, 15, 20, 21, 29, 32, 33, 35, 37, 38, 45, 46, 47, 48-49, 60, 73, 88-89, 104, 105, 108, 110, 111, 112, 115, 117, 167, 168-69, 172, 173-74, 177-78, 180, 181, 182, 184, 185, 187, 188, 189, 191, 192, 193, 195, 201, 203, 208, 209, 210, 211; foreign policy of, 143-65
economic development, 159, 172; Czech, 187-90; Hungarian, 201; German, 12, 20, 21, 22, 154, 176-77, 178-80; Polish, 157; USSR (see, Soviet Union); Yugoslav, 80-81, 91-92
EEC (European Economic Community), 188, 189
elections: in Bulgaria, 39-40, 41, 42; in Hungary, 39; in Rumania, 44
environmental protection, 207
escalation, 113
expansionism, 108, 183

Finland, 46, 111, 112
five year plan, 7, 64, 110
foreign policy (see, individual country)
foreign trade (see, trade, or individual country)
four-power pact, 3-25, 9-10, 15-16, 17, 19, 22 (see also, treaties/pacts)
France, 6, 19, 21, 22, 80, 86, 147, 152, 183, 207
FRG (Federal Republic of Germany), 115, 147, 150-58, 166, 168, 170-71, 173, 175, 176, 177, 178, 181, 184, 185, 186, 190-93, 196, 199, 205, 207, 209; West Germany, 105, 109, 110, 111, 115, 147, 149, 150, 187, 189 (see also, Germany)

GATT (General Agreement on Tariffs and Trade), 205
GDR (German Democratic Republic), 150, 152, 153, 155, 184, 185, 190, 191, 193; domestic policy, 174-75; foreign policy, 166-80, 183; East Germany, 8, 22, 88, 90, 91, 94, 115, 136, 137 (see also, Germany)
Germany, 3-5, 6-11, 12, 13, 14-15, 16, 17, 18, 19, 20-21, 22,

[Germany] 29, 58, 60, 112, 150-51, 152, 153, 157, 160, 165, 175, 177, 184, 185-86, 191, 193, 209 (see also, FRG, GDR)
GFR (German Federal Republic) (see, FRG)
Great Britain, 5, 6, 7, 8, 10, 19, 21, 22, 38, 40, 41, 42, 80, 86, 152, 183
Greece, 79, 81, 82, 83, 93

Hallstein Doctrine, 152
Hungary, 19, 30, 35, 38, 39, 46, 47, 89, 136, 150, 151, 160, 170, 195, 197, 199-213; foreign policy, 200, 203-08; foreign trade, 203-08, 209-10; internal reform, 201-03, 208; NEM (New Economic Mechanism), 201-02, 204, 205

imperialism, 104
India, 116
Indochina, 113
intervention, 89
isolationism, 4, 5
Israel, 178, 210
Italy, 79, 81, 83, 85, 93, 191, 207

Japan, 4, 10, 11, 28, 33, 36, 37, 40, 45, 46, 71, 109, 110, 111, 116

Kremlin, 4, 9, 12, 17, 90, 94, 107, 112, 117, 169

Latin America, 203
Lend-Lease, 29
Lenin/Leninist, 57, 58, 70, 167; Leninist-Stalinist, 68

Manchuria, 49
Marshall Plan, 16, 183
Marxism-Leninism, 62, 64, 68, 70, 171, 176; Marxist, 70, 210
Middle East, 100, 116, 194, 203
militarism, 20, 63, 100, 107, 113, 116 (see also, demilitarization)
military bases, 10, 48; assistance, 81, 86
mutual defense (assistance), 81

NATO (North Atlantic Treaty Organization), 4, 34, 81, 82, 85, 93, 108, 111, 147, 181, 182, 185, 186, 203, 209, 210
Netherlands, 22
Nixon administration, 110, 113, 115, 181, 190
noninterference/nonintervention, 4, 80, 89, 200
nuclear weapons/war, 102, 107, 108, 112, 114, 153

occupation zones/forces, 3, 6, 11, 12, 15, 16, 19, 20, 21, 29, 30, 33, 47, 170, 176, 181, 182

peaceful coexistence, 58, 90, 100, 104, 105, 114, 200, 208
peacetime production, 66 (see also, economic development)
Poland, 4, 15, 16, 19, 29, 30, 31, 32, 46, 49, 89, 136, 148, 149, 150, 151, 152-58, 160, 166, 169, 170, 182, 183, 185, 195, 203
Politburo (see, Communist Party)
Portugal, 191
Potsdam Conference, agreements, 4, 6, 13, 15, 18, 21, 32, 33, 34, 35, 37, 38, 40, 42, 44, 47, 49, 155
printsipnost', 68, 70, 71, 72
propaganda, 20, 64, 91, 192
purge trials, 63; purges, 71

Red Army, 49, 57, 59-60, 61, 67, 74

reparations, 11, 13, 14, 15, 20
repatriation, 16-17
revisionism, 27
Rumania (Romania), 19, 30, 35, 38, 39, 42, 43, 44, 46, 47, 49, 136, 144, 150, 151-52, 159, 160, 169, 183, 197
Russia (see, USSR)

SALT, 112, 115, 193
secret police, 59
security, 3-25, 111, 117, 154, 170-71, 175, 196, 200, 207
Security Council, 4
SED (Sozialistische Einheitspartei Deutschlands), 166, 167, 168, 169, 170, 171, 175-77, 178
Southeast Asia, 116, 194
Soviet-American relations, 26, 31, 32, 40, 50, 57, 99-121, 161, 181, 200
Soviet Party (see, Communist Party)
Soviet Union (see, USSR)
Sovinformburo, 61
spheres of influence, 5, 28, 33, 38, 42, 47-49, 193
Stalinist, 144, 187
state defense committee (GOKO), 60-61
statism, 57-58, 60, 71
superpowers, 90, 101, 116, 117, 160

trade, 22, 106, 114, 122-42, 152, 160, 172, 173, 179-80, 181, 182, 188, 189, 191-92, 194, 196, 197, 203, 204-08, 209
treaties/pacts, 5, 6, 42, 155-56, 157, 177, 183, 187; Austrian State, 19; GDR-USSR, 169; GFR-Czechoslovakia, 192, 196; Munich agreement, 183, 184, 191, 192, 196; Ribbentrop, 183; U.S. draft, 4, 5, 6, 11, 14, 17, 22; objectives, 6; security, 3, 4-5; USSR draft, 22; Warsaw pact/treaty organization, 145, 148, 150, 153, 166, 171, 181, 185, 187, 194, 203
Truman Doctrine, 16, 20
Turkey, 82-83

Ukraine, 16, 206
UN (United Nations), 8, 82, 114, 178, 203
United States, 3-25, 41, 42, 46-47, 63, 79, 82, 99, 103, 105-10, 111, 113, 114, 115, 116, 117, 161, 182, 186, 188, 189, 190, 193-94, 196, 199, 203, 205, 207, 208, 210; aid, 16, 20, 78-96; Cabinet, 4; Defense Department, policy, 3-25, 27, 30, 34-35, 38, 42, 44, 46, 47-48, 49, 102, 106-07, 181, 194; Senate, 4, 6; State Department, 4, 90, 102
USSR (Soviet Union), 3-25, 41, 42, 44, 46, 47-49, 57-77, 79, 85-89, 90, 91, 92, 144-53, 183, 186, 187, 188, 190, 191, 192, 193, 199-200, 202-04, 206-07, 208-11; domestic issues, 58, 66, 104, 106, 197; economic development, 7, 12, 21, 66, 105, 107, 111, 123, 169; foreign policy, 99-121, 144, 183, 184, 200, 203-04, 210; foreign trade, 122-42; internal politics, 103-05, 112, 117; political relaxation, 58-63, 105, 117, 196-97; relations with GDR, 166-80

Vatican, 195-96
Vietnam, 79, 85, 107, 113, 116, 204

war: Indo-Pakistan, 100; Middle

[war] East (1973), 101; production, 12, 17, 59, 61, 67; World War II, 7, 26, 74, 151, 152, 176, 183, 185, 191, 192, 193, 194
Warsaw Pact (see, treaties)
Western Europe, 33, 47, 93, 109, 111, 112, 115, 117, 188, 203, 207
Western powers, 3, 5, 81, 83

Yalta Conference/Declaration, 3, 4, 5, 18, 38, 48
Yugoslavia, 16, 49, 151, 159, 187; foreign policy, 77-96, 144, 150, 205; treaty with Greece and Turkey, 83

ABOUT THE EDITORS AND CONTRIBUTORS

PETER J. POTICHNYJ is Professor of Political Science at McMaster University in Hamilton, Ontario. He is Chairman of the Interdepartmental Committee on Communist and East European Affairs at McMaster and Secretary-Treasurer of the Canadian Association of Slavists. He is the author of *Soviet Agricultural Trade Unions, 1917-1970* (Toronto: University of Toronto Press, 1972), *The Ukraine and Czechoslovak Crisis* (Canberra: Australian National University, 1972), and *Ukraine in the Seventies* (Arlington: Mosaic Press, 1975). He is Editor-in-Chief of *Current Soviet Leaders*.

JANE P. SHAPIRO is Associate Professor of Political Science, Manhattanville College, Purchase, N.Y. She is co-editor of *Communist Systems on Comparative Perspective* (New York: Doubleday, 1974).

WALTER C. CLEMENS, JR., is Professor of Political Science, Boston University; among his works are *The Superpowers and Arms Control* (Lexington, Mass.: Lexington Books, 1973), and *The Arms Race and Sino-Soviet Relations* (Stanford, Calif.: Stanford University Press, 1968).

THOMAS T. HAMMOND is Professor of History at the University of Virginia, Charlottesville; among his books are *Lenin on Trade Unions and Revolution* (New York: Columbia University Press, 1957) and *The Anatomy of Communist Takeovers* (New Haven: Yale University Press, 1975).

WILLIAM O. McGAGG, JR., is Associate Professor of History, Michigan State University, East Lansing, and author of "Jewish Nobles and Geniuses in Modern Hungary" (*East European Quarterly*, 1972).

STEPHEN C. MARKOVICH is Associate Professor of Political Science at the University of North Dakota, Grand Forks. His main interest is U.S. foreign policy toward Eastern Europe.

ROBERT C. HORN is Associate Professor of Political Science, California State University, Northridge. His main interest is in Soviet foreign policy.

STEVEN ROSEFIELDE is Assistant Professor of Economics at the University of North Carolina, Chapel Hill, and the author of

Soviet International Trade in Heckscher-Ohlin Perspective (Lexington, Mass.: Heath Lexington, 1973).

ZVI GITELMAN is Associate Professor of Political Science, University of Michigan, Ann Arbor, and author of Jewish Nationality and Soviet Politics (Princeton, N.J.: Princeton University Press, 1972), and Diffusion of Political Innovation from Eastern Europe to the Soviet Union (Beverly Hills: Sage Publications, 1972).

PETER C. LUDZ is Professor of Political Science, University of Munich, and author of The Changing Party Elite in East Germany (Cambridge, Mass.: M.I.T., 1972).

GEORGE KLEIN is Professor of Political Science, Western Michigan University, Kalamazoo. His main interest is East European politics.

RICHARD C. GRIPP is Professor of Political Science at California State University, San Diego, and author of Patterns of Soviet Politics (Homewood, Ill.: Dorsey Press, 1963, 1967) and The Political System of Communism (New York: Dodd, Mead and Co., 1973).

PUBLICATIONS FROM THE FIRST INTERNATIONAL SLAVIC CONFERENCE, BANFF 1974

I. Volumes in the Social Sciences, published by Praeger Publishers, Praeger Special Studies, New York:

Economic Development in the Soviet Union and Eastern Europe: Reforms, Technology, and Income Distribution, edited by Zbigniew M. Fallenbuchl, University of Windsor.

Economic Development in the Soviet Union and Eastern Europe: Sectoral Analysis, edited by Zbigniew M. Fallenbuchl, University of Windsor.

Education and the Mass Media in the Soviet Union and Eastern Europe, edited by Bohdan Harasymiw, University of Calgary.

Soviet Economic and Political Relations with the Developing World, edited by Roger E. Kanet and Donna Bahry, University of Illinois, Urbana-Champaign.

Demographic Developments in Eastern Europe, edited by Leszek Kosinski, University of Alberta.

Environmental Misuse in the Soviet Union, edited by Fred Singleton, University of Bradford.

Change and Adaptation in Soviet and East European Politics edited by Jane P. Shapiro, Manhattanville College, and Peter J. Potichnyj, McMaster University.

From the Cold War to Detente, edited by Peter J. Potichnyj, McMaster University, and Jane P. Shapiro, Manhattanville College.

II. Volumes in the Humanities, published by Slavica Publishers, Cambridge, Mass.:

Russian and Slavic Literature to 1917, edited by Richard Freeborn, University of London, and Charles A. Ward, University of Wisconsin, Milwaukee.

Slavic Linguistics at Banff, edited by Thomas F. Magner, Pennsylvania State University.

Early Russian History, edited by G. Edward Orchard, University of Lethbridge.

Nineteenth and Twentieth Century Slavic History, edited by Don Karl Rowney, Bowling Green State University.

Reconsiderations on the Russian Revolution, edited by Carter Elwood, Carleton University.

III. Additional Volumes:

"Nomads and the Slavic World," a special issue of *AEMAe Eurasiae Medii Aevi*, 2 (1975), edited by Tibor Halasi-Kun, Columbia University.

Russian Literature in the Age of Catherine the Great: A Collection of Essays. Oxford: Willem A. Meeuws, 1976, edited by Anthony Cross, University of East Anglia.

Commercial and Legal Problems in East-West Trade. Ottowa: Carleton University, Russian and East European Center, 1976, edited by John P. Hardt, U.S. Library of Congress.

Marxism and Religion in Eastern Europe. Dordrecht and Boston: D. Reidel, 1976, edited by Richard T. DeGeorge, University of Kansas, and James P. Scanlan, The Ohio State University.

Detente and the Conference on Security and Cooperation in Europe. Leiden: Sythoff, 1976, edited by Louis J. Mensonides, Virginia Polytechnic Institute and State University.